ENGINEERING WITH LEGO® BRICKS AND ROBOLAB™

2nd Edition

The unofficial guide to ROBOLAB™ version 2.5.4

Eric Wang

Department of Mechanical Engineering
University of Nevada, Reno

In consultation with

Chris Rogers

Department of Mechanical Engineering
Tufts University

College House Enterprises, LLC
Knoxville, Tennessee

Version 2.0: October 2004

College House Enterprises, LLC.
5713 Glen Cove Drive
Knoxville, TN 37919, U.S.A.
Phone (865) 558-6111
FAX (865) 558-6111
e-mail jdally@www.collegehousebooks.com
Visit our web site http://www.collegehousebooks.com

ISBN 0-9723567-9-7

PREFACE TO THE 2ND EDITION

About the book:

It's hard to believe it's been 2 years since I finished the workbook (1st edition). There have been many changes and, of course, the addition of two more chapters. The book has grown from 188 to 342 pages with over 500 examples and images. I've taken what I call the National Geographic approach in the development of this book. Simply stated, a student can get the gist of what's going on simply by looking at the pictures and reading the captions. Of course, the narrative contains more details, but in terms of learning styles, the graphical approach is important because most of us are visual learners.

My original intention was for this book to be used by first year engineering students to introduce them to the design process, engineering fundamentals, and computer programming. However, much to my surprise, many (okay, about half) of the readers have turned out to be K-12 teachers and students. Thus, I've tried to add material that pertains to both teachers and students who may be using this book as a resource to help them conduct science experiments or compete in competitions like the FIRST LEGO® League (FLL).

I was just getting started in the field of *engineering education* when I first met Chris Rogers, the creator of ROBOLAB. In late 2001 the Frontiers in Education conference was held in Reno, and Chris and I hatched the idea for the book over dinner at a local casino. A few months later, I found myself flying to the East Coast to meeting the folks at LEGO® and National Instruments to discuss the book. The result of that meeting was a workbook that contained the first draft of the first four chapters of this book. Released in late 2002, the workbook sold surprisingly well and everyone immediately asked when the full book, which you now hold in your hands, would be done. It took 2 more years but it's finally done. Will the 3rd edition be out soon? Let's just say there are a lot of things that I wanted to include in this edition but didn't have time to write up (multimedia in particular).

There are lots of people, without whom, this book would not have been completed. First off, I'm not sure whether to thank Chris Rogers or blame him for getting me into this. Anyone who has ever worked with Chris knows what I'm talking about. I also want to thank Ryan for lending me his LEGO® bricks (and Bionicles), Sandra at LEGO® for insisting that I just get it done, Jim for his advice on publishing, and Bernard for his excellent editorial comments from the land down under. I also would like to thank my research assistants: Ann-Marie, Victor, Matt, William, and Christian for their willingness to play with LEGO® bricks all day long. Finally, many thanks to Sally, for her inspiration, willingness to spend hours sorting LEGO® bricks, and tolerance for my late nights.

Eric Wang
Reno, NV
October 2004

PREFACE TO THE WORKBOOK VERSION (1ST EDITION)

About the workbook:

This first draft represents a work in progress. The final book will include 8 chapters along with several appendices and on-line reference material. Unfortunately, the completion of the full text is not expected until sometime in the year 2004.

Many people have asked that we publish something while the full text is being completed. To meet this demand, we have produced the first 4 chapters of the book in workbook form, which you are now holding in your hands.

About LEGO® Bricks and ROBOLAB:

I strongly feel that engineering education can, and should be, fun. So when I first heard about using LEGO® bricks to teach engineering, I was instantly intrigued. I had spent way too many hours playing with LEGO® bricks when I was a kid and this sounded like the perfect excuse to start playing with them again. After a couple of terrible initial experiences with the standard Mindstorms programming language and NQC, I hit upon ROBOLAB. It worked great, mainly due to the very short learning curve. The only problem was there wasn't much documentation beyond the Getting Started teacher's manuals.

Thus, the idea for a book was hatched. Chris Rogers, the creator of ROBOLAB, came to Reno for a conference and over dinner we hashed out the skill badge concept and the outline for this book. We were both pretty adamant that the book focus on project based learning. Our experience has shown that hands-on engineering is one of the best ways to learn. Plus, it tends to break down the barriers between the instructor and the student.

With that said, this workbook is intended to be used by first year engineering students, although others may find it is useful as a ROBOLAB reference guide. We've tried to think up design challenges that have no ceiling. You can accomplish the tasks with a moderate amount of effort or you can make it as complicated as you want.

I want to see how far I can push LEGO® bricks and ROBOLAB, both of which were developed for children – not engineering students. I can't speak for Chris, but I think he's of similar mind. We've had to restrain ourselves quite a bit because we keep devising (somewhat diabolically) ever more complex challenges. Fortunately for our students, most of these I have reserved for the last four chapters. On the other hand, if you are somewhat deranged like me, you will just have to wait until 2004 when the full text is released.

Eric Wang
Reno, NV
August 2002

TABLE OF CONTENTS

CHAPTER 1: LEGO® & ROBOLAB Basics

CHAPTER 2: GREEN LEVEL

CHAPTER 3: WHITE LEVEL

CHAPTER 4: BLACK LEVEL

CHAPTER 5: BLUE LEVEL

CHAPTER 6: RED LEVEL

APPENDIX A: Information about LEGO® Kits

APPENDIX B: Tips for Teachers

CHAPTER 1

LEGO® & ROBOLAB Basics

If you are like most people, you probably have not played with LEGO® bricks since you were a child. However LEGO® bricks are wonderful for learning about many physics, engineering, and computer science principles and skills.

The objective of this book is to introduce you to engineering concepts in a fun and challenging way. The assignments in this book take the form of open-ended **design challenges**. The challenges have no ceiling, meaning you can accomplish the required tasks with a moderate amount of effort or you can make it as complicated as you like. This approach permits even the best students to be intellectually challenged.

It is often said that we remember only 10% of what we are told but 90% of what we teach others. There is also an old Chinese proverb that goes something like this:

Tell me and I forget. Show me and I remember. Involve me and I understand.

Combined, these capture the teaching philosophy and the approach we've taken in this book. That is, we fully expect you, the student, to both get involved and to help teach your peers what you've learned.

This book uses ROBOLAB, a graphical programming language, because we want the emphasis to be on the *engineering* with the software side limited to a few mouse clicks. Plus, we have always found it easier to remember the meaning of an icon rather than a function name. You will still learn the basics of computer programming, but ROBOLAB relieves you of the need to memorize lots of syntax and function names.

By the time you have finished this book, you should be able to:
- Describe the design process.
- Read a ROBOLAB program and interpret what the robot will do.
- Apply basic engineering principles and problem solving methodologies.
- Solve open-ended problems given specifications and constraints.
- Apply creative thinking strategies to solve open-ended problems.
- Write complex computer programs that use variables, conditionals, subroutines, and multitasking. More strictly, you will be able to program an embedded microprocessor, which sounds nice on a resume.

1.1 Organization of This Book

Rather than the traditional homework problem set at the end of each chapter, this book utilizes **design challenges.** Each design challenge defines a task that must be completed. It is your job to design, build, and program a robot to accomplish this task given the specifications and constraints. We purposely, and somewhat diabolically, place very few constraints (often called 'rules') on possible solutions so that you have plenty of room to stretch your creative legs.

The real world is full of design challenges and their solutions. Just take a trip down to your local department store and you will find dozens of devices that accomplish the simple task of "toasting a piece of bread." Likewise, you'll find there are several ways to solve the design challenges in this book.

Both you and your instructor will monitor progress in your learning by using a **skill badge** concept. Skill badges are earned for successfully completing a challenge. The skill badges required are indicated at the start of each challenge. How difficult a particular challenge is will depend on how many of the required skill badges you already have earned. In general, you should not try to acquire more than three new skill badges with any single challenge (unless you have an extremely good instructor or have a lot of time on your hands).

The challenges are organized into 5 levels of difficulty: Green (easiest), White, **Black, Blue,** and **Red** (most difficult). At each level we assume you have earned all the skill badges from the easier levels. With this said, however, we are aware that it is possible to skip levels depending on the skill badges sought.

> *Use the Skill Badges as a method of monitoring your own progress.*

Unlike most textbooks, you will not read this book sequentially. We fully expect you to skip back and forth between sections and chapters as you acquire the various skill badges. You will also find that each chapter is organized backwards from a standard textbook; the challenges appear at the beginning of the chapter followed by the sections aimed at teaching a particular skill. In organizing the book in this way, we are encouraging you to develop **self learning skills**, which are crucial to your future success as an Engineer.

The remainder of Chapter 1 deals with the nuts, bolts and electrons of the LEGO® Mindstorms for Schools hardware and the ROBOLAB software. We presume that you have already successfully installed the batteries, installed the software, downloaded the firmware, and perhaps even completed the training missions included on the CD-ROM. If you have not done so or are having trouble, please consult Appendix B for troubleshooting tips.

Chapters 2 through 6 each cover one challenge level and have several challenges at the beginning of each chapter. Figure 1.1 shows the layout of this book and the skill badges associated with each challenge level. There are a total of 28 skills badges that can be earned. Most introduction to engineering courses will cover about 10-12 skills badges.

1.2 Chapter Objectives

In most cases, the learning objectives for each chapter will be to earn the skill badges covered in the chapter. However, on occasion we may throw in some overarching themes that are not so explicit. With that said, upon finishing this first chapter you should be able to:

- List the 5 steps in the Design Process

- List several common creative blocks

- List at least two structured creativity activities

- Be able to design and build a simple LEGO® robot

Figure 1.1. Organization of this book showing the challenge levels and skill badges.

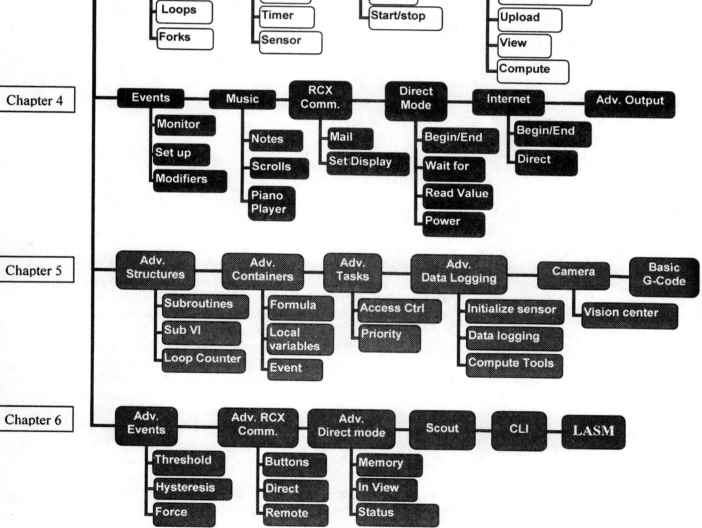

1.3 Engineering and the Design Process

In his many books Henry Petroski, professor of Civil Engineering at Duke University, defines *design* as the obviation of failure. He points out that the design process is often iterative as the engineer struggles to prevent the various modes of failure. You don't learn very much from a design that works the first time around. And even if it works under one specific set of conditions (i.e., at home), that doesn't imply it will work under all conditions (i.e., in class). It's the design that falls apart that teaches you the real lessons. Knowing what went wrong is often more important than not knowing what went right. The point being, ***don't expect to get it right the first time around.*** LEGO® bricks are great because they allow you to improve upon failed designs quickly. Take advantage of this and improve your design through several iterations.

The idea that failure is acceptable is a key component in the **design process**, which has five main steps:

1. Identify the problem, including specifications and constraints

2. Explore alternative solutions

3. Design, build, program, and test your design

4. Optimize and re-design the solution

5. Communicate and disseminate your solution

If you are a writer, then this process should look a lot like the **writing process** (prewrite, draft, revise, edit, and publish). If you are a scientist, this should look similar to the **scientific process** (identify the problem, develop a hypothesis, test it, evaluate the data, and derive conclusions).

The design process is shown graphically in Figure 1.2. The first step is often overlooked as trivial. But it is often the case (especially in robot competitions) that the real problem to be solved is not explicitly stated. In the design challenges in this book, we purposely propose problems which can be solved in a myriad of ways. We encourage you to stretch your "creative legs."

Step 2 involves a lot of creative thinking. You should try to come up with as many alternative solutions as time permits. In Engineering, the "rule of 7" is used quite often, meaning you should think up at least seven alternative solutions before deciding what the "best" design is. Once you've decided what to do, implementing it is actually quite straightforward. As mentioned previously, however, don't expect to get it right the first time. In real life, the difference between a successful product and a total flop is often directly related to the amount of "debugging" the product went through before being released into the marketplace. Thus, expect to spend quite a bit of time optimizing and re-designing your solution.

Finally, it is vitally important for you to communicate and disseminate your solution. When communicating your solution to others, you're basically forcing yourself to justify and explain your design choices. Through this reflective practice you'll learn a lot about yourself and what you've learned. Also try to see how others solved the same problem and compare your solution to theirs. Evaluation is a critical thinking skill that will aid you well in the future. Ask yourself if your design worked better, looked better, used fewer parts, used less programming, etc.

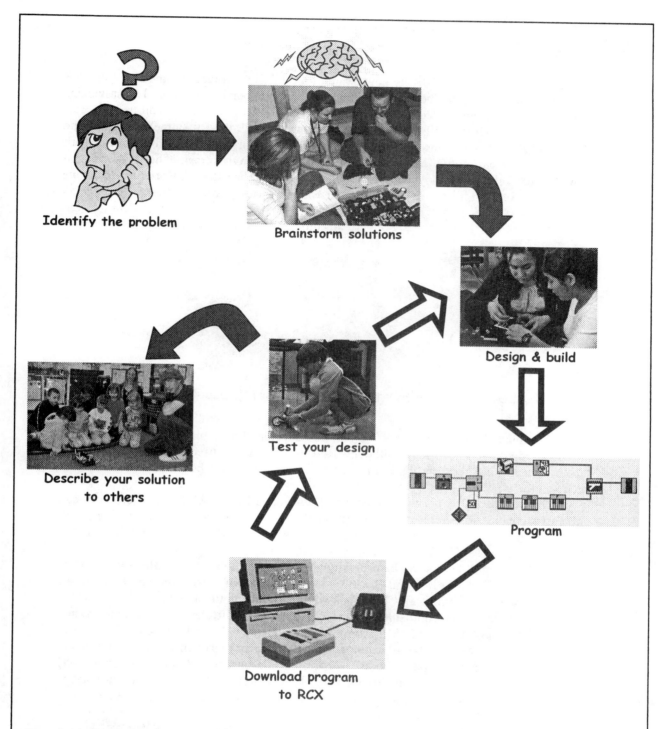

Figure 1.2. "Design is the obviation of failure," which means that failure is not only acceptable but even expected. The white arrows represent the design and optimization cycle, where you will typically cycle around many times as you fix problems and refine the design with each iteration. When everything finally works, you are ready to communicate your final solution to others.

1.4 LEGO® Mindstorms Hardware

LEGO® Mindstorms is a relatively new brand of the LEGO® Group. It came about in 1998 after being inspired by the book *Mindstorms* by Dr. Seymour Papert at the Massachusetts Institute of Technology's Media Lab (Papert, 1999).

The Mindstorms family includes three "smart bricks": the RCX, the Scout, and the Microscout. All three smart bricks contain microprocessors, inputs, and outputs which allow you to create mobile robots that can react to their environment. The RCX evolved from the crickets and handyboard developed at MIT. The book *Robotic Explorations* provides an excellent history of the MIT programmable brick (Martin, 2000).

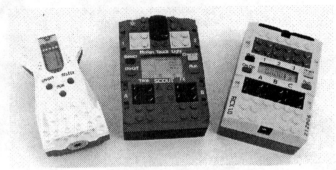

Figure 1.3. LEGO® smart bricks: the Microscout (left), Scout, and RCX (right).

The Scout is based on the RCX but was developed as a platform which does not require a computer to program (although ROBOLAB can be used to program it). Even though LEGO® has recently discontinued the Scout, it can still be purchased at Internet auction sites.

The Microscout is the third smart brick developed by LEGO®. The Microscout can either execute one of seven internal programs or can be programmed via a visible light link (VLL) on a PC or Scout brick. Strangely enough, the Microscout cannot be directly programmed by the RCX; only the Scout brick can do this.

All three smart bricks can be programmed with a wide variety of software programs such as pbforth, NQC, LeJOS and BrickOS, but this book will concentrate on ROBOLAB as the programming environment. This book will also concentrate on the RCX.

Though somewhat confusing, there are actually two different Mindstorms product lines: retail "Mindstorms" and "Mindstorms for Schools," with the later being the product line aimed specifically at the educational market. The primary difference between the "retail" and "Mindstorms for Schools" versions is the absence of the external 9V DC adapter port on the retail version (Figure 1.4). This port is very useful when you want to build a robot that must operate for a long time (e.g. collecting temperature data overnight).

Figure 1.4
The Mindstorms for Schools (left) and retail Mindstorms (right) versions of the RCX.

1.4.1 The Programmable Brick: the RCX

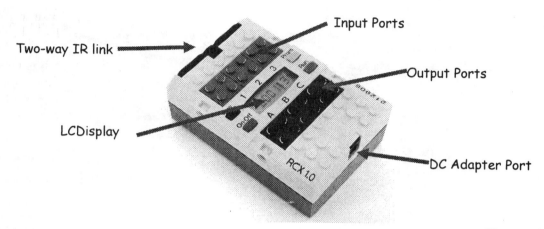

Figure 1.5
The RCX programmable brick.

The Robotic Command Explorer, or RCX, is the brain of the LEGO® Mindstorms kit. There are six ports on the RCX. The three upper ports (1, 2, and 3) are the input ports; connect sensors to these. The three lower ports (A, B, and C) are the output ports; connect motors, lights, and other output devices to these.

The RCX also comes equipped with an liquid crystal display (LCD) for displaying useful information, four buttons for activating the RCX, an internal speaker for playing sounds, and an infrared (IR) communications port. As mentioned earlier, the retail versions of the RCX do not come with the DC adapter port (Figure 1.4), but the version available from LEGO® Education (the educational division of LEGO®) is equipped with the port. We highly recommend purchasing the LEGO® Education version (available online at http://www.legoeducationstore.com/). While an DC adapter cord limits the mobility of the robots built, it makes sensor data and motor output much more reliable and is more environmentally friendly than disposable batteries.

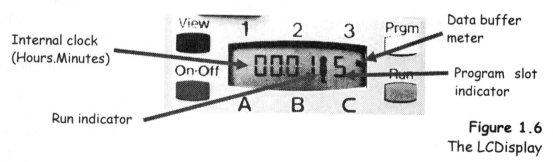

Figure 1.6
The LCDisplay

The RCX display normally displays the internal clock in hour.minutes since it was last turned on. If the display does not show the hours.minutes (i.e. is blank to the left of the run indicator), then you need to install the firmware (see Appendix B). Turning the RCX on and off resets the internal clock. When a program is running, the run indicator is animated and the tiny person looks as if he's running. The Program slot indicator just to the right of the person displays which of the 5 program slots is currently selected. There is also an icon that indicates how full the internal data buffer is (yes, the RCX can function as a data logger to collect and store data).

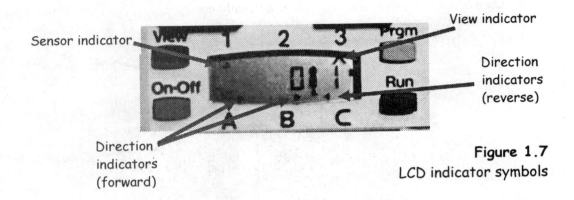

Sensor indicator

View indicator

Direction indicators (reverse)

Direction indicators (forward)

Figure 1.7
LCD indicator symbols

When a program is running, the LCD also shows which sensors are active (sensor indicator) and which direction the motor output is running (direction indicator). By depressing the **View** (black) button, you can also monitor the current sensor reading on any of the 3 input ports or power levels on the 3 output ports.

> Pressing the **View** and **Run** buttons simultaneously turns on output A, B, or C in the forward direction. Likewise, **View + Prgm** will turn A, B, or C in the reverse direction. This can be useful for determining which direction a motor will spin when connected to the output port.

1.4.2 Output and Input Devices

The RCX is also outfitted with an internal speaker for playing sounds and music (in fact there is a music skill badge). External outputs are connected to the output ports A, B, and C. In addition to the motors that come with the Mindstorms kit there are several other output devices. All of the output devices shown in Table 1.1 can be attached to any of the output ports (A, B, or C). As will be discussed in Chapter 2, unlike motors, the sound and light elements are not affected by the orientation of the lead wires.

The Mindstorms kit comes with two touch and, depending on the kit, either one or two light sensors (the different kits available are listed in Appendix A). There are also several other sensors commercially available as shown in Table 1.2. All of the input devices can be attached to any of the input ports (1, 2, or 3). The orientation of the lead wires does not matter. Not shown in Tables 1.1 and 1.2 is the LEGO® capacitor since it is neither an input nor output device for the RCX.

Additionally, there are dozens of input and output devices that you can make yourself if you have some basic electronics skills. These are beyond the scope of this text, but there are several good books and websites (e.g. Martin, 2000; Knudsen, 1999). The ROBOLAB Reference Guide also has a lot of information on defining your own sensors. It's located in the ROBOLAB directory under the Support Material folder in ROBOLAB versions 2.5.1 and higher. There are also several good websites (see section 1.8) that discuss how to connect more than one sensor to a single input port. However, this too is beyond the scope of this text.

A somewhat recent development that has lead to countless headaches by students is the existence of more than one type of internally geared motor. The type of motor is easily determined by noting the part number, located on the bottom of the motor. The "newer" motors (part #43362) don't free spin as easily as the older ones (part #71427-002). The real catch, however, is that **the two motors have different gear ratios** and, thus, turn at different speeds. We've seen countless students trying to get a car to drive straight to no avail.

Figure 1.8. The older (left) and newer (right) motors have different gear ratios and spin at different speeds. You can differentiate the motors by reading the part number (circled).

Table 1.1 Output Devices		
Output Devices		**Notes**
	Motor (internally geared)	Reversing the orientation of the lead wire on either the RCX or the motor will reverse the direction of rotation of the motor.
	Micromotor	Reversing the orientation of the lead wire on either the RCX or the motor will reverse the direction of rotation of the motor.
	9V Motor	Reversing the orientation of the lead wire on either the RCX or the motor will reverse the direction of rotation of the motor.
	Sound Element	Turning the top of the sound element 90 degrees changes the sound produced. Can be connected directly to the output port without a lead wire.
	Lamp Element	Can be attached to the top or bottom of the lead wire. Can be connected directly to the output port without a lead wire. Can also be stacked or placed side-by-side, with two or more elements on one output.
	Other 3rd party devices	There are also few small, independent manufacturers of RCX-compatible output devices (mostly LED's). Our personal favorites are: www.mindsensors.com, www.tenchno-stuff.com and www.hitechnic.com.

Table 1.2 Input Devices

Sensor		Description
	Touch	The wire lead is attached to the front four studs on the top of the touch sensor. The orientation of the lead wire does not matter. Two or more touch sensors can be attached to a single input port; pushing any of them will register as a touch.
	CLI touch	The CLI touch sensor is similar to the standard touch sensor, except the lead wire is integrated into the device.
	Light	The light sensor records values between 1 (dark) and 100 (bright). The units of measurement do NOT correspond to any standard unit of light measurement.
	Rotation	The rotation sensor measures in increments of $1/16^{ths}$ of a rotation. Rotations can be positive or negative depending on which direction the sensor is rotated.
	Temperature	The temperature sensor can measure temperatures between –20 and +50 Celsius (-4 to 122°F). The brick and wire portions of the sensor should not get wet.
	Camera	The camera is the only sensor that is not connected directly to the RCX. The RCX receives the camera sensor readings via the IR port from the computer using Direct Mode. Almost any type web-cam can be used.
	Solar cell	Strictly speaking, the solar cell is not a sensor. However, the voltage produced can be sensed by the RCX. Note, that a lamp element must be used in series with the solar cell since the solar cell has nearly zero impedance.
	Motors	Obviously these are not really sensors. However, by using the motors as generators and sensing the voltage, you have a set of crude speed sensors.
	DCP sensors	Many other sensors can also be used with the RCX with the use of a DCP sensor adapter. DCP sensors include: voltage, humidity, pH, current, temperature, sound, motion, and pressure.
	Other 3rd party sensors	There are many small, independent manufacturers of RCX-compatible sensors (e.g., compass, color, proximity, temperature, tilt, and pressure) and sensor multiplexers. Some of our favorites are www.mindsensors.com, www.techno-stuff.com, and www.hitechnic.com, www.lmsensors.com.
	Homebrew sensors	There is always the option of building your own sensors too. The sensor shown is a CdS sensor, which can be made for less than $1.00. For lots of great information, see http://www.plazaearth.com/usr/gasperi/lego.htm.

1.5 ROBOLAB Software

ROBOLAB is a graphical programming environment that is based on LabVIEW, available from National Instruments. This section provides a brief overview of the ROBOLAB software. Chapter 2 will cover programming techniques in detail.

At this point, we are assuming that you have already installed ROBOLAB on your computer and downloaded the firmware to the RCX. If you have not done so already, please refer to Appendix B for more information. You also may wish to run the Training Missions, which come with ROBOLAB versions 2.5.2 and higher.

ROBOLAB has three different graphical programming modes within it: Pilot, Inventor, and Investigator.

Pilot is the easiest programming mode. It utilizes a serial programming environment to ensure that the program will always compile and execute.

Inventor is the second programming mode. Program icons are "wired" together to create a program. Programs created can contain all the typical programming elements such as constants, variables, loops and functions.

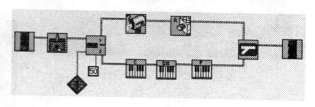

Investigator is the final programming mode. All of the features in Inventor mode are included along with the added feature of data logging and advanced data analysis.

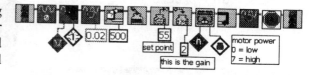

Figure 1.9. ROBOLAB programming modes: Pilot (top), Inventor (middle), and Investigator (bottom).

When you first launch ROBOLAB (versions 2.5.2 and higher), the Splash Screen will start. From here, you can access ROBOLAB itself or view the Training Missions and Setup Tutorials.

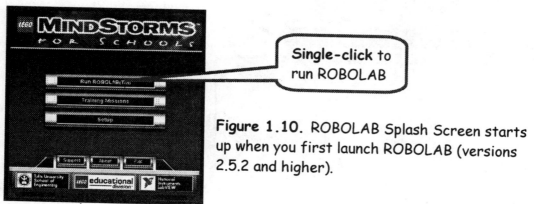

Figure 1.10. ROBOLAB Splash Screen starts up when you first launch ROBOLAB (versions 2.5.2 and higher).

The **Setup Tutorial** will walk you through the installation of the IR tower and the firmware for the RCX (see Appendix B for more information on installing the firmware). You can think of the firmware as the RCX's operating system, like Windows XP for a PC or OSX for a Mac. The **Training Missions** will step you through one programming example each. Within the Training Missions you can access the **Information** area, which is full of troubleshooting tips and tricks. We highly recommend going through the **Training Missions** if you are trying to learn ROBOLAB on your own or if you want to see a quick "refresher" on the basics of ROBOLAB. If you're using ROBOLAB as part of a class, then you'll most likely get the same information from you instructor and can skip the training missions and go straight to using ROBOLAB itself.

Figure 1.11. The setup animation shows you some basic information about setting up the hardware.

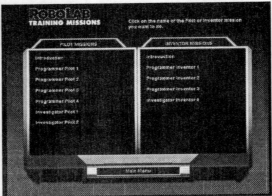

Figure 1.12. The ROBOLAB Training Missions cover Pilot, Inventor, and Investigator programming modes.

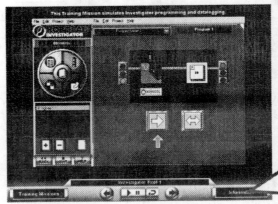

Figure 1.13. Sample Investigator Pilot 1 Training Mission.

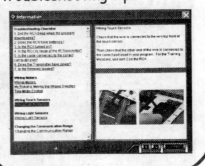

Single-click to access a help area full of troubleshooting tips

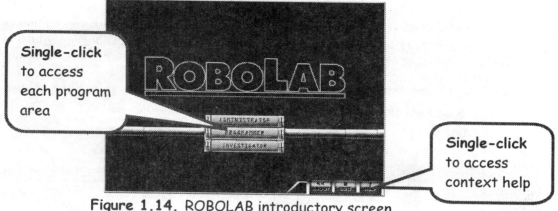

Figure 1.14. ROBOLAB introductory screen.

The introductory screen appears each time ROBOLAB is started. From this screen you can access the three main program areas:

- **Administrator:** this lets you adjust RCX settings, set default file locations, and download firmware. If you do not see the Administrator button, hit function key F5 to make it visible.
- **Programmer:** this accesses both Pilot and Inventor level programming modes. Programmer allows you to create robots that can interact with their environment, but it does not make use of the data acquisition capabilities of the RCX.
- **Investigator:** this accesses the Investigator level programming mode. Investigator level focuses on the data acquisition capabilities of the RCX. Additionally, through Investigator you can gain access to data processing commands.

The help button will open the Context Help window, which provides useful information on whatever the cursor is over.

> WE STRONGLY ENCOURAGE ALL BEGINNERS TO LEAVE THE CONTEXT HELP TURNED ON AT ALL TIMES

1.5.1 Administrator

Administrator has three areas accessed via the tabs at the bottom of the screen.

The **Administrator** tab allows you to setup and test the connection to the RCX and download the firmware.

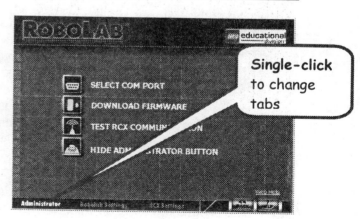

Figure 1.15
Administrator tab.

The **ROBOLAB Settings** tab allows you to add or delete new themes (program groups) and to set the default program paths.

Single-click to toggle between Programmer and Investigator settings

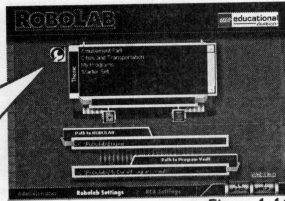

Figure 1.16
ROBOLAB settings tab.

In ROBOLAB version 2.5.0 and earlier, user programs must be stored in the Program Vault directory in order to be opened from within ROBOLAB. If you prefer to store your programs elsewhere (such as a floppy disk or c:\my documents) make sure to change the Program Vault directory.

The **RCX Settings** tab allows you to change several default RCX settings and poll the RCX for current battery level and firmware version. There are three settings which can be adjusted: the IR power setting, the lock on programs 1 and 2, and the powerdown time.

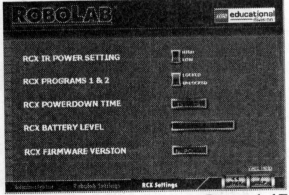

Figure 1.17
RCX Settings tab.

- **IR power setting**: the low setting will not broadcast as far as the high setting but will save battery power. A high setting may be useful for RCX to RCX communication but will consume more battery power.
- **Program 1 and 2 locks**: program slots 1 and 2 by default are locked, meaning you cannot overwrite them. This setting can be used to unlock the program slots 1 and 2, which can be useful if you are trying to store more than 3 custom programs. This setting can also be used to lock one of your custom programs by first unlocking slots 1 and 2, downloading your program to one of these slots, and then locking them again. Good for safeguarding a program you know works!
- **Powerdown time**: this sets the amount of inactive time the RCX will wait before turning itself off. The default time is 15 minutes. You may want to adjust this to a lower setting to conserve battery power.

If you try to download a program to slot 1 or 2 while they are locked, the program will be downloaded to slot 3, overwriting any program in slot 3 in the process.

1.5.2 Programmer

From the Programmer window you can access both the Pilot and Inventor programming modes.

Pilot mode uses program templates to create programs that always compile but are limited in complexity.

In **Inventor** mode you use a graphical programming interface to create programs limited only by your imagination.

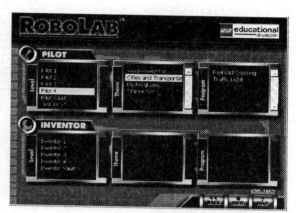

Figure 1.18
The Programmer main window.

1.5.3 Investigator

In Investigator mode, you can create programs that make use of the data acquisition capabilities of the RCX. You also have access to advanced programming and data analysis tools.

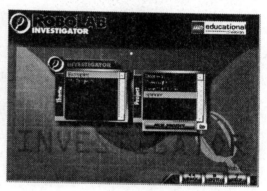

Figure 1.19
The Investigator main window.

1.5.4 ROBOLAB Version 2.5.4

This book was specifically written for the latest version of ROBOLAB, which is currently version 2.5.4. So naturally, we are assuming that's the version you have installed. With that said, however, most of the information in this book can be used for earlier versions as well.

ROBOLAB versions 1.0 and 1.5 started it all but only had Pilot and Inventor programming modes. In version 2.0, Investigator mode was added to exploit the data acquisition capabilities of the RCX.

More recently, version 2.5 was created to take full advantage of the new RCX firmware. It added camera support and advanced control. Version 2.5.2 fixed some minor bugs in version 2.5 and added the training missions. Version 2.5.4 uses the new LabVIEW 7.0 engine. Because of this change, Investigator programs written in 2.5.4 cannot be opened in earlier versions of ROBOLAB, but version 2.5.4 can open all older file types.

You can download patches (bug fixes) for ROBOLAB at http://www.ceeo.tufts.edu/ROBOLABatceeo/.

1.6 Design Skills

You may have played with LEGO® bricks as a child, but if you are like most of our students, you are bound to find out that contemporary LEGO® bricks are not quite like the ones you used to play with. There are lots of strange looking pieces and a myriad of ways to put them together, some better than others.

In this section, we've compiled a series of hints and tips on how to build with the LEGO® Mindstorms kit. In doing so, we've used <u>many</u> references for inspiration. For those interested, we suggest the following references: the LEGO® Mindstorms Constructopedia (versions 1.0, 1.5, and 2.0); the LEGO® Extreme Creatures Constructopedia, the LEGO® RoboSports Constructopedia, *Robotic Explorations* by Martin; *Building Robots with LEGO Mindstorms* by Ferrari, Ferrari, and Hempel; *Jim Sato's LEGO Mindstorms* by Sato; *LEGO Mindstorms Idea Book* by Nagata; and *Creative Projects with LEGO Mindstorms* by Erwin.

1.6.1 Tips for Building with LEGO® Bricks

Before we get into the details, let's establish some of the nomenclature for LEGO® bricks. Clockwise from the top, left in Figure 1.20 we have a 2x4 plate, 1x6 plate, a 1x5 throw arm, a 1x6 beam, a 1x2 axle brick, and a 2x4 brick.

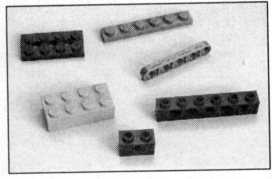

Figure 1.20
Common LEGO® bricks.

Just as bricks and plates are denoted by the number of studs, LEGO® axles are referred to by their length in studs. Figure 1.21 illustrates axles of length 4, 6, and 8.

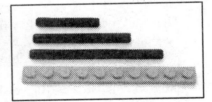

Figure 1.21
LEGO® axles with lengths 4, 6 and 8.

You may have noticed that a 1x1 LEGO® brick is not a cube – it is slightly taller than it is wide. In fact it is exactly 6/5 (1.2) times taller than wide. If we designate the width of a 1x1 brick as the standard Unit, then the height is 1.2 Units.

You may also have noticed that takes 3 LEGO® plates to equal the height of one brick. Thus, a plate is 0.4 Units thick (i.e., 1.2 ÷ 3). Doing a little math, it's pretty easy to see that the height of 1 brick + 2 plates equals 2.0

Figure 1.22
A 1x1 LEGO brick is 1 Unit wide and 1.2 Units tall.

Units. Likewise, 3 bricks + 1 plate = 4.0 Units and 5 bricks = 6.0 Units.

The somewhat strange LEGO® brick dimensions turns out to be the key in understanding how to connect vertical LEGO® beams to your creations. The vertical spacing between holes has to be an integral number of our LEGO® Units in order for the holes to line up. Figure 1.23 illustrates assemblies with 2, 4, and 6 Units.

Why use vertical beams? The great modularity of LEGO® bricks also is their largest drawback – they tend to fall apart easily. Strengthening LEGO® structures with vertical beams is commonly referred to as **bracing**. To build a strong robot, which is very important in head-to-head competitions, you will need to get proficient at bracing structures.

Figure 1.24 shows several additional methods for bracing your LEGO® creations. Note that the cam is the only piece that comes in the ROBOLAB Team Challenge kit that can be used to brace beams stacked directly on top of each other.

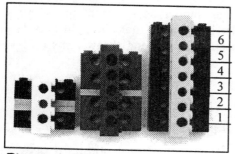

Figure 1.23
Vertical LEGO® spacing: 2 Units (left),
4 Units (middle), and 6 Units (right).

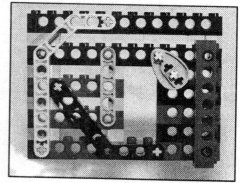

Figure 1.24
Bracing methods.

In addition to bracing, it is also a good idea to use at least 2 studs to join LEGO® bricks. As depicted in Figure 1.25 overlapping bricks by only one stud (left) can lead to structures which can twist and deform. Much better is to overlap by at least 2 studs, as shown on the right.

Figure 1.25
Building stiff LEGO® structures.

And while we're on the subject of building strong structures, we should talk about the plethora of connectors available: pins, bushes and joiners. Figure 1.26 is a photograph of the more common pins. In the top row from left to right: long friction pin, friction pin, pin, ¾ pin, ½ pin, and axle pin. Bottom row: long axle pin, long pin w/bush, bush, ½ bush, and double pin. Figure 1.27 shows the more common LEGO® joiners. From left to right: axle joiner, perpendicular axle-pin joiner, perpendicular axle joiner, perpendicular axle-axle pin joiner, long perpendicular axle-pin joiner, #1, #2, #3, #5 and #6 joiners.

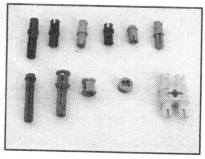

Figure 1.26
LEGO connector pins and
bushes.

Figure 1.27. LEGO® axle and pin joiners.

What is the difference between the black friction pins and light gray pins in Figure 1.26? The black friction pins are slightly larger in diameter than the gray pins, which makes them good for forming rigid connections. For example, in Figure 1.23 we used the black friction pins to hold the assemblies together. The gray pins being slightly smaller make good pin joints for when rotation is desirable as shown on the right in Figure 1.28. Similarly, the dark gray ¾ pins are slight smaller in diameter than the light gray ½ pins, which makes the ¾ pins good pivots for connecting beams and throw arms (1/2 width beams) as shown on the left in Figure 1.28.

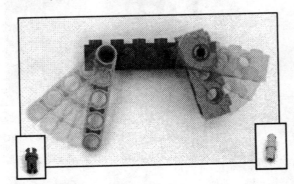

Figure 1.28
Dark gray ¾ pins and light gray pins are used as pivots between beams and throw arms (left) and beams (right) respectively.

In addition to bracing and pivots, being able to build sideways at right angles is also a handy skill. Figure 1.29 shows two methods for doing this. On the right we have used a right angle plate and on the left we have employed a few light gray ½ pins. The configuration on the left works because the stud end of the ½ pin has the same dimensions as the studs on the top of a standard brick. Neat, eh?

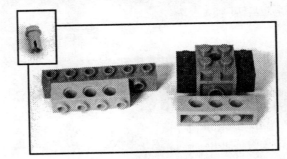

Figure 1.29
Two methods for building at right angles.

1.6.2 Gears and Axles

A thorough knowledge of gears and axles is also crucial to building a LEGO® robot. At full power, the standard LEGO® motor (Table 1.1) spins at approximately 350 rev/min, which may be fine for some designs but is probably too fast for most applications. Gears are used to change the rotational speed (rev/min) and torque between shafts or axles.

Figure 1.30. Common LEGO® Gears (left to right):
Top row: 40T spur, 24T spur, 16T spur, 8T spur, differential
Middle row: 24T crown, 24T double bevel, 12T double bevel, 12T bevel
Bottom row: 24T clutch, linear rack, worm, 16T idler, 4T axle, 8T knob.

Strictly speaking, an axle is not a gear, but we have used them as 4 tooth gears in a pinch. Likewise, the 8T knob is not meant to be a gear but can be used if necessary.

Figure 1.31. Types of gears.
Left to right: crown, bevel, spur and double bevel. Only the 12T bevel gear is ½ a Unit thick; all the other gears are 1 Unit thick.

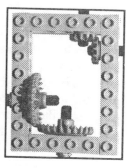

Figure 1.32. Turning corners.
Both crown and bevel gears are used to transfer power between two axles that are perpendicular to each other.

Turning corners is only one use for gears. More commonly, engineers use gears to trade **torque** for **angular velocity**. If you are not familiar with these *engineering* terms, you can think of torque as the twisting force on a gear or axle and the angular velocity as the rotational speed (e.g. revolutions per minute). For example, you apply torque with your hand to turn a doorknob or a screwdriver. When you ride your bicycle, the wheels spin around at a certain angular velocity while your bicycle moves forward at a certain linear velocity.

If we ignore friction (which isn't always such a good assumption, but we'll proceed anyway), we can express the relationship between the product of **number of teeth**, n, and angular velocity, ω, at one gear to the number of teeth and angular velocity of a second gear as:

$$n_1\omega_1 = n_2\omega_2 \qquad \text{(eq. 1.1)}$$

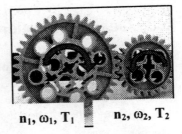

$$n_1, \omega_1, T_1 \qquad n_2, \omega_2, T_2$$

Figure 1.33
Gear relationships

If the big gear is driving the little gear, this is called "gearing up" because the small gear will spin faster than the big gear. Conversely, when a little gear is driving a big gear, this called "gearing down." As shown in figure 1.33, the 40T gear will spin 0.6 times as fast as the 24T gear.

There is also an equation that relates the product of the **torque**, T, and **angular velocity**, ω, at one gear to the torque and angular velocity of a second gear. The torque and angular velocity of two mating gears are related by the following equation:

$$T_1\omega_1 = T_2\omega_2 \qquad \text{(eq. 1.2)}$$

This equation turns out to be quite important for engineers. It basically says that if you want to increase torque, you have to decrease angular velocity. Likewise, if you want to increase angular velocity, you have to decrease torque. Thus, if we wanted to make a car that could climb a really steep hill, we would choose gears such that the wheels are spinning very slowly (low angular velocity, high torque). This same combination would be good for a SumoBot that would have a lot of "pushing power." Combining Equations 1.1 and 1.2 leads to:

$$T_1 n_2 = T_2 n_1 \qquad \text{(eq. 1.3)}$$

Since $n_1 = 40$ and $n_2 = 24$, the torque on the little gear's axle will be 0.6 times the torque on the big gear's axle in Figure 1.33.

Figure 1.34. Gear ratios.
Both arrangements shown use 8T and 24T gears.
LEFT: low speed, high torque. The output shaft on the bottom will turn 1/3 as fast as the motor. Because the arrangement can produce a lot of torque, we've used the white clutch gear to prevent stalling the motor (which drains the batteries very fast).
RIGHT: high speed, low torque. The output shaft spins 3 times as fast as the motor but will produce very little torque.

Figure 1.35. *Gear radii and gear trains.*
The 40T, 24T, and 8T gears are 2.5, 1.5, and 0.5 Units in radius respectively. When used together, their centers are an integer number of Units apart and can be easily meshed on a single LEGO® beam. Conversely the 16T gear (not shown) has a radius of 1.0 Units and, thus, will only mate to another 16T gear when used on a single LEGO® beam.

Using Eqn. 1.1, the 8T gear will spin 3 times as fast as the 24T and 5 times as fast as the 40T gear. Note the 24T gear will spin in the opposite direction as the others. The 8T gear will require 1/5 the amount of torque to turn as the 40T gear according to Eqn 1.3.

Figure 1.36. *Compound gear trains.*
On axle #2 we have used both a 24T and an 8T gear. In doing so we have created two joined gear trains, one between the axles 1 and 2 and the second between axles 2 and 3. This is called a **compound gear train**. Using Eqn 1.1 we find that $\omega_1 = (^{24}/_8)\omega_2$, thus, the 8T gear on axle #1 will spin 3 times faster then the 24T on axle #2. Both the 8T and the 24T gears on axle #2 will spin at the same angular velocity since they share the same axle. Again using Eqn 1.1, $\omega_2 = (^{40}/_8)\omega_3$. Combining these results we find that the 8T gear on axle #1 spins 15 times faster than the 40T gear or $\omega_1 = 15\omega_3$.

Using Eqn 1.3 twice, we also find that $T_1 = (^1/_{15})T_3$.

Figure 1.37. *Too much torque.*
Here's a good argument for using the white clutch gear. Through the use of compound gear trains, it is not very

difficult to get an axle which is spinning extremely slowly and, thus, capable of producing a lot of torque. In this figure, the LEGO® axle was obviously subjected to more torque than it could handle.

Figure 1.38. *Worm gears.*
Worm gears are a special type of gear in which the axles are perpendicular to one another. The worm gear is a 1 tooth gear and is commonly used to greatly reduce the angular velocity and greatly increase torque. Another feature about a worm gear is that the worm gear can drive the pinion (the spur gear), but the pinion cannot drive the worm gear - it binds up.

LEGO® makes a neat little gearbox (right), but it's also fairly easy to build one yourself if you want to use a worm gear. As shown, the worm gear will spin 24 times slower than the spur gear.

Figure 1.39. Aligning multiple worm gears.
If you want to stack several worm gears in a row, make sure you have the orientation correct or it won't work. In the figure we have shown a correctly (top) and incorrectly (bottom) aligned pair of worm gears. It's hard to see, but the pair on the bottom don't quite line up correctly in the center.

Figure 1.40. Linear motion parallel to axle.
The worm gear can be used to convert rotational motion into linear motion. Each complete revolution of the axle will advance the rack one tooth. Notice that the rack will move parallel to the axle when a worm gear is used.

Figure 1.41. Linear motion perpendicular to axle.
Linear motion can also be accomplished with a rack and pinion set up. Unlike the worm gear, the motion is both perpendicular to the axle and much faster.

Figure 1.42. The differential.
The differential is unique in that it is a gear train with 3 input/output axles. In your car, axle 1 would be driven by the motor and the wheels would be connected to axles 2 and 3. The differential allows the two wheels to spin at different velocities as your car goes around a corner (the outside wheel must spin faster since it travels a farther distance). The book, *The Way Things Work*, and the accompanying website (www.waythingswork.com) provide an excellent description of a differential.

Figure 1.43. Pulleys and belts.
Pulleys act very much like gears with the exception that slipping may occur between the belt and the pulley. One of the biggest advantages of using pulleys is that the various sizes and elasticity of the belts affords a lot of flexibility in locating the axles. You are not restricted to spacing pulleys an integral number of Units apart, as is the case with gears. Eqn 1.1 works if you replace the number of teeth, n, with the diameter, d, of the pulley. Eqn 1.2 holds true up until the belt starts to slip on one of the pulleys.

NOTE: Belts are NOT rubber bands. They are not intended to be stretched very much and will break easily if stretched even moderate amounts.

Stalling a motor will drain the batteries FAST. To prevent stalling a motor you may want to use pulleys and belts instead of gears. The 24T clutch can also be used (figure 1.30)

1.6.3 Getting Around on Wheels

Let's now turn our attention to the art of moving around. The two most basic methods of building robots that move are to use either wheels or legs. Creating robots with wheels is much easier for most people, so we'll start there first.

Figure 1.44. Common LEGO® wheels and tank tread.
LEGO® provides a literal plethora of wheels to work with. Shown here are some of the wheels that are commonly found in Mindstorms kits.

Figure 1.45. Tank treads.
Tank treads are commonly used for locomotion. The typical setup involves using a 16T spur gear inside the white tread hub. The upper photo shows an 8T spur gear mounted on the motor output shaft driving a 24T spur gear. The 16T spur gear is mounted on the same shaft as the 24T gear.

Vehicles that use two tank treads can turn by spinning the treads in the opposite direction. This is commonly called "skid steering."

Figure 1.46. Triangle tank treads.
Here's an alternative arrangement that uses three tread hubs. It also makes a nice conveyor belt.

Figure 1.47. Four wheel drive.
The biggest drawback of the skid steering is that it has a lot of friction and, as a result, tends to be very slow. However, the tank treads can be replaced with closely spaced wheels, which results in a very maneuverable and fast method of locomotion. It's still skid steering, but it's better than tank treads.

Figure 1.48. Skid steering.
Turning the motors in opposite directions results in a robot that turns on the spot (zero turning radius).

Figure 1.49. Turning on the left motor while stopping the right will result in right turn that pivots about the right wheels.

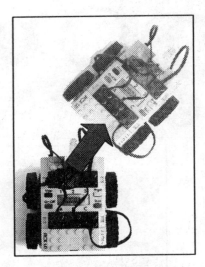

Figure 1.50. Running the left motor faster than the right results in a large radius right turn.

Figure 1.51. Caster wheels.
Caster wheels are the type of swiveling wheels on the front of a shopping cart. Caster wheels are useful for making two wheel drive robots. Several typical arrangements are shown.

Figure 1.52. Friction button.

Even better yet, the caster wheel can be completely replaced with a friction button and only two wheels are needed for the car.

Figure 1.53. Sample two wheel chassis.

This figure shows top and bottom views of a simple two wheel chassis that uses two friction buttons for balance. Because the wheels are connected directly to the motors, this vehicle is very quick.

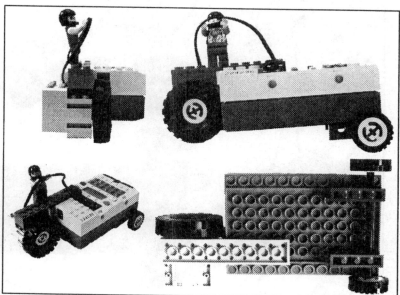

Figure 1.54. The 9-piece car.

This figure shows three orthogonal views (back, side, and bottom) and a 3D-view (lower left) of a simple car we use all the time. This car can be built with only nine pieces, not including the RCX, motor, wire lead and mini-fig (which is optional, but cool). The car can be built in less than 5 minutes regardless of prior LEGO® experience. You can use different size wheel combinations to make the car go slower or faster.

Figure 1.55. Another easy car.

This figure shows a variation of the 9-piece car. It also uses only a handful of pieces, but this variation uses a 24:8 (or 3:1) gear ratio to make the car move much slower. It would be easy to exchange the gears and make a car that is really fast. This car is one of our personal favorites because it is so easy to build.

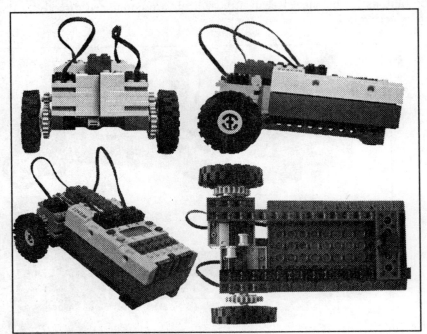

Figure 1.56. Simple two wheel car.

This figure shows yet another variation of the 9-piece car. This time we've used two motors so that the car can turn (for a line follower, for example). A simple friction button supports the front of the car. This car also has a 3:1 gear ratio so that it moves reasonably slow. The motors are offset so that the axles can be supported on both ends, which increases the structural soundness of the design.

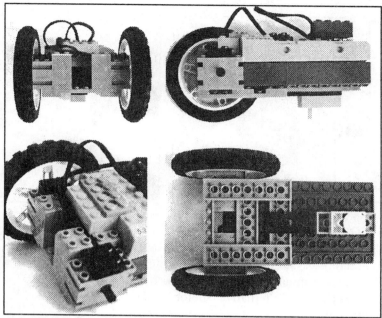

Figure 1.57. Another two wheel chassis.
This figure shows three orthogonal views and a detail view of the motor mounts for another simple two wheel chassis. Again a friction button (white) is used for balance.

Figure 1.58. One last steering method.
This figure shows one last method for steering a vehicle. It uses a motor to drive a rack-and-pinion steering mechanism. The steering motor can be controlled by the RCX or, if you want to actually drive it around by hand, by another motor. The motor attached to the 40T green gear acts as a generator, which causes the motor on the car to turn. Makes for a fun remote controlled car.

Figure 1.59. Belt Drive.
Unlike gear trains, pulley and belts allow for a variety of arrangements because the belts are flexible (don't stretch them too far). Pulley and belt drives also don't require very rigid motor mounting. Belts also have the advantage of being twistable, so that two axles don't have to be parallel.

Figure 1.60. Mounting motors.

The LEGO® motors are surprisingly powerful. Mounting a motor securely can be accomplished with the 1x2 motor mount plates as shown in the upper two figures. An alternative motor mount, shown on the right, utilizes 2x6 plates both above and below the motor.

Figure 1.61. One motor turning.

If you use two motors for driving, that doesn't leave many options for claws. One solution to this dilemma is the use of the differential. As shown, one motor is used for both driving and turning. When the car goes forward (to the right) it drives straight. When it backs up, the ratchet locks the bottom right wheel and the car turns.

Figure 1.62. Output selector.

In this photo, we've used the differential and 2 ratchets, like the one shown in Figure 1.61, to ensure both axles never spin at the same time. When the motor spins forward, only one of the output axles turns. Reversing the motor direction causes the other output axle to turn. Viola, you now have two outputs with one motor! We've seen plans for a 5 output selector, but it's a bit beyond the scope of this book.

1.6.4 Getting Around on Legs

Vehicles with wheels are more prevalent than vehicles that utilize legs, mainly because legs tend to be more difficult to implement. However, we have found that it's the robots with legs that people find most intriguing. To help you develop your leg-building skills, this section will cover some of the more common techniques used.

An important concept to remember is that when a leg lifts off the ground, the robot must either balance on the other leg(s) or have some kind of support. In figure 1.63, we have employed stationary supports behind the legs. On the other hand, in figure 1.64 we haven't used any supports and the robot will roll on the gears resulting in an awkward combination of walking and rolling.

Figure 1.63. Basic legs.

The legs will appear to move in an elliptical path. Supports must be used to keeps the robot balanced when the feet lift off the ground.

Figure 1.64. Variation on the basic legs.

Here we've introduced a cosmetic change to the basic legs. These legs behave the same as the legs in the previous figure, but look very different. No supports are shown, but must be used for balance.

Figure 1.65. Four-bar linkage legs.
Slightly more complicated than the basic legs, four-bar linkage legs can be used to create a wide variety of leg motion. Here we use a parallelogram-type design. The foot will move in a circular path. The gears on the back keep the links synchronized.

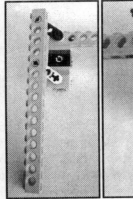

Figure 1.66. Unequal link lengths.
This four-bar linkage design utilizes 4 links of different lengths (the 40T gear serves as one of the links). The resulting motion is elliptical.

Figure 1.67. Reciprocating legs.
This leg design is similar to the piston-cam mechanism in most cars. The "foot" follows an elliptical path. The length of the leg, the diameter of the gear, and the distance to the brace all affect the foot path. At least three legs are needed for each side of a robot for balance. The Internet is filled with various hexapod (6-legged) robot designs based on this basic format.

Figure 1.68. Hexapod.
To build a hexapod, timing of the legs is critical. With each step, the robot must lift up 3 legs at a time. In this figure, only the center leg is lifted. On the opposite side of the robot, only the center leg would be down (2 legs off the ground).

Figure 1.69. Putting it together.

As an example of putting it all together, we've constructed a simple eight-legged robot. Notice the vertical bracing on the inside of the chassis (far left figure). This robot lifts 4 legs at the same time (2 on each side).

Figure 1.70. Best legs contest.

Here are some ideas for decorating your robot's legs.

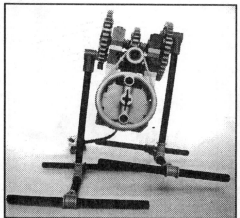

Figure 1.71. Balancing robot.

Although we've left off the RCX, this simple single motor robot can balance on one leg as it lifts the other. The result is a very realistic gait. A worm gear has been used to gear down the motor output.

1.6.5 Bumpers and Sensors

Being able to make a robot that reacts to its environment is one of things that makes the Mindstorms product line so interesting. In this section, we present some ideas for bumpers using the touch and light sensors.

Figure 1.72. Simple bumper.
The figure shows a simple bumper that uses a single axle to activate the touch sensor.

Figure 1.73. Guided bumper.
This simple bumper uses two axles as guide pins to prevent twisting and turning. Note the ½ bush used on the lower guide axle to retain the bumper.

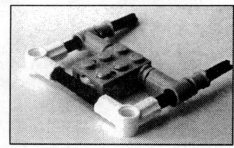

Figure 1.74. Guided bumper #2.
Here's another simple bumper that uses an axle passing through the axle hole in the touch sensor and two #1 pin joiners as guides.

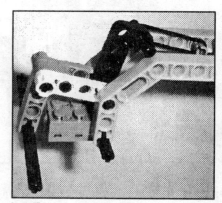
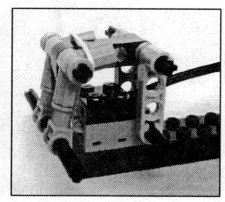

Figure 1.75. Lever bumpers.
The figures show two examples of lever-arm type bumpers. Both bumpers utilize rubber bands to hold them open rather than relying on the internal spring inside the touch sensor.

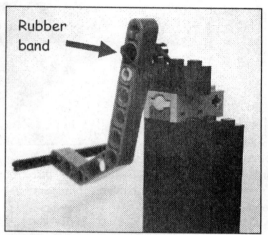 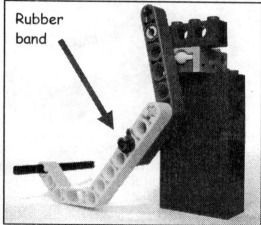

Figure 1.76. Lever arm bumpers.
Left: a lever arm activates the touch sensor when it swings back. A rubber band is used to return the arm to the neutral position shown.
Right: a bumper that reacts to both bumps and dips. A rubber band between the two arms provides the return force.

Figure 1.77. Front Bumper.
This figure shows the right side of a lever arm bumper that can be used on the front of a vehicle. A rubber band stretched between the two lever arms keeps them open. The 2x4 black plate serves as a positive stop for the lever arm.

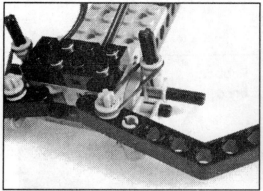  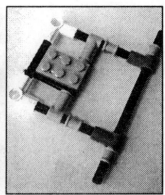

Figure 1.78. Normally closed bumpers.

Most bumpers rely on the touch sensor being pressed to activate. These three bumper designs rely on the touch sensor being released to activate. All three bumpers rely on a small rubber band to keep the touch sensor normally closed.

Figure 1.79. Light sensor bumper.

Need an extra touch sensor? Here's how to use a light sensor as a touch sensor. This only seems to work well for dark colored lever arms.

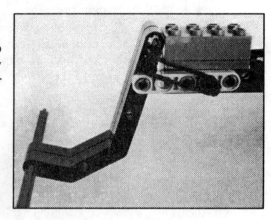

Figure 1.80. Light rotation sensor.

Here we've used the light sensor to measure rotation. With six positions, this sensor has a resolution of 60 degrees.

Figure 1.81. Touch rotation sensor.

The touch sensor can also be used to sense rotation. Here a cam is used to activate the touch sensor once per revolution.

Figure 1.82.

Generator sensor.

No the motor isn't connected to the wrong port in this picture. By using a motor as a generator, you can make a crude speed sensor. Note, that the motor can easily generate 9V, but the RCX can only read in a maximum of 5 Volts.

1.6.6 Multiplexing Sensors

Connecting more than one sensor to a single input port is called *multiplexing*. Students always end up running out of sensor ports to use, so multiplexing would alleviate this problem. There are several ways to connect two or more sensors to a single input port if you are willing to be a little creative and understand the basic operation of the LEGO® sensors.

Figure 1.83. Two touch sensors.

By connecting two (or more) touch sensors to the same input port, pressing either touch sensor will register as a press. In engineering terms, this arrangement is a logical OR gate (i.e. pressing the left OR the right will register as a touch).

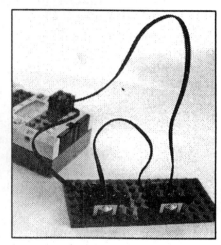

Figure 1.84.

Logical AND using two touch sensors

As documented on Gasperi's website (which is a VERY good one, located at: www.plazaearth.com/usr/gasperi/lego.htm), a fellow named Tom Schumm figured out the arrangement shown in Figure 1.84, which is equivalent to a logical AND gate, meaning a press is not registered unless the left AND right touch sensors are pressed at the same time.

Figure 1.85.
Light and touch sensor.
If the input port is setup as a light sensor, then it is possible to stack a touch sensor on top of the light sensor. When the touch sensor is pressed, the port will register a light value of 100. Since a light sensor value of 100 never occurs in normal use, you can monitor for this special condition.

Figure 1.86. Touch sensor schematic.
The standard LEGO® touch sensor is a switch in series with a resistor. When the yellow button is pressed, the switch is closed. The 500 Ohm resistor causes a small voltage drop when the switch is closed. If we could

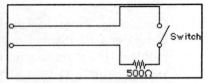

somehow manage to change the resistor value, then the voltage drop would change. If each touch sensor had a different voltage drop, then we could connect them to the same input port and look for the different voltage drops corresponding to each of the touch sensors. If only real life were so simple!

Figure 1.87. Two touch sensors.
In this case, we're in luck because it appears LEGO® has unknowingly provided us with touch sensors with different resistor values! On the bottom of each touch sensor there is a two-digit code (probably the manufacturing lot number). Touch sensors with different lot numbers have different resistor values. You may have to test a couple, but it's pretty easy to find a pair (or triplet) of touch sensors that have very different resistor values. This arrangement only works well if the touch sensors are pressed and held in for at least a second (i.e. rapid presses won't be registered as different).

In order to make use of this, you need to know how to set up the input port to use the **Sensor Adapter** functions to read a generic, unpowered sensor instead of a touch sensor. This is covered briefly in section 2.7.5 and an example using two touch sensors is shown in section 3.2.3.

Figure 1.88. Two touch sensors and a lamp brick.
If you are unlucky enough to only have touch sensors with the same lot number, then you will be glad to know that LEGO® has provided us with a resistor in the form of a lamp element (see Table 1.1). Figure 1.88 shows two touch sensors, one having been modified with a pair of lamp elements to add to some resistance.

Again, in order to take advantage of this arrangement, you will have to use the **Sensor**

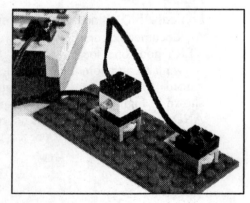

Adapter functions. Additionally, the lamp element doesn't add much resistance, so the difference between the sensors will be small (the lamps may change the reading by 5 whereas we've found touch sensors which result in differences of more than 100).

Figure 1.89. CyberMaster touch sensors.

The LEGO® CyberMaster kit has been discontinued for quite some time, but you can still find them occasionally on auction websites. If you can get a CyberMaster kit, you will find it includes three touch sensors with different resistor values. Thus, all three can be connected to a single input port. Note that while they are compatible with the RCX, the CyberMaster touch sensors are slightly different in operation since the resistor is in parallel with the switch instead of in series as in Figure 1.86 (i.e. the resistor spans the two wires instead of being inline with only one of the wires). Nonetheless, it is a pretty easy way to connect three touch sensors to a single input port.

Figure 1.90. Third party multiplexers

By far the easiest way to multiplex sensors is to simply buy a sensor multiplexer that is sold by many third party (i.e.; non-LEGO®) companies such as www.techno-stuff.com or www.hitechnic.com.

1.6.7 Stepper Motors

Wouldn't it be nice to have a motor that rotated exactly once (360°) each time you turned it on? Wouldn't that make turning *exactly* 90° or driving *exactly* 3 inches forward easier?

At first, you will probably try to use time. Only after having tried (and failed) several times are you likely to review this section more carefully.

What you've probably found out (the hard way) is that the LEGO® motors are not very consistent. You could always use a LEGO® rotation sensor or build your own encoder (Figure 1.80),. but this has the disadvantage of using up some of your input ports. Engineers use a **stepper motor** when accurate positioning is required. A **stepper**

Figure 1.91. Stepper motor. Due to the tension in the rubber band, the motor will make only whole rotations when the motor is switched on and off quickly.

motor will turn a specific angle each time it is turned on.

One of the keys to making a good stepper motor is that you need to use a rubber band (not a belt), that is strong enough to overcome the motor. Using the *float* instead of the *stop* function is also a must when using stepper motors (see section 2.7.1).

Figure 1.92. Stepper motor #2.

We've left the motor out of the photo but this stepper motor is extremely simple. A small bias is required, meaning you need to keep the motor on at a low power level to keep the axle from turning.

Figure 1.93. Stepper motor #3.

This stepper motor doesn't require any motor bias. Since there are 4 positions, each pulse of the motor will result in a 90° turn of the axle. In our tests, we only had to turn on the motor for about 0.05 seconds (always use a *float* instead of a *stop* to turn off the motor).

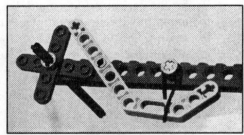

Figure 1.94. Stepper motor #4.

Another simple 90° stepper motor.

Figure 1.95. Stepper motor #5.

This stepper motor has six positions giving it a 60° increment.

Figure 1.96.

Simple car with stepper motor.

Here's an example of a car with a stepper motor. We've taken the car from Figure 1.55 and added a four position stepper, like the one shown in Figure 1.93. When programmed correctly (see section 3.2.2), the rear wheel will move exactly ¼ a revolution each time the motor is pulsed for 0.1 seconds.

1.6.8 Grippers and Claws

Now that you know how to move around and sense that you've bumped into something, we will discuss how to grab onto things. There are two main types of claws/grippers: motor actuated and over-the-center actuated. Motor activated claws use, not surprisingly, a motor to provide the gripping force. Over-the-center grippers use a rubber band that is triggered by some kind of switch.

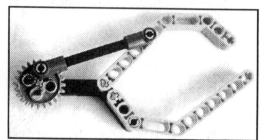

Figure 1.97. Basic gripper.
The typical gripper uses a gear or cam, powered by a motor, to open and close the claws.

Figure 1.98. Scissor claw.
This claw uses the classic scissor mechanism actuated by a 40T gear. Changing the lever arm lengths will affect the range of motion of the jaws.

Figure 1.99. Modified scissor gripper.
This gripper is mechanically equivalent to the scissor claw, but uses lever arms instead of beams. We also used the 24T white clutch gear so that the motor isn't stalled when we grab things (stalling a motor drains the batteries very fast).

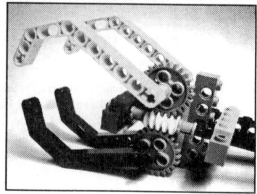

Figure 1.100. Worm-gear claw.
This claw is actuated by a worm gear. The two spur gears also serve to keep the upper and lower jaws synchronized. Because of the high gear reduction, this jaw can produce a lot of gripping force to destroy your opponents!

Figure 1.101. Synchronized gripper.
This gripper has two unique features. First, it uses 3 gears to synchronize the motion of the upper and lower jaws (far right). Second, it uses a rubber band to hold the gripper either open (center) or closed (left).

Figure 1.102. Over-the-center claw.
With an over-the-center claw, the jaws are held open by a rubber band. A throw arm acting against a pin keeps the jaws from opening too far. The claw closes when the trigger is pressed. This causes the upper jaw to rotate slightly and then the rubber band snaps the jaws closed.

Figure 1.103. Another OTC claw.
This over-the-center claw is a much cleaner design and utilizes a linear-motion trigger. Again, the rubber band changes from holding the jaw open to snapping it closed when the trigger is pressed.

1.6.9 Check your progress

We've covered a whole bunch of material already. If you haven't done so already, this is a good time to stop and evaluate your building skills. Try constructing one of the simple cars shown in Figures 1.54, 1.55, 1.56 or 1.57. Then try adding a bumper, like the one shown in Figures 1.72-1.78. Like everything in life, it takes practice to get good at something. Building with LEGO® bricks is not exception.

1.7 Creativity & Aesthetics

Creativity and aesthetics are often overlooked in engineering, but both play a crucial role in the design process (see section 1.3). First off, creative thinking goes a long way in the search for alternative solutions. Secondly, the truth of the matter is that how well a product does in the market is often more governed by its form than its function. While we don't support designing for looks alone, it certainly cannot hurt to have it in mind during the design process. Furthermore, creative designs typically cost less and do better in the marketplace than non-creative ones. For an example of how creative thinking can affect a product, just look at the multitude of tooth brushes that have recently hit the marketplace (note, the function of the toothbrush hasn't changed since it was first invented).

And, contrary to popular belief, both creativity and aesthetics are not innate skills reserved for only the "artistic." There are several good references that discuss structured creative thinking processes such as **brainstorming**. The point being, you can learn creativity just like any other skill. All you need is a little practice and room to play.

The Art of Innovation by Tom Kelly is very good at providing some insight as to the importance of creativity and aesthetics. The book discusses the way IDEO, probably the most famous "innovative" design firm in the world, goes about its business. IDEO is responsible, among other things, for the original Apple computer mouse, the Polaroid i-Zone instant camera, and the Palm V personal digital assistant. IDEO is a very successful company (by almost any measure of success) because it fosters and rewards creative thinking and demands attention to aesthetics from its employees. And by the way, IDEO is also largely responsible for starting the revolution in toothbrush design.

1.7.1 Creative Blocks

So how do you go about thinking creatively, even if you don't consider yourself creative? **Structured creative thinking.** *Conceptual Blockbusting* by James Adams and *A Whack on the Side of the Head* by Roger von Oech are both excellent books that cover techniques for creative thinking. Both books spend a great deal of time emphasizing ways to overcome "creative blocks." Adams defines creative blocks as:

> *"mental walls that block the problem-solver from correctly perceiving a problem or conceiving its solution."*

Creative blocks are necessary for surviving everyday life. The concept of driving on the left hand side of the road in the U.S. may be creative, but not very safe. Seeing someone walking out of a hospital wearing scrubs usually leads to the conclusion that he works at the hospital. We reach this type of decision without all the facts everyday. The truth, however, may be that he is a mental patient trying to escape!

Anyone who has children quickly realizes that children are both extremely creative and extremely accident prone. We think the two go hand in hand. When was the last time you tasted something to determine its function?

Oechs lists ten common creative blocks:
1. Looking for the one "right answer"
2. Being too logical
3. Following the rules
4. Being too practical
5. Believing play is frivolous

6. Sticking to your own area of expertise
7. Being afraid to look foolish
8. Avoiding ambiguity
9. Believing "to err is wrong"
10. Believing you're not creative

Looking for the "right answer" is a great way to stifle creativity because you presume there is only one solution. However, the most obvious solution is usually not the best. Earlier we mentioned the "rule of 7." One way to get a good solution is to think of seven possible solutions and then pick the best one.

Being too logical tends to elicit comments like "that won't work because…" or "that doesn't make sense because…" In order to think creatively, you often have to examine what initially seems outrageous or implausible.

Following the rules is usually a good habit. However, most rules have a gray area and it is these areas which can be exploited to achieve creative solutions. In our class, we encourage as much "cheating" as possible in the design competitions. By interpreting the rules as loosely as possible, you'll have more solutions available to you. However, be forewarned that you always run the risk of being disqualified for breaking the rules!

Work should be fun. A great brainstorming session is always punctuated by lots of laughter. Have fun at the start of the design process. Think of lots of crazy ideas. Then use logic and math (your engineering skills) to reduce those ideas to a workable solution.

Recruiting the opinion of someone from the outside is a great way of spurring creative solutions because they don't know what the "correct" solution is or "how it's always done." Likewise, when you are working outside your area of expertise, you don't know what is and isn't possible. That's one reason why kids can be so creative – they don't know what's impossible!

We mentioned earlier that laughter is a sure sign of a good brainstorming session. It goes without saying this means you have to be comfortable having your ideas laughed at once in a while. It's often the laughable concept that ends up being the best in the end.

Engineering and science disciplines stress eliminating ambiguity – precision is important. However, during the initial design phases, ambiguity is cherished because it doesn't constrain a solution. "Let's use a big shaft" doesn't specify the size of the shaft. Only once the detail design phase starts do we want to start getting that specific.

"You learn from your mistakes." It's okay to make mistakes once in a while. Brainstorming sessions are not about pointing out technical infeasibilities – they are about generating creative solutions.

If you don't truly believe you're creative, you won't be. Everyone can be creative with a little practice.

1.7.2 Structured Creativity

Brainstorming is the most popular form of structured creativity. The goal of the brainstorming session is to generate as many solutions to the problem as possible. A typical brainstorming session only lasts about 5 minutes. The rules for a brainstorming session typically look like the following:

- No criticizing. Don't judge anyone's ideas during the brainstorming session.
- No hesitating. No idea is to be considered too outrageous, ridiculous, or "wacky."
- No holding back because you have "too many" ideas. The more the better.

- No owning of ideas. If you can build upon or improve upon someone else's idea, write it down.
- No sticking to your own field of expertise. Think globally across disciplines.

Brainstorming may be the most common structured creative thinking technique, but it is far from the only one. **List making** in one form or another is also popular technique. For example, if you are trying to find new uses for a brick (the kind used for fireplaces, not the LEGO® ones), listing all its attributes (red, brittle, rough, heavy, etc) and then determining ways to exploit each individual attribute will lead you to lots of "creative" uses. In one of my classes we were brainstorming uses for extra bricks and one student suggested selling them on the Internet at www.protestersupplies.com.

By using some form of structured creative thinking, you can overcome creative blocks. When this happens, a whole new class of solutions is possible. I witnessed a great example of creative thinking (not on my part unfortunately) at a workshop I attended for new faculty. During one part of the workshop we were asked to make a device using LEGO® bricks. I won't get into the specific objectives of the task, but suffice to say it required some creative solutions given the limited assortment of LEGO® bricks we were provided with. Someone on another team got the brilliant idea to cut the teeth off an 8T spur gear to make a watch-like mechanism. The photo shows a gear train with a 40:1 gear ratio that has intermittent motion. The concept of destructively modifying a LEGO® gear never occurred to me. However, once the other team overcame this creative block, a whole new class of solutions was available to them. As you can imagine, this provided them with a distinct competitive advantage because they had a function that nobody else had.

Figure 1.104
Creative modification
of an 8T LEGO gear.

1.8 Additional Resources

Students often ask about the difference between the retail and LEGO® educational versions of the Mindstorms kits. As we mentioned back in section 1.3 (see Figure 1.4), the retail version is the Mindstorms RIS (Robotics Invention System) kits that you can buy at toy stores. It costs about $200 and includes simple RIS programming software. The Mindstorms for Schools kit is sold by LEGO Education and is specifically designed for use with ROBOLAB and has the same $200 price tag.

Figure 1.105. Left: Mindstorms RIS retail version. Right: Mindstorms for Schools version from LEGO® Educational.

There are also a lot of very good websites that you can also visit to get more information. Here are just a few sorted by topic.

1.8.1 The Robotics Academy Video Trainer

If you are trying to learn ROBOLAB on your own, then we highly recommend getting yourself a copy of the **ROBOLAB Video Trainer**, available for about $50 from the Carnegie Mellon Robotics Academy (http://www.rec.ri.cmu.edu/education). It probably isn't for you if you already have some ROBOLAB experience or are learning ROBOLAB as part of a class, but for a ROBOLAB newbie, it is hands-down the best self-help resource currently available for ROBOLAB (with the exception of this book of course).

If you are a K-12 teacher trying to get started with ROBOLAB in your classroom, then we would also recommend seriously considering using one the Robotics Academy curriculum CDs, like the **Robotics Explorer**. Similar to the video trainer, they are great resources, complete with multimedia clips and well planned activities.

1.8.2 Official ROBOLAB Materials and Information

- Official Mindstorms for Schools Website -
  http://www.lego.com/eng/education/mindstorms. This web site features information on ROBOLAB products as well as links to official downloads and support resources.

- Tufts University, the makers of ROBOLAB - **http://www.ceeo.tufts.edu/ROBOLAB**

- Download software patches and other resources at
  http://www.ceeo.tufts.edu/ROBOLABatceeo

- National Instruments, the makers of LabVIEW
  http://www.ni.com/company/robolab.htm

- **Using ROBOLAB**, is the official "user's manual" for ROBOLAB. It's a great resource and reference book and is now available on a CD with ROBOLAB. If you're feeling a bit uncomfortable just diving into this book, then we highly recommend getting a copy of **Using ROBOLAB**.

- **ROBOLAB Quick Start Guide** – download this 25 page document for free at http://www.legoeducationstore.com. It has installation, programming, and building tips.

- ROBOLAB software on CD-ROM retails for about $70. For engineering students, this is a real buy since it includes LabVIEW, which you'll probably need for later classes anyway.

1.8.3 Where to buy

- In the United States, the only place to get ROBOLAB is from the Pitsco LEGO® - Education Store - **http://www.legoeducationstore.com.** The Pitsco LEGO®-Education store is the official retailer of all LEGO® educational materials in the United States. ROBOLAB can be purchased from here by any consumer (teacher, parent, individual etc.)

- LEGO® World Shop – **http://shop.lego.com**

The official LEGO® online store.

- Mondo-tronics, inc – **http://www.robotstore.com**
  Robot Books.com – **http://www.robotbooks.com**
  Two great source of all things robotic

- Unofficial Online LEGO® shops where you can buy extra bricks
  - **http://www.bricklink.com**
  - **http://www.brickshelf.com**

- Unofficial Online shops where you can buy RCX-compatible sensors and outputs:
  - **http://www.hitechnic.com**
  - **http://www.techno-stuff.com**
  - **http://www.mindsensors.com**
  - **http://www.lmsensors.com**

1.8.4 Groups

- LUGNET (Lego Users Group Network) - **http://www.lugnet.com**
  LUGNET has fabulous LEGO® resources ranging from pieces in sets to a wide array of discussion groups on robotics, education, ROBOLAB and more.
    Discussion group on LEGO® education - **http://news.lugnet.com/edu/**
    Discussion group on LEGO® dacta - **http://news.lugnet.com/dacta/**
    Discussion group on LEGO® robotics - **http://news.lugnet.com/robotics/**

- MIT's Epistemology and Learning Lab - **http://el.media.mit.edu/**
  Check out where the whole programmable brick idea came from and see where it might go next.

1.8.5 Resources
- NQC (Not Quite C) - **http://bricxcc.sourceforge.net/nqc/**
  If you want to program the RCX with a C-like syntax then NQC is an excellent alternative to ROBOLAB.

- LEGO® SDK **http://mindstorms.lego.com/sdk/SDK.asp**

- Java **http://lejos.sourceforge.net/**
  New Java interface for programming the RCX

- LegOS, **http://legos.sourceforge.net/**

- NASA's Robotics Education site - **http://robotics.arc.nasa.gov/**

- NASA's LEGO® Data Acquisition and Prototyping System - **http://ldaps.arc.nasa.gov/**
  See the precursor to ROBOLAB and lots of interesting projects.

1.8.6 Examples, Ideas and Cool Projects

- Boulette's Robotics in Luxemburg (**http://www.convict.lu/Jeunes/RoboticsIntro.htm**).
  A fabulous site that features high end robotics and ROBOLAB projects with great

descriptions and the code used. You'll also find information on Ultimate ROBOLAB here, which is the next-generation version of ROBOLAB that makes full use of the RCX by allowing you to write your own firmware with ROBOLAB. Be forewarned, this is not for use by the novice. Ultimate ROBOLAB gives you enough rope to hang yourself! I found myself taking the batteries out the RCX to reset everything a lot.

- Michael Gasperi's excellent page on "extreme mindstorms," including great tips on building sensors - **http://www.plazaearth.com/usr/gasperi/lego.htm**

1.9 References and Further Reading

- Adams, James (2001), **Conceptual Blockbusting: A Guide to Better Ideas**, Perseus Publishing, New York.

- Erwin, Benjamin (2001), **Creative Projects with LEGO Mindstorms**, Addison Wesley, Boston, MA.

- Ferrari, Mario, Ferrari, Giulio, and Hempel, Ralph (2001), **Building Robots with LEGO Mindstorms: The Ultimate Tool for Mindstorms Maniacs**, Syngress, Rockland, MA,

- Petroski, Henry (1992), **To Engineer is Human: The Role of Failure in Successful Design**, Vintage, New York.

- Petroski, Henry (1994), **Design Paradigms: Case Histories of Error and Judgment in Engineering**, Cambridge University Press, Cambridge.

- Petroski, Henry (1994), **The Evolution of Useful Things: How Everyday Artifacts - from Forks and Pins to Paper Clips and Zippers – Came to be as They are**, Vintage, New York.

- Kelly, Tom (2001), **The Art of Innovation: Lessons in Creativity from IDEO, America's Leading Design Firm**, Currency, New York.

- Martin, Fred (2000), **Robotic Explorations: An Introduction to Engineering Through Design**, Prentice Hall, Upper Saddle River, New Jersey.

- Nagata, Joe (2001), **Joe Nagata's LEGO Mindstorms Idea Book**, No Starch Press, San Francisco, CA.

- Papert, Seymour (1999), **Mindstorms: Children, Computers, and Powerful Ideas**, 2nd Ed., Basic Books, New York.

- Sato, Jim (2002), **Jim Sato's LEGO Mindstorms: The Master's Technique**, No Starch, San Francisco, CA.

- von Oech, Roger (1998), **A Whack on the Side of the Head: How you can be more creative**, Warner Business, New York.

1.10 LEGO® Design Challenges

In developing the design challenges for this book, we've assumed you are working together on small teams. By working on small teams, you discuss, argue, and fight about the solutions. This interaction gets you directly involved in the learning process and makes you think about your approach. The instructor becomes more of a facilitator than a teacher.

As for putting the challenges at the beginning of the chapter (with the exception of this first chapter), we realize most students start by reading the problem and then commence scanning the chapter for the equations they need. We've cut to the chase by putting the challenges at the beginning of the chapter and then listed the skills required for each challenge. We've organized the book by skills so you can skip right to the section you need to complete the challenge.

The skills badge approach also has one unique advantage over the traditional problem set. In a "normal" homework set, perhaps 95% of the comments you get back are negative in nature, highlighting your errors. The design challenges are meant to let you show off the skills you have learned, which we think is a much more constructive method of teaching. Plus, its way more fun!

1.10.1   Team Communication

Challenge: Develop oral communication skills by building a LEGO® sculpture aided only by verbal instructions.

Skill Badges: None

Procedures:
Experimental Setup: Each pair of students should receive an identical set of LEGO® bricks.

Robot Design:
- This is an exercise for two people. Check to make sure your LEGO® pieces match identically (size, shape, and color).
- Select one of the people to be the leader for this exercise.
- The two participants should sit back to back.
- The leader should design and construct a LEGO® object (anything he/she wants). As the leader is building the object he/she is to explain to their partner how to assemble the same object using verbal instructions only
- The second partner is not to speak or gesture in any way if there is mis-understanding – no peeking! Example: if the second partner missed the color description s/he is not allowed to say "what color?", or gesture with an elbow to repeat the comment.

The second partner cannot talk or ask questions by any means.

- Once the objects are completed the partners are to face one another and discuss the differences of appearance (if any).

Program: None

Analysis: Answer the following questions:

- How did your team decide who would be the leader?

- Did you feel confident and comfortable during the exercise?

- What were the main reasons for error?

- Did you get better as you went along?

- What might you do differently next time?

- How might you use what you've learned from this exercise in the future?

1.10.2   Drag Race

Challenge: Design and build a vehicle powered only by a rubber band.

Skill Badges: None

Procedures:

Experimental Setup: All that is needed for this project a stopwatch for timing.

Robot Design:
- This is a three-phase, timed in-class design competition.
- Your score will be based upon a combination of time to market and distance traveled.

Phase I:
- You have 30 minutes to design, build and test a rubber-band powered vehicle. The official rubber-bands will be supplied by the instructor.
- The time to market is defined as the time you 'release' your design to the rest of the class. Your vehicle must be on public display at front of class until the competition starts. No modifications are allowed once a design is 'released'. Copying of released designs is encouraged!
- The winner is determined as the longest distance traveled. The distance traveled is defined as distance from the start line to the LEGO® piece closest to the starting line.

Phase II:
- You have 5 minutes to re-design your vehicle. Pay attention to designs that did well!
- The winner is determined as the longest distance traveled.

Phase III:
- You have 5 minutes to re-design you vehicle once more.
  The winner is determined as the longest distance traveled.

Program: None.

Grading:

Your grade will be based 40% on time to market, 40% on distance traveled and 20% on creativity and aesthetics.

Time to market	Distance traveled	Creativity & Aesthetics
A+: First to market.	A+: Moved the farthest	A+: Best of show
A: Within 3 minutes	A: Moves 15+ feet	A: Outstanding
B: Within 5 minutes	B: Moves 10+ feet.	B: Good
C: Within 10 minutes	C: Moves forwards.	C: Okay
D: Within 15 minutes	D: Moves backwards.	D: Nothing special
F: Didn't finish	F: Didn't move	F: Divert your eyes!

This challenge is based on the Biodiometer challenge developed by Prof. Sheppard at Stanford University

1.10.3   South Pointing Chariot

Challenge: Design and build a south pointing chariot. Your cart must navigate a figure-eight course, all the while pointing south.

Skill Badges: None

Procedures:

Experimental Setup: A figure-eight course and a compass are required for this project.

Robot Design: The photo shows a South Pointing Chariot, which was invented in China in the third century AD and is the first known use of a differential gear.

A figure was mounted on the two-wheel carriage which always pointed south, no matter how the carriage turned as it moved. The figure was set to south and then a differential driven by the wheels turned the figure in the opposite direction to the carriage so that it still pointed south.

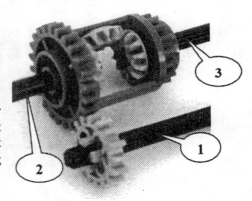

Unlike most gear trains which have only two axles (an input and an output), a differential has 3 axles. In most applications that use a differential, like your car, a motor (the input) turns axle #1 and the wheels (the outputs) are connected to axles #2 and #3. For the south pointing chariot, the wheels will be connected to axles #1 and #3 and the pointer will be connected to axle #2. Try building up just the differential and playing with it to see how it works. Try holding one axle, while turning another.

Program: None

Grading:

Your grade will be based 80% on accuracy and 20% on creativity and aesthetics.

Accuracy	Creativity & Aesthetics
A: Always points south	A+: Best of show
B: Turns the right direction, but doesn't track due south	A: Outstanding
	B: Good
C: Pointer turns	C: Okay
D: You build something with wheels	D: Nothing special
F: You don't show up to class	F: Divert your eyes!

1.10.4　Heavy Lifting

Challenge: Design and build a LEGO® crane.

Skill Badges: None

Procedures:

Experimental Setup: The only specialized components required are various calibrated weights. Your instructor will indicate how the crane is anchored (if at all) to the table.

Robot Design: Gear trains and vertical bracing will be important construction skills to learn.

Program: None

Grading:

Your grade will be based 80% on the weight lifted and 20% on creativity and aesthetics.

Weight lifted	Creativity & Aesthetics
A+: Most lifted	A+: Best of show
A: More than 3 lbs	A: Outstanding
B: 1.0 – 3.0 lbs	B: Good
C: 0.5 – 1.0 lbs	C: Okay
D: Less than 0.5 lbs	D: Nothing special
F: You don't show up to class	F: Divert your eyes!

1.10.5   Crash Test Dummy

Challenge: Design and build a LEGO® car that can survive (not fall apart) a fall from waist high onto a hard floor.

Skill Badges: None

Procedures:
Experimental Setup: No specialized set up needed.

Robot Design: Your team must design and build a LEGO® car that can survive a fall from waist high and not fall apart. For the purpose of this challenge, "waist high" is defined as the height of your waist. Here's one of those rare occasions where being short is an advantage!

Since creativity will be based on the appearance of your car you may want to add people (crash test dummies), headlights, and other amenities. Of course, these are the parts of the car most likely to fall off during the test. Engineering is all about making trade-offs, so you might as well get used to it.

Program: None

Hints: Bracing is the key to building strong LEGO® structures. You should also get used to prototyping – testing early designs before the real test.

WARNING: DO NOT DROP AN RCX AND/OR MOTORS! You'll end up doing significant damage. The short stubby axle on the motor can be sheared off very easily and will render your $25 motor useless.

Grading:

Your grade will be based 80% on performance and 20% on creativity and aesthetics.

Performance	Creativity & Aesthetics
A: Survives the fall totally intact	A+: Best of show
B: Nothing structural breaks off	A: Outstanding
C: Car still rolls, despite missing some parts	B: Good
D: Hits the ground and shatters	C: Okay
F: You don't show up to class	D: Nothing special
	F: Divert your eyes!

1.11 Summary

If you only remember one thing in this chapter, please make it the steps in the design process. If you don't remember them, please go back and look at Figure 1.2. Understanding that problem solving is an iterative process is a key concept that you will need to demonstrate throughout this book as you take on the design challenges and acquire the skill badges.

We'll also take a moment to remind you that the skill badges are really meant to provide you (the student) with a means for evaluating your own progress. Most students think the skill badges are used by the instructor to grade you. However, the instructor will grade you by evaluating your solution to the design challenges. If you didn't learn a particular skill it will be obvious and, more importantly, too late. Thus, it is imperative that you get used to monitoring your own progress so that you can get help before it is too late.

CHAPTER 2
GREEN LEVEL

Skill badges available in this Chapter

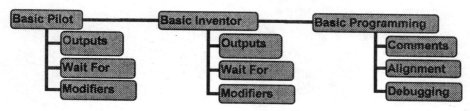

2.1 Green Challenges

The green challenges cover the basic pilot, basic inventor, and basic programming skills.

2.1.1   Going the Distance

Challenge: Using Pilot mode, design, build, and calibrate a car that can travel a specified distance.

Skill Badges: Basic Pilot   or   Basic Inventor

Procedures: Basic Programming

Experimental Setup:
> In class: the instructor will need a line (electrical or masking tape), a tape measure, and an area clear of obstacles to run the robots. The instructor will also supply a computer with ROBOLAB installed to program the cars in class.
> At home; you will need a tape measure to *calibrate* your car (distance vs. time). Make sure to ask the instructor what type of floor surface the Challenge will be conducted on in class (e.g. carpet or tile).

Robot Design: Design and build a motorized car using the RCX. If this is your first design challenge, we suggest building a simple car like the one shown above. Using this model is totally acceptable; after all, you aren't being graded on your building skills in this competition.

Program:
1. Program your car to travel for different amounts of time in PILOT (level 2 or higher) and record the distance it travels for a motor power level of 1. Depending on your design, the time will typically range from 0-5.5 seconds, which corresponds to approximately 0-10 feet.
2. *Calibration* of distance versus time: Using Excel, create a graph that shows how far your RCX car travels (in inches or centimeters) when programmed for a given amount of time.
   - The data collected should be shown as data points.
   - You should add Trendlines (linear regression) for each data set – make sure you display both the equation and r^2-value on the chart.

   Repeat steps 1 and 2 for motor power levels 3 and 5 and plot them on the same graph.

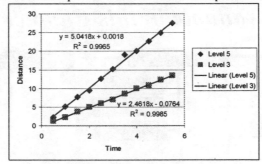

Sample calibration graph

3. Class Competition
   - Bring your car AND calibration graph to class.
   - The in-class competition will be to see who can get the closest to the line without crossing it.
   - The distance to be traveled will not be revealed until class time (you should check with the instructor about the type of floor the competition will be held on).
   - The instructor will provide a computer and ROBOLAB for programming your car in class.
   - Your grade will depend on how close you get to the line.

Hints:
   - Use the AC power adapter to make sure the results are not dependent on battery level.
   - Think about how the speed of your car affects the accuracy of your calibration curve.
   - Try to get an estimate of the repeatability and accuracy of your calibration curve. After you have created your calibration curve, try testing it out by using the regression equations to predict the distance traveled.

Grading:

Your grade will be based 100% on accuracy.

Accuracy
A+: You get the closest
A: You get within 6 inches
B: You stop short by more than 6 inches
C: You go over the line
D: Your car runs when turned on
F: You don't show up to class

Like always, you must receive a "B-" or better to earn the Skill Badge.

2.1.2   The Steepest Incline

Challenge: Using Pilot level 4 or Inventor Level 4, design and build a vehicle that is activated by a touch sensor and can climb the steepest incline.

Skill Badges: [Basic Pilot]   or   [Basic Inventor]   [Basic Programming]

Procedures:

Experimental Setup: All you need for this challenge is an adjustable slope incline such as wide board and some bricks. Getting to the 'top of the hill' is defined as progressing up the slope a given distance (e.g. 12 inches) that will be specified by the instructor. Each attempt will last a maximum of 10 seconds.

Robot Design: Design and build a motorized vehicle using the RCX. The vehicle should start running once touch sensor on input port 1 is pressed (by the instructor). The only construction restriction is that at most two motors can be used and that the vehicle must not leave anything behind. The cars shown in Figures 1.55 & 1.56 are good places to start. With only a little effort you can change the gear ratios.

Design factors to consider include gear ratios, friction, and center of mass of your robot.

Program: The program for this challenge is fairly simple; the program should wait for a touch sensor on input port 1 to be pressed before turning on the motor(s).

Hints: use the AC power adapter to prevent rapid use of batteries (stalling a motor will quickly drain a battery).

Grading:

Your grade will be based 100%.

Performance
A+: The hill climb champion
A: Climbs at least a 30 degree incline
B: It moves uphill
C: Motors turn on when touch sensor is pressed
D: You have something resembling a vehicle
F: You don't show up to class

Like always, you must receive a "B-" or better to earn the Skill Badge.

Optional: This design challenge can be altered by including a flat section before the hill (which shouldn't be too steep in this case) and then using the time to traverse the entire course as the performance criteria. This is a great alternative because it requires a combination of speed and torque, meaning the car with the lowest gear ratio probably won't win.

2.1.3   Tug-of-War

Challenge: Design and build a tug-of-war robot using Pilot Level 4 or Inventor Level 4 to program the robot. The objective is to pull the opposing robot over the centerline. The battle commences when both the robots are activated by a single touch sensor.

Skill Badges: [Basic Pilot]   or   [Basic Inventor]   [Basic Programming]

Procedures:

Experimental Setup: The required materials for this Challenge include a line (electrical or masking tape) on the floor, two pieces of 6-inch long string, each with a paper clip at one end, and a touch sensor with two long lead wires.

During the competition, the opposing robots are tied together by the connecting the paper clips on the ends of the string. The paper clips are positioned over the line. The lead wires from the touch sensor are connected to Input Port 1 on both RCX's. The battle starts when the instructor presses the touch sensor (one touch sensor triggers both RCX's).

A single elimination contest will be used to determine which design wins. A draw will be declared after 10 seconds elapses without any progress.

Robot Design: The only three restrictions are:
> 1) Input Port 1 must be accessible to connect the touch sensor lead wire to.
> 2) You may use a maximum of two motors.
> 3) Your robot must permit a piece of string to be attached (you decide how).
> 4) Your robot must fit inside a cube 9 inches on a side.

Design factors to consider include gear ratios, friction, and center of mass of your robot.

Program: The program for this project is fairly simple. Your robot must wait until the touch sensor on Input Port 1 is pressed before turning on the motor(s).

Hints: Use the AC power adapter to prevent rapid use of batteries (stalling a motor will quickly drain a battery).

Grading:
Your grade will be based 75% on performance and 25% on creativity and aesthetics.

Performance	Creativity & Aesthetics
A+: Undefeated champion	A+: Best of show
A: You win more than once	A: Outstanding
B: You put up a good fight	B: Good
C: Motors turn on when touch sensor is pressed	C: Okay
D: You have something to connect the string to	D: Nothing special
F: You don't show up to class	F: Divert your eyes!

Like always, you must receive a "B-" or better to earn the Skill Badge.

2.1.4   Tunnel Vision

Challenge: Using Pilot Level 4 or Inventor Level 4, design, build, and program a vehicle that automatically turns its headlights on when it enters a dark tunnel. You can use either Inventor or Pilot mode, which will determine the Skill Badge you earn.

Skill Badges: | Basic Pilot | OR | Basic Inventor | | Basic Programming |

Procedures:

Experimental Setup: This Challenge requires a tunnel of sufficient size for a robot/vehicle to drive into. Lamp elements (see Table 1.1) are needed to serve as the headlights. If no Lamp elements are available, a sound can be played instead. Note, the sound output is not available in Pilot mode.

Robot Design: Design and build a motorized car using the RCX that has a light sensor on it. The cars shown in Figures 1.54-1.57 all will work just fine.

Program: Your robot should move forward when turned on. When the light sensor detects dark, you should turn the lamp element on (or play a sound if no lamp elements are available) while continuing to move forward (i.e. your car should not have to stop to turn its lights on). When it emerges from the other end of the tunnel, the lamp should turn off.

Hint: The amount of ambient room light can make a big difference when using light sensors. You might want to practice in the classroom to determine the proper light sensor threshold setting. Also, if you are using Inventor Mode, you will have to choose between the *wait for dark* and *wait for darker* commands.

Grading:

Your grade will be based 100% on performance.

Performance
A: Turns lights on & off properly
B: Turns lights on when entering the tunnel
C: The lights go on and off (anytime)
D: Your car runs when turned on
F: You don't show up to class

Like always, you must receive a "B-" or better to earn the Skill Badge.

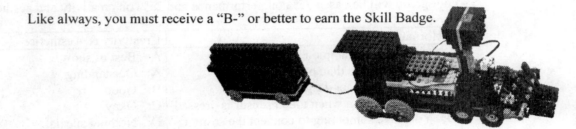

2.1.5   Wallace & Gromit™

Challenge: Design and build a device that can deliver a person (LEGO® mini-fig) from a bed on the 2nd floor to the seat at the kitchen table on the 1st floor. The system should be activated by the rising sun (simulated by a flashlight). You can use either Inventor or Pilot mode, which will determine the Skill Badge you earn.

Skill Badges: [Basic Pilot]   OR   [Basic Inventor]   [Basic Programming]

Procedures:

Experimental Setup: We highly suggested watching the Wallace & Gromit animated feature *The Wrong Trousers* as an introduction to this Challenge. Both a flashlight and the first floor of the house, including the table and chair, will be supplied by the instructor.

Robot Design: The only restriction is that the device used to transport the mini-fig must not be touching the mini-fig at the end of the challenge (i.e. you must let go at the end). You must build the second floor of the house, including the bed. This Challenge is more build-intensive than program-intensive.

Program: Your program must be activated by a light sensor. The program will most likely consist of turning motors on and off at specified times.

Grading:

Your grade will be based 70% on performance and 30% on creativity and aesthetics.

Performance	Creativity & Aesthetics
A: In the chair, not touching the floor	A+: Best of show
B: Touching the chair and/or table	A: Outstanding
C: Somewhere on the first floor	B: Good
D: In bed upstairs	C: Okay
F: You don't show up to class	D: Nothing special
	F: Divert your eyes!

Like always, you must receive a "B-" or better to earn the Skill Badge.

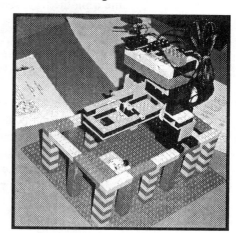

2.1.6   Line Follower

Challenge: Design and build a robot that can follow a black line. You can use either Inventor or Pilot mode, which will determine the Skill Badge you earn.

Skill Badges: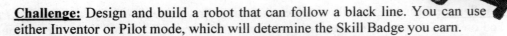

Procedures:

Experimental Setup: The course should be constructed using black electrical tape on a white background. The line will curve gently and be approximately 3 feet long. The instructor will use a stop watch to time how long it takes your robot to follow the line.

Robot Design: For this exercise you need to design and construct a basic car with at least two wheels and a light sensor facing down.

Program: There is a very simple **algorithm** that will make a robot follow a line. Actually, this **algorithm** doesn't really follow a line as much as zigzag back and forth over the line. Assuming you start on the line:

```
Turn left motor on
Wait for bright
Turn left motor off
Turn right motor on
Wait for dark
Turn right motor off
Repeat
```

> An **algorithm** is an outline of the major steps required to solve the problem

By alternating the left and right motors, the robot will pivot about the wheel which is stopped and slowly crawl forward on the right side of the line. While this algorithm is very robust (works nearly every time), you will quickly find that this method of line following is pretty slow. To speed up your robot you can leave the motor on at a low power level rather than turn it off completely. If you set the motor power too high, the robot will tend to loose the line. You should try experimenting with the motor power levels to get a good combination of reliability and speed.

Hints: Ambient light levels can drastically affect the performance of the line follower. Try shielding the light sensor from all ambient light to increase reliability (see Fig. 2.12).

Grading:

Your grade will be based 75% on performance and 25% on creativity and aesthetics.

Performance	Creativity & Aesthetics
A+: You follow the line the fastest	A+: Best of show
A: You follow the entire line	A: Outstanding
B: You follow the line more than 1 foot	B: Good
C: You car zig-zags	C: Okay
D: Your car runs when turned on	D: Nothing special
F: You don't show up to class	F: Divert your eyes!

2.1.7   Speed Walking

Challenge: Design and build the fastest walking robot you can. Just to make things interesting, you will be racing over a pebble surface. You can use either Inventor or Pilot mode, which will determine the Skill Badge you earn.

Skill Badges: Basic Pilot   OR   Basic Inventor   Basic Programming

Procedures:

Experimental Setup: This challenge is typically run over a pebble course in a single elimination format with the winner of each race advancing to the next round. Typically the race course is about 4 feet long.

Robot Design: For this exercise you need to design and construct a robot that can walk (crawling may also be permitted) over a mildly uneven surface. Creativity is worth 75% and will be based largely on the walking/crawling mechanism employed.

The only restriction is that you cannot intentionally trip another robot.

Program: Most likely your program will simply consist of turning motors on and off. This a build-intensive, not program-intensive, challenge.

Grading:

Your grade will be based 25% on performance and 75% on creativity and aesthetics.

Performance	Creativity & Aesthetics
A+: You are the fastest walker	A+: Best of show
A: You walk and win at least once	A: Outstanding
B: You walk, but don't win	B: Good
C: You walk but don't make it to the finish line	C: Okay
D: You move, but don't walk	D: Nothing special
F: You don't show up to class	F: Divert your eyes!

2.1.8   How Fast is That?

Challenge: Design and build a robot to measure the torque versus RPM of a LEGO® motor.

Skill Badges: | Basic Inventor | | Basic Programming |

Procedures:

Experimental Setup: This Challenge requires the use of a LEGO® rotation sensor (see Table 1.2). The instructor will supply calibrated weights for you to use. You will also need a timing device such as a stop watch. This Challenge is done completely as homework.

Robot Design: For this exercise you need to design and construct a robot that can wind up a string with a weight on the end. Using a stop watch, you will measure the length of time it takes to reach the specified number of rotation units – this will allow you calculate the approximate RPM (revolutions per minute) of the LEGO® motor. By varying the weight on the string and/or the diameter of the hub you wind the string on, you can vary the torque applied to the LEGO® motor. You should acquire approximately 15-20 data points.

You must submit a copy of your program, the torque-RPM curve, and a digital photograph of the robot used.

Program: You should program your robot to turn on a motor for a specified number of rotation units (16 rotation units = 360 degrees).

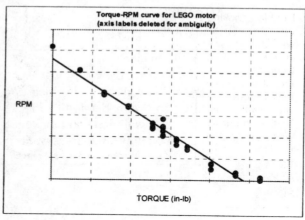

Bonus (extra half-grade): Most electric motors exhibit **asymmetry**, meaning they have different characteristics in the forward and reverse directions. Measure the torque-RPM in both directions for an extra half-grade.

Grading:

Your grade will be based 90% on performance and 10% on creativity and aesthetics.

Performance	Creativity & Aesthetics
A: You submit all 3 items.	A+: Best of show
B: You submit 2 of the 3 items.	A: Outstanding
C: You submit only one of the 3 items: torque-rpm curve, program or digital photograph.	B: Good
	C: Okay
D: You submit documentation of a valiant attempt to complete the Challenge	D: Nothing special
F: You submit someone else's graph, program or digital photograph	F: Divert your eyes!

Like always, you must receive a "B-" or better to earn the Skill Badge.

2.2   Pilot Basics

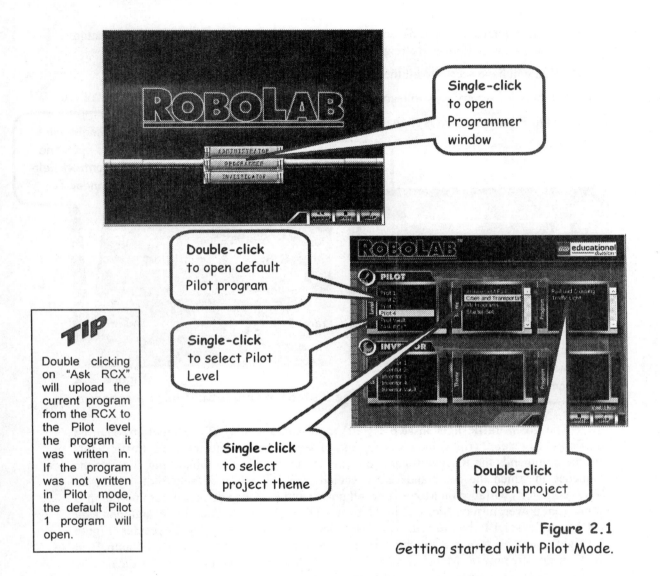

Single-click
to open
Programmer
window

Double-click
to open default
Pilot program

Single-click
to select Pilot
Level

Single-click
to select
project theme

Double-click
to open project

TIP

Double clicking on "Ask RCX" will upload the current program from the RCX to the Pilot level the program it was written in. If the program was not written in Pilot mode, the default Pilot 1 program will open.

Figure 2.1
Getting started with Pilot Mode.

Pilot mode is the easiest of the 3 programming modes in ROBOLAB. Pilot mode can be accessed from the Programmer window. Pilot mode is very useful for getting familiar with the RCX, outputs, and sensors because all Pilot mode programs will *always* execute. They may not do exactly what you intended, but they will always compile and execute.

Pilot programs are sequential, meaning the commands are executed one after another in a fixed sequence. If you are familiar with computer programming already, you will notice that loops, functions (subroutines), and other programming structures do not exist in Pilot mode.

Pilot Mode has four levels, with Pilot 1 being the simplest and Pilot 4 the most complex. Pilot 3 and 4 each have several Themes with sample Programs.

2.3 The Basic Pilot Badge Basic Pilot

This section provides information on the skills needed to earn the Basic Pilot skill badge. Rather than start with Pilot 1, we're going to get started with Pilot 4 for two reasons:

1) You will have access to all the functions and

2) Pilot mode is very easy to learn (we have full confidence in you).

The default Pilot 4 program is shown below in Figure 2.2.

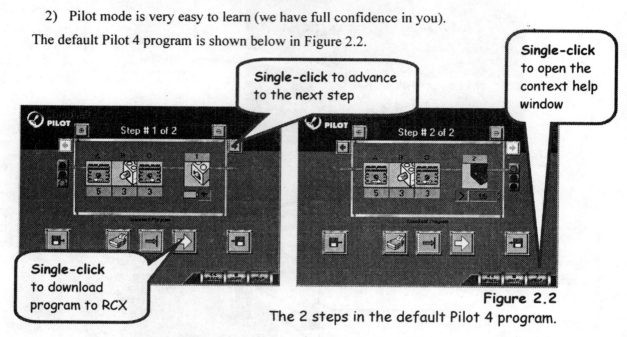

Single-click to advance to the next step

Single-click to open the context help window

Single-click to download program to RCX

Figure 2.2
The 2 steps in the default Pilot 4 program.

The green traffic light in step 1 (left) represents the start of the program. The red traffic light in step 2 (right) indicates the end of the program. Between the 2 traffic lights are the commands the RCX will carry out (i.e. the program). The pink string controls the sequence in which the commands are executed. Step 1 of the default Pilot 4 program (Figure 2.2-left) will turn on Motor A at full power in the reverse direction, turn on Lamp B at medium power, turn on Motor C in the forward direction at medium power and then *wait for* Touch Sensor 1 to be pressed. After the touch sensor is pressed step 2 executes (Figure 2.2-right): turn on Motor A in the forward direction at full power, turn on Lamp B at medium power, turn on Motor C in the reverse direction at medium power, *wait for* the reading from Light Sensor 2 to exceed 55 and then stop.

Clicking the large white arrow icon will download the program to the RCX. Make sure the RCX is turned on and the IR sensor on the front RCX is directly facing the IR transmitting tower attached to your computer. Use the **Prgm** button (gray) to select which of the 5 program slots to use. A task meter will indicate download progress (Figure 2.3-left).

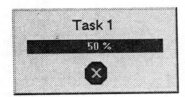 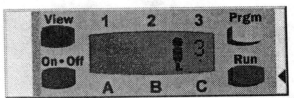

Figure 2.3

Download progress (left) and *download complete* (right) indicators.

Once the download is complete, a window indicating the program slot used will appear (Figure 2.3 – right). Note that if you attempt to download to program slots 1 and 2 while they are locked, program slot 3 will be used. See Chapter 1.5.1 for information on how to unlock program slots 1 and 2.

2.3.1   Outputs

Clicking on a motor or lamp icon opens a pop-up window which allows you to select one of four output commands: *motor reverse*, *motor forward*, *lamp on*, or *stop output*. The *stop output* command is used when you either want to turn a motor or lamp off or when there is no output device connected to a port. The power level is shown below the motor/light icons and will be discussed later in Section 2.3.3.

Single-click to open the Output pop-up window

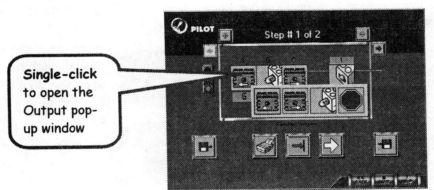

Figure 2.4

Output selector pop-up window.

While the commands are called *motor forward* and *motor reverse*, the actual direction the motor spins will depend on the orientation of the lead wires. Since there are 4 orientations a lead wire can be attached and there are connections at both the motor and the RCX, there are 16 possible ways to connect a motor to the RCX. Fortunately, many of the orientations have the same result. Shown below are pairs of connections that cause the motor to rotate in the same direction. In general rotating a connector 180 degrees will reverse the motor direction.

Rotating the lead wire 180 degrees at either the motor or the RCX will always flip the direction of rotation.

Figure 2.5
Motor connections that result in the same output.

Figure 2.6
RCX connections that result in the same output.

Finally, while only the geared motor and lamp element are listed as output devices in ROBOLAB there are actually several useful LEGO® output devices that you can buy. A complete list of output devices is shown in Table 1.1 in Chapter 1.

2.3.2 The "Wait For" Functions

The *wait for* command is probably the most commonly used command in ROBOLAB. Clicking on the touch sensor icon opens a pop-up window (Figure 2.7) where you can select one of three *wait for* conditions: time, touch, or light.

TIP

Clicking on the **help** button opens the context help window – one of the most useful windows in ROBOLAB.

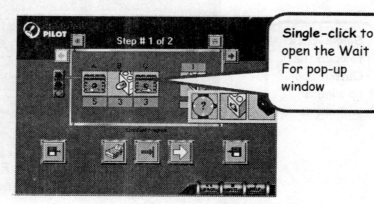

Single-click to open the Wait For pop-up window

Figure 2.7
Wait for selector pop-up window.

As shown in Figure 2.8, the *wait for time* command can either be set for a specified time or a random time (between zero and specified maximum). The *wait for touch* command can be set to wait for either a press or a release. Finally, the *wait for light value* command can be set for wait for either dark or light (100 = bright, 0 = dark).

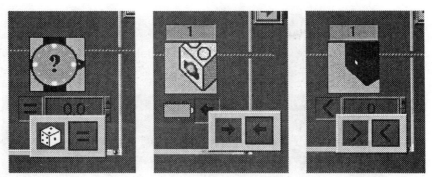

Figure 2.8
Pilot 4 *wait for* modifiers.

2.3.3 Modifiers

Modifiers allow you to select which port a sensor is connected to or at what power level to run a motor (see Figure 2.9). Modifiers also allow you specify the *wait for* conditions like length of time or light threshold value (see Figure 2.8).

In Pilot level programming the *power level modifiers* are located below the motor and light icons. They indicate the power level being supplied to each of the output ports. Clicking on the modifier allows you to change the power level of each port. Level 5 is the highest level (brightest light or fastest motor) and Level 1 is the lowest level.

Similarly, the number above the touch and light sensor *wait for* command is the *input port modifier*. Clicking on it allows you to specify the input port to which the sensor is connected.

The most common mistake for beginners is to connect a sensor to the wrong input port. For example, Input Port 1 is specified in the program, but the sensor is connected to Input Port 2 on the RCX.

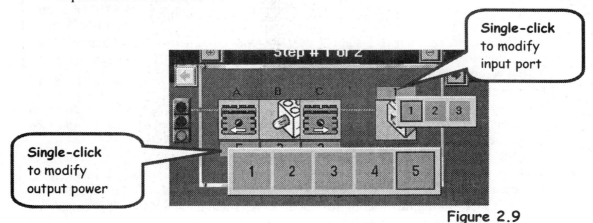

Figure 2.9
Power level and input port modifiers.

> Strictly speaking, modifiers adjust motor power not motor speed. While more power can lead to more speed, if the robot is extremely overpowered, adding more power will not affect speed very much. Thus, power level 1 does not always result in a slower robot than power level 5 (see Chapter 4.7 for more details on power versus speed)

2.3.4   Sample Pilot Level 4 Programs

Here are two sample Pilot 4 programs which will help you understand how to create your own Pilot programs.

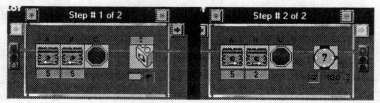

Figure 2.10
Sample Pilot program.

This first program is two steps long. The program starts at the green light (far left) and then turns on both Motors A and B in the reverse direction at full power (level 5) and then waits for the touch sensor on Input Port 2 to be pressed. Then Motor A is turned on in the forward direction at full power and Motor B is turned on in the forward direction at power level 2 and then waits for 10.0 seconds before stopping at the red stop light (far right).

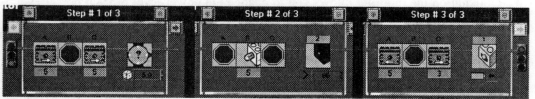

Figure 2.11
Sample pilot program with three steps.

The second program is 3 steps long. First, Motors A and C are turned on in the forward direction at full power (level 5) and then the program waits a random amount of time (0-5 seconds). Then in step 2, Motors A and C are stopped while Lamp B is turned on at full power. The program then waits for the light sensor value on Port 2 to exceed 65 (100 = bright, 0 = dark) before proceeding to step 3. In step 3, Motors A and C are turned on again in opposite directions (A reverse, C forward) while Lamp B is turned off and then waits for the touch sensor on Port 1 to be pressed before stopping.

The actual turning of motors on and off only takes a fraction of a second. Thus, most of the time in a program is spent at the *wait for* commands. It is important to note that the *wait for* command does nothing more than make the program pause until the specified condition is met. During this waiting period, all sensors and outputs will be active; motors will continue to run and sensors will continue to function.

2.3.5   Notes About Using the LEGO® Light Sensor

Not surprisingly, the light sensor works by measuring the intensity of light (in both the visible and infrared wavelengths). The light source can either be external (e.g. a flashlight) or internal (i.e. the red LED). In practice, you will use the light sensor in one of two ways: to measure either the amount of light reflected by a surface (reflective mode) or the intensity of an external light source (ambient mode). Probably the two most common uses for the light sensor represent these two modes: line following (reflective mode) and finding the brightest spot in a room (ambient mode).

REFLECTIVE MODE: measuring the amount of light reflected by a surface utilizes the internal red LED. In this measurement mode, the red LED emits light that bounces off a surface and the amount of reflected light is read by the light sensor. The amount of light reflected by the surface will depend on lots of things. For example, a rough white surface far away can result in the same amount of reflected light as a smooth black surface close up.

We've seen many students yelling at a computer because they can't get the light sensor to reliably sense color during a line following exercise. The root of their frustration is that ***the light sensor doesn't measure color*** – it measures the amount of light. Color, surface roughness, distance to the surface, angle of incidence, and amount of ambient light will all affect the amount of light reflected. Black will reflect less light than white. A rough surface will reflect less light than a smooth one. Surfaces close up will reflect more light than surfaces far away. Surfaces perpendicular to the light sensor will reflect more light than those at an inclined angle. And finally, ambient light (both visible and infrared) is the largest source of error (you measure it, but don't want to).

If this sounds complicated, it's because it is. However, it's the large number of contributing factors that also makes the light sensor so versatile. In practice, you should try to measure the effect of just one factor, such as color, while keeping all other factors constant. For example, if you want to sort LEGO® bricks by color, make sure all the bricks are the same distance from the light sensor and that they are all presented to the light sensor at the same angle and there is no ambient light.

On the other hand, if you want to measure the distance to a surface (a proximity sensor), along with minimizing ambient light you should make sure the surface is perpendicular to the light sensor, and that color and surface roughness are uniform.

In general, we can use the light sensor to measure any of the factors mentioned above: color (color sensor), surface roughness (roughness meter), distance (proximity detector), and angle of incidence (inclinometer). The only caveat is that we minimize the amount of ambient light because ambient light is the greatest source of error.

If the amount of ambient light was constant, it would simply cause our measurement of reflected light to be a little too high. However, in reality the amount of ambient light changes drastically as your robot moves around in and out of shadows. The effect of changing ambient light levels is usually larger than the effect of the factor you are trying to measure.

If you could use the light sensor in complete darkness, the repeatability of the readings would be quite high. This is the ideal condition but isn't very practical. To simulate complete darkness you can place the light sensor under the robot where it is shaded from most external light sources. In this way, it wouldn't matter if the room lights were on or off – the light sensor will be using the red LED as the only light source. You can also isolate the light sensor as shown in Figure 2.12. This doesn't block all ambient light, but helps quite a bit. Even better is the light sensor "sled" shown in Figure 2.13. Not as versatile as the using the 1x2 brick, but it does a much better job of blocking out all ambient light.

The light sensor has both a light source (red LED) and a sensing unit on it. The best way to make sure that your light sensor readings are consistent is to make the LEGO® light source the only light source. This can be accomplished by isolating the light sensor from any ambient light. One creative way to is by using a 1x2 beam placed at the end of the light sensor as shown.

Figure 2.12
Isolating a light sensor from ambient light.

Figure 2.13. Light sensor "sled."
This light sensor "sled" can be pulled behind or pushed in front of a robot and does a good job at isolating the light sensor from nearly all the ambient light.

AMBIENT MODE: measuring the intensity of an external light source is another common use for the LEGO® light sensor. However, it is also much harder to do reliably than most people realize because of two things: the red LED and infrared (IR) sources.

Because the red LED is so close to the light detecting element (a phototransistor), it can make measuring weak external light sources nearly impossible. Even in complete darkness the light sensor will read around 20. Put your finger over the light sensor in an attempt to cover it up and you'll get a reading around 45. Any objects within a few inches will also cause the LED's reflected light to become significant.

In addition to the LED, light sensor readings can go awry due to interference from IR sources. The LEGO® light sensor is actually very good at measuring the intensity of IR light sources which, unfortunately, we can't see. And the news gets worse, because IR sources are everywhere: light bulbs (incandescent and florescent), remote controls, heat sources, handheld computers, and the IR tower used to program the RCX.

Fortunately, the most common light source people try to detect is a standard flashlight, which happens to be both very bright in comparison to the surroundings and puts out a lot IR as well as visible light.

 Don't forget you can use the **view** button on the RCX to see what the current light sensor reading is.

Figure 2.14. Light sensor flipper.

One challenge that students often face is how to use the light sensor to both find an object (or an opponent) and keep an eye on the ground (to see the tournament boundaries). One solution is to use a differential to flip the light sensor up and down. In the photos shown, when moving forward the light sensor flips down. When reversing, the light sensor flips up to a horizontal position (not shown). Black friction pegs serve as positive stops.

2.3.6   Steps, Run Mode, Printing, and Saving

So what are all those other buttons on the Pilot screen? In case you haven't figured it out by playing with them, let's briefly go over the functions of the various buttons.

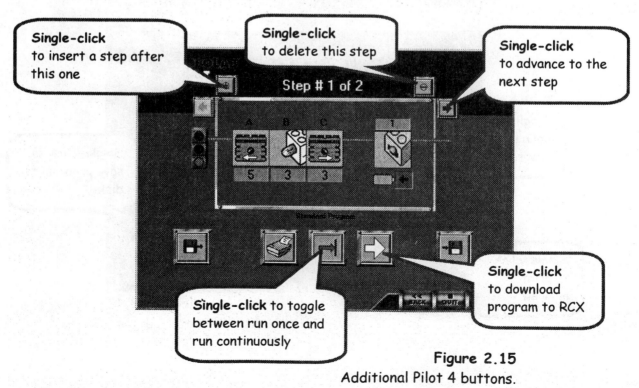

Single-click to insert a step after this one

Single-click to delete this step

Single-click to advance to the next step

Single-click to toggle between run once and run continuously

Single-click to download program to RCX

Figure 2.15
Additional Pilot 4 buttons.

Steps

Program steps are like frames in a movie. Each step is executed sequentially one after the other to make up the entire program. Pilot 4 allows you to create longer programs by adding steps. You insert or delete steps using the "+" and "-" icons at the top of the screen. You scroll backwards and forwards through the steps by using the red arrow icons on the top left and right of the Pilot window.

The sample program in Figure 2.10 has 2 steps. The sample program in Figure 2.11 has 3 steps. The maximum number of steps is unlimited.

Run Mode

The run mode button (pink arrow) toggles between *run once* and *run continuously*. If you select the *run continuously* option and run your program on your RCX, your program will start over and repeat until you stop it by pressing the green **run** button on the RCX again. This can be very useful for making a robot repeat a simple behavior.

Figure 2.16
Run mode.

If run continuously, the program in Figure 2.10 could be used to make a robot avoid obstacles. The robot would drive forward until it bumped into something, backs up and then goes forward until it bumps into something again. Because the motors are at different power levels in Step 2, the robot would tend to turn as it backed up.

Once you've selected the run mode, you still must download your program to the RCX using the large white arrow (run icon).

Printing & Saving

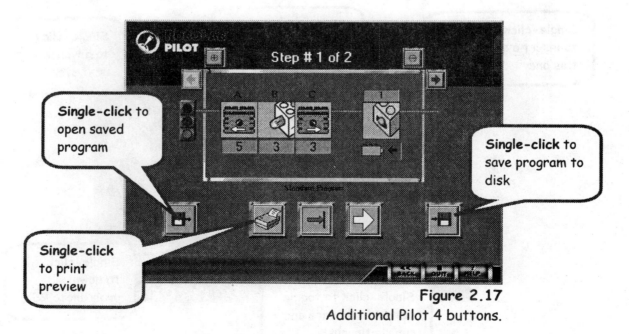

Figure 2.17
Additional Pilot 4 buttons.

Clicking on the printer icon in Figure 2.17 will open the print-preview window shown in Figure 2.18. Click on the Print icon to print the image or click on the Back button to cancel the print job.

Clicking on the Save Program button (lower right in Figure 2.17) will allow you to save your Pilot program to disk. Pilot Level 4 programs are saved as *filename.pi4*.

Similarly, the **Load Program** button allows you open previously saved Pilot programs.

Figure 2.18
Print preview window.

2.4 Relation to Text-Based Programming

The icons in ROBOLAB correspond to *functions* in a text-based programming language and modifiers correspond to *arguments*. Figure 2.19 shows a 2 step Pilot Level 4 program.

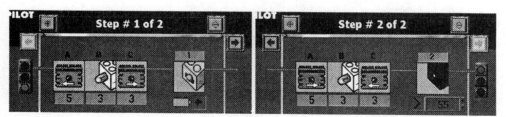

Figure 2.19
Sample Pilot program.

In step 1 the program begins by turning on Motor A at full power in the reverse direction, Lamp B at medium power, and Motor C at medium power in the forward direction. Next, the program waits (with motors and lights on) until the touch sensor connected to input port 1 is pressed. The program then proceeds to step 2, which starts by turning on Motor A in the forward direction at full power, Lamp B at medium power, and Motor C in the reverse direction at medium power. The program then waits until the light sensor connected to input port 2 registers a light level greater than 55 (100 = bright, 0 = dark) before stopping.

If we were to convert this program into a text-based programming language, it might look something like this:

```
Start;
     Rev_A(5);
     Fwd_B(3);
     Fwd_C(3);
     Wait_for_touch(press);
     Fwd_A(5);
     Fwd_B(3);
     Rev_C(3);
     Wait_for_light(greater_than,55);
End;
```

Note that the wait for light function is the only function that has two arguments, which correspond to the two modifiers in ROBOLAB (greater/less than and the threshold level).

For the novice programmer the main advantage of using ROBOLAB over a text-based programming language (such as NQC) is that you don't have to deal with syntax errors. Instead of worrying about spelling errors ("Rew_B" instead of "Rev_B") or which comes first in the argument list ("greater_than" or "55") you can focus on the logic of the program. You also don't have to worry about whether "55" is an integer, a floating point number, or a character string – you just use it.

In case you're interested, ROBOLAB actually converts the icon program you write into a text based program for use in LASM, the LEGO® Assembly language, which is covered in Chapter 6. ROBOLAB does the conversion for you so that you don't have to worry about syntax.

2.5 Limitations of Pilot Programming

The great strength of Pilot Mode is that all programs will run (compile and execute). However, it's the sequential organization of Pilot programs, which makes it impossible to write a program that won't run, that is also the main limitation of Pilot mode.

Pilot mode does not contain any program *control structures*. In computer programming lingo, a *control structure* is a command which allows looping and/or branching in the program. In other words, *control structures* allow you to jump around in the program in a non-sequential manner. For example, if you wanted a robot wait for 2 seconds if touch sensor 1 is released (not pressed) and run Motor A for 10 seconds if touch sensor 1 is pressed, you couldn't do this in Pilot mode because it requires a *conditional statement*, which does not exist in Pilot Mode.

We need to step up to Inventor Mode to access conditionals and other advanced *control structures*. Shown below is a non-sequential program that would accomplish this simple task. Notice that the *arguments* are now "wired" to each *function*.

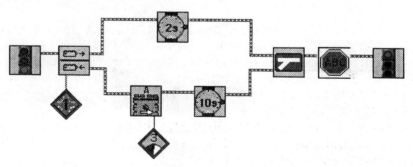

Figure 2.20
Sample conditional statement implemented in Inventor Mode.

In a text-based programming language, this program might look something like this:

```
Start;
      If_touch(1) = release then;
            Wait_for_seconds(2);
      Else;
            Fwd_A(3);
            Wait_for_seconds(10);
      End_if;
      Stop_ABC;
End;
```

2.6 Inventor Basics

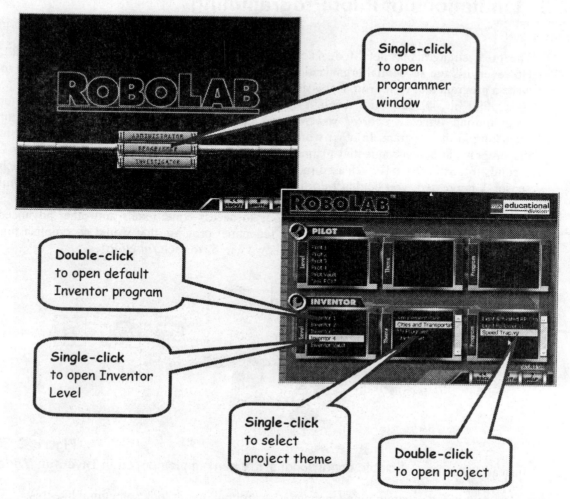

Single-click to open programmer window

Double-click to open default Inventor program

Single-click to open Inventor Level

Single-click to select project theme

Double-click to open project

Figure 2.21
Getting started with Inventor Mode.

Inventor mode is the second of the three programming modes in ROBOLAB: Like Pilot mode, Inventor mode is accessed from the Programmer window (see Figure 2.21). Also just like Pilot mode, there are 4 levels of Inventor mode with Inventor 1 being the simplest and Inventor 4 being the most powerful.

The major differences between Pilot and Inventor modes are that you can make use of variables, structures, and subroutines in Inventor mode. Additionally, in Inventor mode you have to "wire" the icons together yourself. These additional features add complexity, but it also allows you to create very powerful programs.

This section will cover a few of the basics needed to get around in Inventor mode: the windows, tools palette, and function palette. The next section will cover the nuts and bolts of programming with Inventor.

When you open an Inventor program, three windows open. The upper window is the **front panel**, the lower window is the **block diagram**, and the floating window is the **Functions Palette**. All your programming will be done in the **block diagram**.

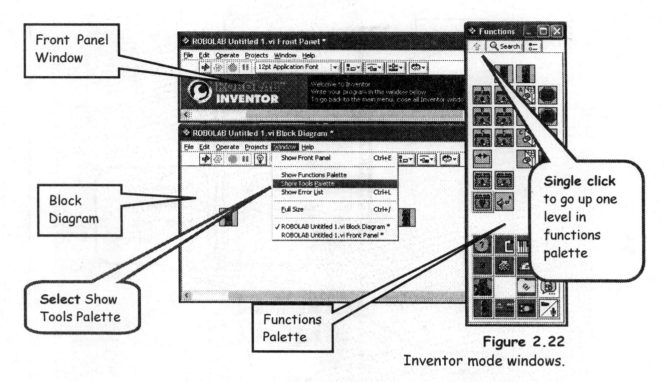

Front Panel Window

Block Diagram

Select Show Tools Palette

Functions Palette

Single click to go up one level in functions palette

Figure 2.22
Inventor mode windows.

Remember the big white arrow in Pilot that was used to send your programs to the RCX? Well, its still here in Inventor, its just not as big anymore. You can find the **Run** button at the upper left hand corner of the **block diagram.**

The run continuously will NOT cause the program to restart. Instead it will cause the program to download to the RCX over and over and over…. (not a nice thing to do).

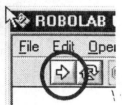

Figure 2.23
Run button.

2.6.1 The Functions Palette

The **functions palette** contains the programming icons used in ROBOLAB. Icons are picked from the **functions palette** and placed into the **block diagram**.

At the top of the functions palette are the green and red traffic lights (the begin and end icons). Just like in Pilot mode, every program must start with the green traffic light and end with the red traffic light.

The upper portion of the **functions palette**, as shown in Figure 2.24, contains all the output functions, most of which should look familiar from Pilot mode. The lower portion of the palette contains several sub-palettes. In this chapter, we will discuss the *wait for* sub-palette and the *modifiers* sub-palette.

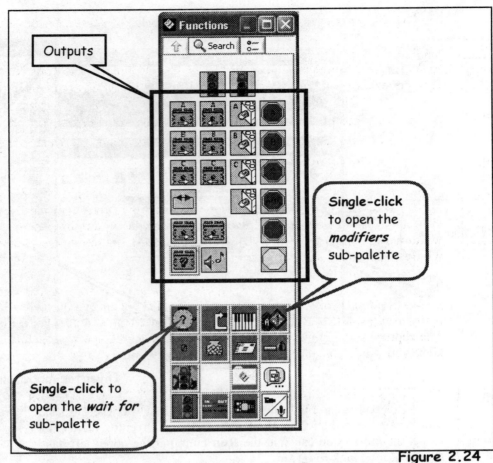

Figure 2.24
Inventor 4 Functions Palette.

2.6.2 The Tools Palette

The Tools Palette is not shown by default but is very useful for beginners. To show the Tools Palette, select "Show Tools Palette" from the Windows Menu (see Figure 2.22).

- The String Tool is used to "wire" icons together. Get familiar with it, because you will use this tool a lot.

The Select Tool lets you pick and place or drag icons around. The Select tool can also be used to resize text boxes (see the Text tool below). The Select and String tools are the most commonly used tools.

Figure 2.25
Tools Palette.

> **TIP**
>
> Pressing the SPACE BAR toggles between the Select and String tools.

This is the Operate Tool. With this, you can change numeric values.

The Text Tool lets you change values, just like the Operate Tool. However it also lets you add text boxes to your program – which is very useful for **commenting** your program.

> In computer programming lingo, **commenting** is the process of adding text comments to your program so that others can understand what you are doing.

- The Placement Tool lets you move around the contents of the diagram window. It also can be used to pick and place icons from the **functions palette** to the **diagram window** (just like the Select Tool). You can also use the scroll bars to move the **diagram window** contents around.

- Shortcut Tool. This is the same as right-clicking on an icon. In ROBOLAB, the only really useful shortcut is **replace**. Deleting an icon often causes broken wires (Figure 2.26). The **replace** shortcut allows you to substitute one icon for another, which comes in handy since you won't have to re-wire any connections.

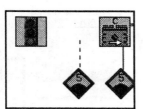

Figure 2.26
Example of a broken wire.

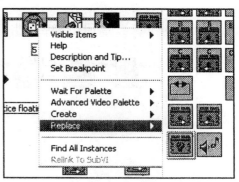

Figure 2.27
The **replace** shortcut.

 **Wiring**

Many of the icons in Inventor mode look familiar from Pilot mode. However, in Pilot mode you never had to deal with wiring the icons together. Since ROBOLAB is a graphical programming language, we need a way of telling the computer in which order to compile our program. We do this by wiring it with the pink string.

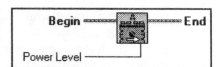

Figure 2.28
Wiring terminals.

Figure 2.28 shows the general layout of a ROBOLAB function. The **End** terminal of one function is wired to the **Begin** terminal of the next function. **Begin** and **End** terminals are always wired with the pink wire. *Modifiers* will be wired with blue, green or orange wires.

Sometimes you need to use a circuitous route for the wire. By clicking anywhere other than on an icon with the String Tool, you can create bends in the wire as shown in Figure 2.29. If you need to stop wiring for any reason, hit the ESC key. Another neat trick is to hit the space bar to flip the wire corner.

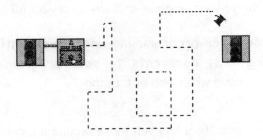

Figure 2.29.

Create bends in a wire by clicking on any blank space.

Figure 2.30 is an example showing how wiring, not the layout of the icons, controls the order of execution. Notice how the three **comments** (text boxes) that were created with the Text Tool help you understand the program.

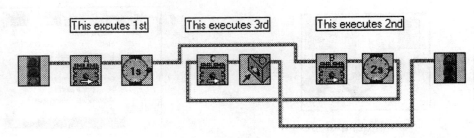

Figure 2.30

Wiring example.

Autowiring

A new feature since ROBOLAB 2.5 is **autowiring**. When you pick a program icon from the **functions palette** and place it onto the **block diagram** it attempts to automatically wire itself to the closest icon. This is usually very helpful, but sometime it wires itself to the wrong icon or terminal.

By hitting space bar once while you are dragging an icon around, the icon will attempt to autowire itself to the nearest icon (note, you must already be dragging the icon around before pressing the space bar). This is useful for autowiring icons that are already in the **block diagram**.

2.6.3 Getting Help

The context help window is the most beneficial feature of ROBOLAB for beginners. You can access Context Help from the **Help** menu as shown in Figure 2.31, by clicking on the question mark icon on the right hand side of the toolbar, or by typing CTRL+H.

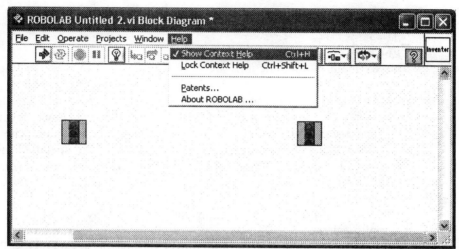

Figure 2.31. The context help is accessed from the **Help** menu.

Context Help provides information on where to wire the functions. All of the different connection points (called terminals) are color coded for easy identification. For example port modifiers are connected to functions using green colored wire. Integer numeric constants use blue wire. Floating point numeric constants use orange wires.

The help window also lists all the **default values** for a function. The default values are the values used when no modifiers are wired to the function.

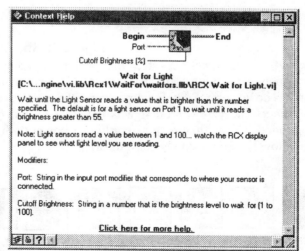

Figure 2.32. The context help window is <u>very</u> useful. When active, placing your cursor over any ROBOLAB icon will lead to detailed help.

2.7 The Basic Inventor Badge   Basic Inventor

The purpose of this section is to provide you the information necessary to earn the Basic Inventor skill badge. Like Pilot Mode, we are going to jump right to Inventor Level 4.

2.7.1   Outputs

Figure 2.33. Motor outputs.
The six main motor functions are basically identical to those in Pilot mode. As will be discussed in section 2.7.3, the only difference is that a *power level modifier* has to be wired to the motor icon as shown in Figure 2.28. If a *modifier* is not wired to a motor, it will by default run at full power (power level 5).

There are also several new motor functions in Inventor. The first is *flip direction* which reverses the direction of rotation of the specified motor(s). The next two functions are the generic *motor forward* and *motor reverse*. Both the power level and the output port(s) are specified using *modifiers*, as will be discussed in Section 2.7.3.

Using the *play sound* function you can also play one of six sounds on the internal speaker.

Finally, the *advanced output control* sub-palette has its own skill badge and will be covered in Chapter 4.

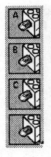

Figure 2.34. Lamp Outputs.
The *Lamp A, B, C* outputs are similar to the Motors in that the *power level* modifier should be wired to them. If no modifier is used, they default to power level 5 (full power) In addition to the *power level* modifier, the generic *Lamp* output also requires that you wire the *output port* modifier. If no modifiers are wired, the default is to turn on all ports (A, B, and C) at full power.

Figure 2.35. Output Port Stops.
Stop A, B, C functions stop the Motor or Lamp connected to the corresponding output port. The *Stop ABC* function stops all three output ports. The generic *Stop* function stops the ports specified by the *port modifiers*. The yellow stop sign is the *float output* function. Unlike the stop functions, the float output simply cuts power to the output port, which will allow motors to slowly coast to stop.

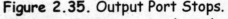

Figure 2.36.   Start/stop motors example. Note, the default values are used since no modifiers are wired.

The program in Figure 2.36 turns on Motor A in the forward direction waits for 1 second, flips the direction of Motor A, waits for 1 more second, and stops Motor A before ending.

Note that no modifiers were used (Inventor mode modifiers will be discussed shortly). In ROBOLAB, all functions have **default values** that are used if no modifiers are wired to them (the default values are always listed in the Context Help window as shown in Figure 2.32). In this case, the default power level for Motor A is full power and the default was to flip the direction of all output ports.

Figure 2.37. The motors won't stop when program ends!

Note the importance of the final *Stop A* in figure 2.36. Without it Motor A would continue to run even though the program ended. For example, in figure 2.37, both Motors A and B will continue running until either the **prgm** button on the RCX is pressed or the RCX is turned off. This program will also execute in essentially no time (a few milliseconds).

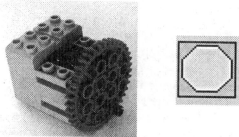

Figure 2.38. This motor demonstrates the behavior of the *float* function.

The difference between *Stop* and *Float* functions is best exemplified with a couple of little experiments. Figure 2.38 shows a motor with no lead wire attached to it. Try spinning it and notice how easily it turns and continues to spin for little while, coasting to a stop. This is equivalent to the *float* function.

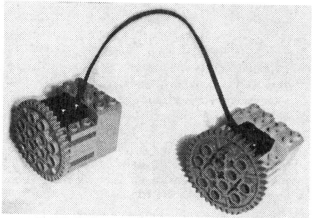

Figure 2.39. Using a LEGO® motor as a generator.

Now let's try a second experiment. Figure 2.39 shows two motors connected together with a lead wire. Turn one of the motors and the other will miraculously turn! What's going on? The motor you turn is acting as a generator and the power is being used to active the other motor. In the first experiment (Figure 2.38) the motor also acted as a generator, but there wasn't any *load* (i.e. nothing was using the power generated) so we didn't notice that we generated any power. The orientation of the lead wires will also determine the direction the motor turns; see if you can get the motor to turn the same direction and the opposite direction as the generator.

Figure 2.40. This motor demonstrates the behavior of the *stop* function.

Our last experiment illustrates the concept of an electric brake, which is what happens when you use the *stop* function. In Figure 2.40, both ends of the lead wired are stacked at 90°. Try spinning it and you will notice that it is very hard to turn. What going on? In this experiment we are using the motor as both a generator and a motor *at the same time*. By spinning the motor we generate electricity. The electricity passes though the wire and powers the motor to spin – in the opposite direction. The end result is an electric brake.

When you use the *stop* function, the RCX cuts the power to the motor AND short circuits the motor to create an electric brake, just as we did in the third experiment (Figure 2.40). When you use the *float* function, the RCX cuts the power but leaves motor circuit open, just as we did in the first experiment (Figure 2.38).

2.7.2   The "Wait For" Functions

Figure 2.41. Time wait for functions.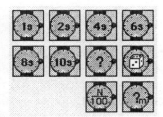
The first six *wait for time* functions specify the time the program will wait in seconds before proceeding to the next function. For the watch icon with the question mark, the number of seconds is specified by wiring a *numeric constant* modifier to the function. Similarly for the *wait for random time* function, the *numeric constant* modifier specifies the maximum time to wait. The last two *wait for time* functions allow you to specify the time in hundredths of a second and minutes respectively (again using the *numeric constant* modifier).

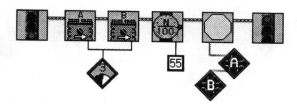

Figure 2.42. Example using the wait for time function.

The program in Figure 2.42 will turn on both Motors A and B in the forward direction at power level 3, wait for 0.55 seconds, and then float Motors A and B. Because the *float output* function was used, the motors will slowly coast to a stop when the program ends. Note we have taken a little bit of liberty here because we've used several *modifiers*, which will not be fully explained until section 2.7.3 in this chapter.

Figure 2.43. Touch sensor wait for functions.

The *wait for push* function is nearly the same as in Pilot mode. The two exceptions are that 1) you have to wire the *port* modifier to specify the port and 2) you can also specify the number of pushes to wait for with a *numeric constant modifier*. For example, you may want to wait for 3 pushes before proceeding to the next function, as shown in Figure 2.44. The *wait for release* function requires only the port modifier.

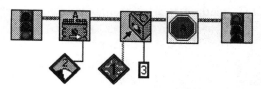

Figure 2.44. Sample wait for multiple push program.

Figure 2.45. Light sensor wait for functions.

The *wait for light* function waits until the light sensor value is higher than the specified value, which is defined by using a *numeric constant* modifier (100 = bright, 0 = dark). Similarly, the *wait for dark* function waits until the light sensor value is less than the specified value.

The *wait for lighter* and *wait for darker* functions wait until the light sensor reading is brighter or darker than the <u>current</u> value. Both the *input port* modifier and the amount of change must be wired to these functions.

It is important to note that the first two functions are based on absolute light sensor values whereas the later two functions are based on relative changes in the sensor values. This is important for accommodating varying ambient light conditions. For example, at home you may be dealing with one ambient light level and at school another. If you used the wait for light or dark functions you will probably get very different behaviors at home and school because of the difference in ambient light levels.

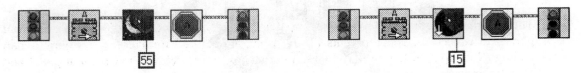

Figure 2.46. Wait for dark (absolute) and wait for darker (relative change) functions.

The program on the left of Figure 2.46 turns on Motor A in the forward direction at full power (the default value), waits for the light sensor on input port 1 (the default value) to drop below 55 before turning off Motor A and ending. The program on the right is nearly the same except that it waits for the light reading to drop by 15 before turning off Motor A and ending. Again, in both programs we've taken advantage of the default values built into the ROBOLAB functions to avoid having to wire *modifiers* to them. See Figure 2.79 at the end of this chapter for more info on using the *wait for brighter/darker* functions.

One interesting feature of the *wait for light* functions is that the LCD will switch from showing the clock to viewing the light sensor reading. This is also true for both the *wait for temperature* and *wait for rotation* functions (see below). This can be very helpful when trying to debug your programs.

The next two sets of wait for functions require the temperature and rotation sensors, which are not included in the standard ROBOLAB Team Challenge set but can be purchased separately.

Figure 2.47. Temperature sensor wait for functions.
The *wait for decreasing* and *wait for increasing temperature* functions cause the program to pause until the temperature is below or above the specified temperature respectively. Either Celsius or Fahrenheit temperature scales can be used. All four functions require both the *input port* and *numeric constant* modifiers to be wired to them to specify the sensor input port and temperature. A sample program using a pair of temperature wait for functions is shown at the end of this chapter in Figure 2.61.

Figure 2.48. Rotation sensor wait for functions.
The *wait for rotation* function waits for the rotation sensor to exceed the number of rotation units specified. There are 16 rotation units per revolution. Similarly, the *wait for angle* function waits for the angle to exceed the specified value. Since there are 16 divisions per revolution, the angular resolution is 22.5 degrees. The last rotation wait for function, *wait for rotation w/o reset*, is similar to the wait for rotation function except that the rotation sensor is not zeroed each time. Both the *input port* and *numeric constant* modifiers are used in conjunction with all rotation sensor wait for functions.

Figure 2.49. Sample wait for rotation function.

The program in Figure 2.49 turns on Lamp A and then waits for the rotation sensor on input port 1 to exceed 16 rotation units (1 full rotation) before turning off the Lamp A and ending. Note no modifiers were wired to the function so the default values, input port 1 and 16 rotation units, were used.

Figure 2.50. Other wait for functions.
The rest of the wait for functions and sub-palettes will be covered in Chapters 3, 4 and 5.

2.7.3   Modifiers

We've used modifiers several times in Pilot mode and in the examples above, but we still need to formally introduce them and explain their use in Inventor mode. Modifiers are used to specify input ports, output ports, power levels, and numeric constants. Modifiers are picked and placed from the **functions palette** to the **block diagram** just like other ROBOLAB icons.

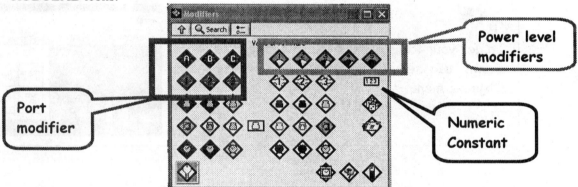

Figure 2.51. The modifiers sub-palette. For now, we'll only be using a few of the icons.

You won't find an orange numeric constant on the **modifiers** sub-palette; the integer numeric constant will change from blue to orange automatically when a floating point number is entered.

Figure 2.52. Examples of bad wiring.
Left: the modifiers are wired to the wrong terminals, which leads to broken wires.
Right: an input port modifier (1, 2, 3) is wired where an output port (A, B, C) should be, which does not lead to a broken wire (less obvious mistake).

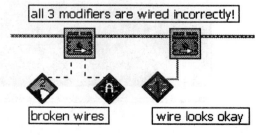

Figure 2.53. Broken Run Arrow.
If you have wiring errors, the Run arrow (upper left) will appear broken. Clicking on the broken arrow will open a pop-up window listing all the errors.

Figure 2.54. Integers and floating point numeric constant modifiers.
Both *wait for* functions will pause for the same length of time, 0.31 seconds. The first *wait for* uses an integer numeric constant modifier (blue) while the second uses a floating point numeric constant modifier (orange).

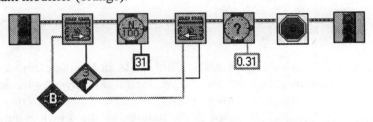

TIP

To get your icons aligned like the examples we've shown, use select the icons and use the **Align Objects** menu.

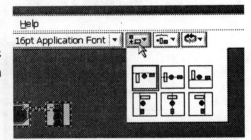

2.7.4 Getting to the Source

If you're interested, you can get to the source code for any of the ROBOLAB functions by double clicking on any function, as shown in Figure 2.55.

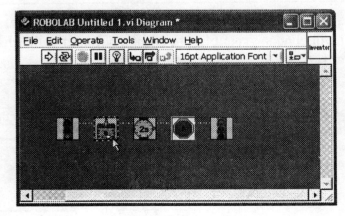

Figure 2.55. Double click on any icon to access the source code. In this example, we're opening the *Motor A forward* function.

Double clicking an icon will open the **panel** for that function. Figure 2.56 shows the **panel** for the *Motor A Forward* function. To see the **block diagram** (which is where we normally do all the wiring), select **Show Diagram** from the **Window** menu.

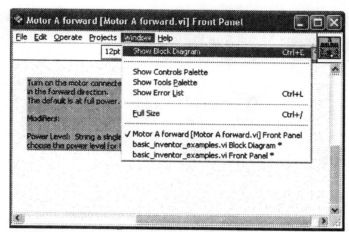

Figure 2.56. On the Window menu, select Show Block Diagram.

Once the diagram window is open, you can see how the function is put together and where the modifiers come into play. What you are seeing is the LabVIEW G-Code, which is covered in Chapter 5.

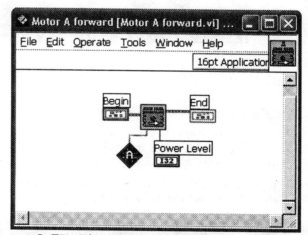

Figure 2.57. The *Motor A Forward* block diagram.

2.7.5 Sample Programs

The following 5 programs will help you gain an understanding of basic Inventor programming. If you can read and understand what they do, you should have no problem earning the Basic Inventor skill badge.

Figure 2.58. Example #1.

This program turns on Motor A in the forward direction at power level 3 until the rotation sensor reads a value greater than 24 rotation units (1.5 revolutions) at which time it turns off Motor A and ends.

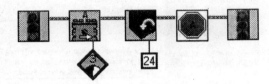

Figure 2.59. Example #2.

Here we've redone the Pilot program in Figure 2.11 in Inventor mode.

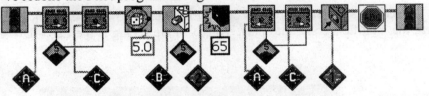

Notice floating point numbers are orange and integers are blue

Figure 2.60. Example #3.

This program turns on Motors A and B in the forward direction at full power until the touch sensor on input port 1 is pressed. Then it reverses both motors for 1 second, stops both motors and then turns on Motor A in the forward direction at power level 3 for a random amount of time (up to 2 seconds). Motor A is then stopped and the program ends. It is always good programming etiquette to stop the motors before ending the program.

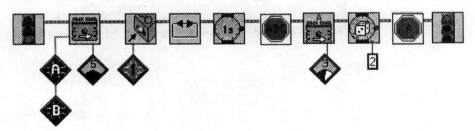

Figure 2.61. Example #4: simple feedback control.

This program uses a *jump/land* pair of functions that you haven't seen yet that form a loop. When the program reaches the *jump*, it "jumps" backwards to the *land*, thus causing everything between the *jump* and *land* to repeat over and over (indefinitely in this case). This program could be used to control a set of fans which maintains the temperature between 75 and 80 degrees Fahrenheit.

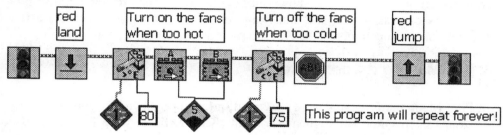

Figure 2.62. Example #5: Sun tracker.

This program is also a crude method of feedback control. It was meant to help a LEGO® solar panel track the Sun. The motor slowly turns the solar panel until the Voltage reaches 2V, indicating that it is pointing towards the Sun (the Voltage was determined by trial and error). The motor stays off until the Voltage drops to below 1.25V. The program then repeats. Since there is no wait for specifically for the solar panel, we've used one of the **sensor adaptor** generic voltage wait fors.

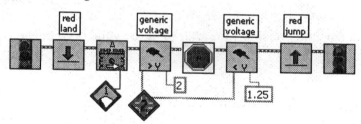

2.7.6 What's Next?

Thus far, we are still using Inventor to perform sequential programming. We have not made use of the ability to implement **control structures** yet. This will be the focus of Chapter 3.

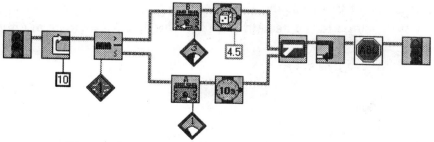

Figure 2.63. Inventor control structures.

2.8 The Basic Programming Badge [Basic Programming]

In this section we're going to show you how to arrange and document your programs so that others can easily read and understand them. After that, we'll provide a few tips for avoiding the most common ROBOLAB pitfalls and some debugging hints.

2.8.1 Making it Look Nice

In Pilot Mode the programs were very nice and well organized. If you've made your own programs in Inventor Mode, then you know that things can get a bit messy. If you're an instructor, then you know what it's like to try and grade a program with wires running everywhere. Below is a step-by-step guide showing you how to make your programs look nice (even if they don't behave nice).

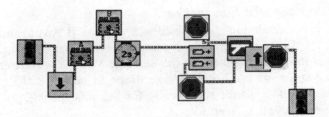

Figure 2.64. Programs can easily start looking like a mess. Try to figure out what this program is for and you'll get an idea of what your instructor faces a hundred times a day!

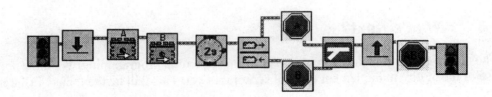

Figure 2.65. Start by arranging the icons in a generally linear fashion. If you program is very long, start a second line (see the Event examples in Chapter 4).

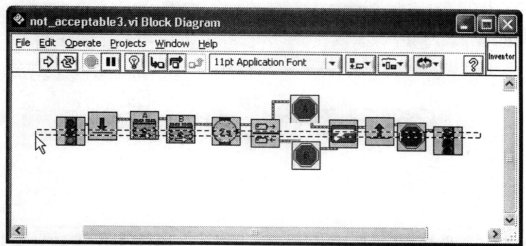

Figure 2.66. It is not necessary to draw a selection box *around* the icons you want to select. When you draw a selection box with your cursor, any icon that touches the box is selected. Here we didn't want to select the **Stop A** and **Stop B** icons.

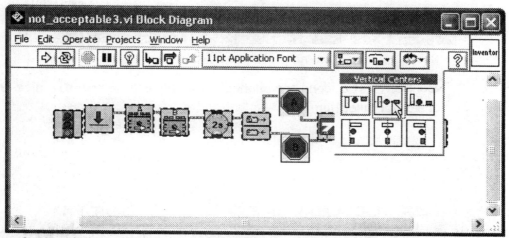

Figure 2.67. Click on the Align Objects button and select one of the six alignment options. Here we are using "vertical centers."

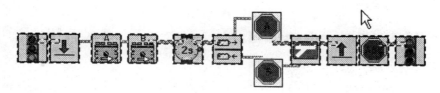

Figure 2.68. The result looks pretty nice, but icons are still a bit squished together.

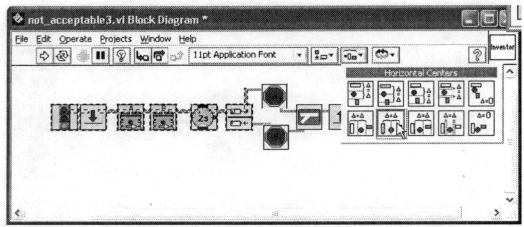

Figure 2.69. By selecting just the first six icons and clicking on the Distribute Objects button (just to the right of the Align Objects button), we can apply "horizontal centers."

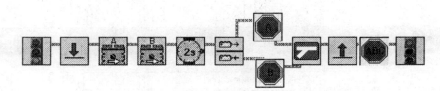

Figure 2.70. Now the first 6 icons are aligned vertically and distributed nice and evenly in the horizontal direction.

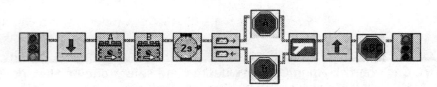

Figure 2.71. Doing the same thing to the last four icons and moving the fork wires around a bit results in a masterpiece! Compare this Figure 2.64.

2.8.2   Making it understandable

Have you figured out what this program is for yet? Now that we've got to the point that the program looks nice, we are still faced with the difficult task of understanding what the program is supposed to do.

Computer programmers use *comments* to, not surprisingly, make comments. The act of commenting your program is a habit you should get into. In ROBOLAB, comments are added using the *text tool*, which can be found on the Tools Palette (see Figures 2.25 and 2.72).

To enter text, simply click on the place you want the text to appear and start typing away. To stop entering the comment, simply click somewhere else or hit the TAB key to change tools (you can't use the spacebar to change tools since a space is a valid text character). The pointer tool can be used to resize or move your text boxes.

Figure 2.72. The text tool is located on the tools palette

Figure 2.73 shows our final program, complete with comments. It not only looks nice, but we can actually start to understand what the programmer was trying to do. We say "trying" because there is still at least one fatal flaw in the logic of the program. Can you spot it? The program will run just fine, but it probably won't do exactly what the programmer wanted.

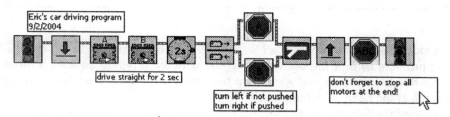

Figure 2.73. Adding comments to your program with the text tool makes it much easier for someone else to understand.

2.8.3   Figuring out What Went Wrong

If you expect all your programs to work the first time you download them, then you are going to get disappointed – often. Figuring out what went wrong, or debugging, is where most of the lessons are learned. It's a critical part of the design process (Figure 1.2). In the next few pages, we'll first discuss some of the most common mistakes we see students make. Then we'll go on to include a few tips for debugging programs.

As shown in Figure 2.74 it is entirely possible (in fact it's quite easy) to wire the **begin** and **end** terminals together on a single icon (left icon). This would result in obviously bad wires, as shown in the middle icon. Shown on the right, however, is an icon that has the **begin** and **end** terminals wire together *behind* the icon. The bad wire is not visible, because it's hidden behind the icon!

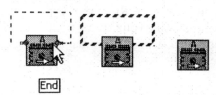

Figure 2.74. It is possible to wire the **begin** and **end** terminals of one icon together.

When you try to use an icon that has the **begin** and **end** terminals wired together, you get more bad wires, as shown in Figure 2.75. This simple, non-obvious, problem has caused countless hours of frustration for our students. Manually deleting the bad wires in Figure 2.75 doesn't help. Using CTRL+B, however, removes all the bad wires, including the hidden one, and solves the problem.

Figure 2.75. You can't wire an icon with hidden bad wires to anything

 If you are having wiring problems, try removing all bad wires (CTRL+B).

Once you get the program all wired correctly and downloaded to the RCX, there is still the problem of figuring out what's wrong with the program because 9 times out of 10, the robot doesn't do what you wanted on the first try. Figuring out what's wrong with your program is at the heart of debugging.

One of the first things to look for is whether or not the run icon (the little person) is still running. Remember, the run icon should be moving when your program is running. Often your program has ended, but the motors are still on because you have forgotten to explicitly turn them off (see Figure 2.37).

Figure 2.76. Make sure the run icon is moving when your program is running.

Often your program will produce unexpected results. The key to debugging is to develop the ability to step through the execution of the program like the RCX does. In the examples below, the commands directly following the *wait for touch* are not apparent, meaning it will seem like the RCX didn't execute them. Sit down and "read" the programs to yourself. Keep in mind that the RCX will execute the programs as fast as it can, never pausing or waiting unless you explicitly instruct it to. It only takes a few milliseconds to execute each command, so a string of commands will be over in a blink of an eye.

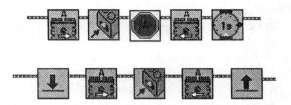

Figure 2.77. In the upper example, the *stop motor A* function is not apparent. In the lower example, the *Motor A reverse* is not apparent.

Initially getting to used to the behavior of the *wait for brighter* and *wait for darker* commands always ends up causing headaches for students. First, let's recall how the wait for brighter/darker functions work. When the program encounters the *wait for brighter* function, it takes a light reading (the current light level) and then waits for the light level to get higher by the amount specified with the *modifier* (the default is higher by 5). Figure 2.78 shows the actual "guts" of the function. It fills container #47 with the current light sensor value, adds 5, and then *waits for light* (containers are covered in Chapter 3).

If you want to see what's inside for yourself, simply double click on the function as described earlier in Section 2.7.4 (to create your own functions, see the section on subVI's in Chapter 5).

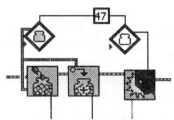

Figure 2.78. The "guts" of the *wait for brighter* function.

Let's say you wanted to make a simple robot that drives forward until the light sensors see something bright. It then stops, beeps, and starts driving again. Figure 2.79 shows a program that seems like it would accomplish this task. If you try it, you will find it works fine for the first bright spot, but never seems to react to additional bright spots.

Figure 2.79. A robot can be "blinded" by the wait for brighter function.

The problem is the robot gets "blinded" by wait for brighter function. Remember how the function works (Figure 2.78). When you first run the program it almost immediately takes a light reading and then waits (driving forward all the while because you already started the motor). When it encounters a bright spot, it indeed stops, beeps and then starts moving again. After it beeps, chances are you don't drive very far before the wait for brighter function takes another light reading (the current light level). You are then waiting for a spot brighter than the first bright spot you encountered (i.e. the robot gets "blinded" by the first bright spot).

Again, the problem arises because the RCX executes the *jump*, *land*, and *motor A forward* commands so fast. At this point you know what caused the problem. The next logical question is how to fix the problem. We'll leave that up to you.

Here's another common problem that occurs when you first start using loops (Chapter 3). In Figure 2.80 we show a simple line following program. At least that's what it's supposed to do. If you download and run this program you'll find the robot only runs for about 2 seconds, making 1 or 2 turns at most. How can this be possible when we've specified 100 turns?

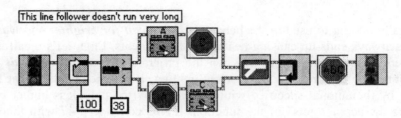

Figure 2.80. This line following program only runs for about 2 seconds. Since there are no *wait for* commands the loop **only** takes about 20 milliseconds to execute.

Since there are no *wait for* commands, the program plows through the commands one at a time, never pausing. Each command only takes a few milliseconds to execute, so the entire loop ends up taking roughly 20 milliseconds to complete. In other words, 100 loops only takes about 2 seconds.

The fatal flaw in the logic is that the programmer wanted to make 100 turns, not 100 hundred loops. One loop does not translate into one turn as it does for a line follower that utilizes *wait fors* (e.g. design challenge 2.1.6).

One of the easiest tricks to help you debug your program is to add a little beep to your program. In the figure below we've added beeps to each of the fork paths. When we run the program, we not only have an audible indication for how fast the loop executes, but we also know which fork path is executing. Of course, the beeps slow down the loop speed quite a bit. But once you have the program debugged, you would obviously remove the beeps to speed things up.

Nonetheless, students often can figure out if a certain part of their program is working by putting a short beep in various places. This can help you figure out where you are in the program.

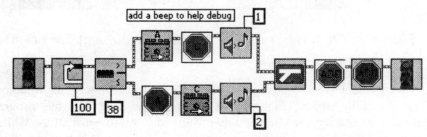

Figure 2.81. Adding beeps can help you debug your program.

As will be discussed in Chapter 4, the *Set Display* function is also quite handy for debugging your programs. Here we've decided to display the value of the sensor port 1 (the light sensor in this case) so that we can see the current value.

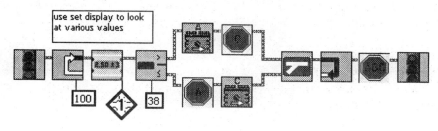

Figure 2.82. The *Set Display* function is another handy debugging tool.

CHAPTER 3

WHITE LEVEL

Skill badges available in this Chapter

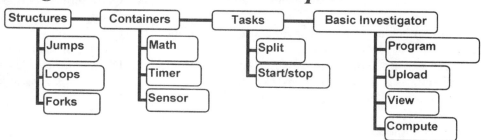

3.1 White Challenges

All of the White Level Design Challenges presume that you have already earned all the Green Level skill Badges.

3.1.1   LEGO® Cockroach

Challenge: Design, build, and program a robot that mimics the behavior of a cockroach: moves around in the dark and runs away when the lights turn on.

Skill Badges: | Structures | AND | Containers |

Procedures:

Experimental Setup: No special setup is required, just plenty of room to let the robots roam and the ability to turn on and off the lights.

Robot Design: The basic design will be a vehicle with 2 or more wheels and a light sensor (which direction you point the light sensor is up to you).

Program: Examples of LEGO® cockroach programs are shown in Figures 3.12 and 3.33. Your program will need make use of containers so that your cockroach can "learn" the difference between lights-on and lights-off and your program should utilize loops instead of the jumps that are used in the examples (because it's better programming etiquette to use loops).

The instructor will start with the room lights on, so your cockroach should store the light sensor value that corresponds to "lights-on" just before running away. When the lights go off, your cockroach should be smart enough to know the lights are off and should start hunting for food. Use loops so that your cockroach doesn't run forever (i.e. it should get tired eventually and stop).

Grading:

Your grade will be based 50% on performance & program and 50% on creativity and aesthetics.

Performance & program	Creativity & Aesthetics
A: Your cockroach acts like the real thing and your program is all your own (uses both containers and loops)	A+: Best of show
	A: Outstanding
	B: Good
B: Your program uses both containers or loops, but doesn't quite work all the time	C: Okay
	D: Nothing special
C: You use a slight modification of one of the example programs (uses containers or loops, but not both)	F: Divert your eyes!
D: You use one of the example programs to make your cockroach react to light and dark (uses neither containers nor loops)	
F: You don't show up to class	

3.1.2 Wall Follower

Challenge: Design, build, and program a robot that can navigate a maze. You are not allowed to use dead reckoning as the method of navigation. The instructor may give you additional instructions concerning the type of program you must use.

Skill Badges: | Structures |

Procedures:

Experimental Setup: The Challenge obviously requires a maze. A typical maze is constructed out of 2x1 wood boards nailed to a 4x4 piece of plywood. The course is more like a twisting corridor than a maze (which may have forks and dead-ends).

Robot Design: The basic design will be a vehicle with 2 or more wheels. Depending on your approach, you may also use more than 2 sensors. Both turning radius and speed should be considered. The faster you go, the more likely you are to get lost, so consider wheel size and gear ratio carefully. The only restrictions are that your vehicle must be completely autonomous and carry everything (i.e. leave nothing behind).

Program: **Dead reckoning** is the simplest but least reliable method of navigating a known maze, but you are not allowed to use this method for this Challenge. Dead reckoning is accomplished by navigating based on time. For example, when you know the layout of the maze, you can program your robot to go forward for 2 seconds, turn left, forward for 1 second, turn right, etc. The problem with this method is that mistakes are compounded. If a wheel slips early on, the robot may think it's going straight, when it actually may be veering off to one side.

For this Challenge you will use **wall following.** You can navigate some mazes by following either the left or right wall the entire time. Wall following can be accomplished using 2 sensors (either the light and a touch sensor or 2 touch sensors), one on the front of the robot and one on the side. If we designate the front sensor as `front` and the side sensor as `left` (assuming we want to hug the left wall), a flowchart for the basic algorithm is as follows:

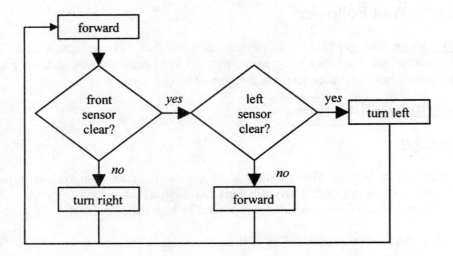

This approach uses a nested *If* function. *If* functions are *forks* in ROBOLAB. The repeat function is a *loop* or *jump* in ROBOLAB. If you use this approach, you will earn the Structures skill badge.

Grading:

Your grade will be based 75% on performance and 25% on creativity and aesthetics.

Performance	Creativity & Aesthetics
A+: You make it through the fastest	A+: Best of show
A: You make it to the end	A: Outstanding
B: You make it more than ½ way	B: Good
C: You seem to headed in the right direction	C: Okay
D: You wander aimlessly	D: Nothing special
F: You don't show up to class	F: Divert your eyes!

3.1.3   Remote Controller

Challenge: Using at most 2 sensors, design and build a tethered controller for remotely operating an RCX vehicle. You will use your controller to drive your vehicle through an obstacle course or maze as fast as you can.

Skill Badges: | Structures | AND | Tasks |

If more than one sensor is used, you will most likely earn the Tasks skill badge in addition to the Structures skill badge. Your instructor will determine which skill badges you get based on an examination of your program.

Procedures:

Experimental Setup: The tethers consist of long wire bricks (the black lead wires). LEGO® sells 10 foot long versions, or several shorter ones can be connected in series. An obstacle course or maze is also required for students to demonstrate controlled driving of the vehicle.

Robot Design: Nearly any vehicle will suffice for this Challenge. You should consider designing a controller that can control both speed and direction. The only constraints are that the RCX must be on your vehicle (i.e. no holding it in your hand) and you may use at most 2 sensors on the remote control. Non-LEGO® parts, such as paper and tape, may be allowed at the instructor's discretion.

Program: Your program will consist of **sensor forks**. You will also most likely use **loops** or **jumps** in your program to continually monitor the sensor(s). If you use more than one sensor and wish to monitor both of them simultaneously, you will also have to use **tasks**.

Grading:

Your grade will be based 80% on performance and 20% on creativity and aesthetics.

Performance	Creativity & Aesthetics
A+: You make it through the fastest	A+: Best of show
A: You make it to the end	A: Outstanding
B: You make it more than ½ way	B: Good
C: The robot is under your control at some point in time	C: Okay
	D: Nothing special
D: You wander aimlessly	F: Divert your eyes!
F: You don't show up to class	

3.1.4   LEGO® Brick Recycler

Challenge: Design, build and program a machine for sorting LEGO® bricks based on color.

Skill Badges: | Structures |

Procedures:

Experimental Setup: The only items required for this Challenge are a few LEGO® 2x4 bricks: 4 black, 4 white, and 2 blue. The blue bricks are the "challenge" bricks – the hard ones to sort.

Robot Design: The operator (the instructor) will place the bricks into your machine in a random order. Your machine should move the bricks in front the light sensor and then sort them into one of three bins based on color. More creativity points will be given to designs that do not require the operator to load or orient the bricks in a special way.

You will use the light sensor and one or more motors for this Challenge. You may also consider using a touch sensor.

Program: Forks and loops will be used to complete this Challenge. In order to sort all three colors, you will need to use nested forks.

Hints: The LEGO® light sensor is very sensitive to ambient light levels. You may want to consider shielding the light sensor from the room lights as in Figures 2.12 and 2.13 or even under some kind of shield. Also, taking multiple (repeated) light readings will increase accuracy.

The light sensor is also very dependent on the distance between the sensor and the brick (it is actually a very good proximity sensor). For example, a black brick very close to the sensor will look like a white brick that is far away.

Grading:
Your grade will be based 75% on performance and 25% on creativity and aesthetics.

Performance	Creativity & Aesthetics
A+: Sort the most bricks correctly the fastest	A+: Best of show
A: Sort 9 bricks correctly	A: Outstanding
B: Sort 6 bricks correctly	B: Good
C: Sort 4 bricks correctly	C: Okay
D: Move the bricks around	D: Nothing special
F: You don't show up to class	F: Divert your eyes!

3.1.5   Stupid Robot Tricks

Challenge: Construct, completely from your LEGO® kit, an autonomous robot capable of staying within a square denoted by four lines taped on the floor. While inside the box, your robot is to perform the most interesting task possible.

Skill Badges: | Structures |

You may earn additional badges, depending on your program. Your instructor will decide.

Procedures:

Experimental Setup: All that is required is four lines of a contrasting color to the floor. Black electrical tape on a white tile floor works well. The instructor will specify the location of Challenge so that you know what color the floor is.

Robot Design: In order to perform useful tasks, a robot must be able to properly navigate its way through its surroundings. In order to move through its environment, a robot may be called upon to avoid obstacles, detect changes in light or heat, or find its way through a maze of hallways. The American Nuclear Society held a competition several years ago specifically designed to test a robot's navigation and object detection abilities. They mapped out a grid of white tape on a black floor to aid the robot in its navigation. Those who could take advantage of these contrasting lines were able to move about the arena more easily.

There are many ways to stay inside the box, the most obvious of which is to mount a LEGO® light sensor on your robot. Where and how you mount your sensor(s) is entirely up to you. There is no limit on the weight or size of the robot, although originality and creativity will inevitably win you praise (but not necessarily points) from the judges. The only restriction is that your robot may not stop moving for more than two seconds. In other words, a robot that never moves will perform the task (i.e. it will never leave the box), but will earn you a D grade.

You are also responsible for **programming** your RCX to perform this task. Some suggestions for interesting tasks:
- **Run and Stop** - Drive towards one line on the floor, stop once you reach it, turn around and run again until you reach another line. (B)
- **Line-Following** - Start your robot in any orientation, find one of the lines on the floor and follow it all the way around the perimeter. Simple. (B+)
- **Obstacle avoidance** - Start in any orientation you wish, and perform the run and stop algorithm while avoiding some light-colored objects placed within the box. (A)
- **Your Imagination** - Impress us with something more complex? (A+)

Program: It's totally up to you!

Grading:

Your grade will be based 100% creativity and aesthetics. Your grade will depend entirely on how impressed the instructors are! If your robot doesn't complete any task but stays in the box you will get a D for the Challenge.

3.1.6   Fetch the Light

Challenge: A flashlight will be placed somewhere on the floor pointing in the direction of your robot. Find this light and get as close as possible to it and stop before running into it. Simple.

Skill Badges: | Structures |

Procedures:

Experimental Setup: Bring your own flashlight. This is critical, since you will be testing with your own flashlight at home. We will have one, but the chances of your robot performing equally well with two different light sources are slim.

Robot Design: A national Fire-Fighting robot competition is held at Trinity College each year in which the entries are required to find and extinguish a fire somewhere in a house. The fire is actually a candle and the house is little more than a simplified maze so the task may seem easy. The trick is that once the robot has identified the room containing the fire, it must get within 12 inches before trying to extinguish it. Generally, the closer you can get to the candle without touching it, the better. If a robot is running LEGO® motors and fans, for instance, the closer it can get to the candle, the better chance it has of putting it out.

We will turn the lights off in the room so that the point of greatest light should be the flashlight, but there is no guarantee that the room will be completely free of natural light. This competition will not be run as a group, so leave the claws of death at home. Everybody will have an unobstructed path to the light source. If you can solve this problem with obstacles, you get an extra half-grade (A+ max).

Program: Simple code always triumphs. Think of some motions your robot could do to solve a simpler problem (say, aim at the brightest spot in the room) and loop through those motions until you have reached a maximum value.

Grading:
Your grade will be based 75% on performance and 25% on creativity and aesthetics.

Performance	Creativity & Aesthetics
A+: Stops less than six inches away	A+: Best of show
A: Your robot stops within one foot of the flashlight	A: Outstanding
	B: Good
B: Your robot stops within 3 feet of the flashlight	C: Okay
	D: Nothing special
C: Your robot moves towards the light	F: Divert your eyes!
D: Your robot is light-shy	
F: You don't show up to class	

3.1.7   Robot Zoo

Challenge: This is not a competition in the normal sense. Rather, we want you to build your interpretation of an animal with LEGO® bricks. If you visited a zoo full of LEGO® animals, what would they look like? How would they move? Be creative. Your imagination is the only limitation this week.

Skill Badges: | Structures |

Procedures:

Experimental Setup: All you need is a large enough area to let all your animals roam free.

Robot Design: Some things to think about:
- Most animals don't move with wheels. If yours has legs in real life, it should probably have them in LEGO® life.
- If your animal moves with legs, how does its gait look?
- Does this animal have knees? Elbows? Shoulders?

Just like in nature, Darwinism applies. We will have all of your creations have a go at each other in a full-on mass competition where survival of the fittest is the only rule.

Program: You will most likely use structures in this Challenge, if for no other reason than to make the program loop over and over. You may earn other skill badges based on the complexity of your program (you instructor will decide).

Grading:
    Your grade will be based 20% on performance and 80% on creativity and aesthetics.

Performance	Creativity & Aesthetics
A+: Top of the food chain!	A+: Best of show
A: You play fair & have fun	A: Looks like the real thing
B: You play fair	B: Looks like an animal
C: Your animal moves and makes noise	C: Something moves around
D: You animal moves	D: Looks like it was once alive
F: You don't show up to class	F: Put it out of its misery!

3.1.8 Edge Detector (a.k.a. Barcode Reader)

Challenge: Design and build an edge detector than can sense the transition between black and white. Your device should play one sound for a black-to-white transition and another sound for a white-to-black transition.

Skill Badges: [**Structures**] AND [**Containers**] AND [**Music**]

Note: For information on the Music skill badge, see Chapter 4.

Procedures:

Experimental Setup: A strip of white paper with black stripes of varying thickness and spacing is required. The instructor will provide the dimensions of the paper strips to be used. A variation (to add difficulty) is to include several shades of gray, which also must be detected.

Robot Design: Your device will have to either pull the paper strips in, move the light sensor over a stationary strip of paper, or a combination of both. The only restriction is that you are not allowed to manually move the paper or light sensor (i.e. the device must be fully automated).

Program: The basic algorithm is to read in the current light sensor value and compare it to the last reading. If there is no difference, then there has not been a transition between colors. If it is different, then a transition has occurred and we should play a sound. You will have to determine what constitutes "no difference" between readings.

Hints: Shading the light sensor from the ambient light condition will result in the most consistent light reading.

The light sensor is also very dependent on the distance between the sensor and the brick (it is actually a very good proximity sensor). For example, a black stripe very close to the sensor will look like a white stripe that is far away.

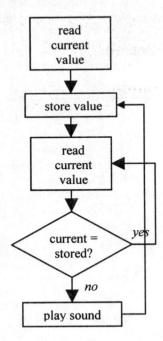

Grading:

Your grade will be based 80% on performance and 20% on creativity and aesthetics (pay attention to the sounds your device makes). The instructor will provide 4 different strips of paper, each with different complexity of transitions. The "A" strip will the most complex, with many transitions. The "D" strip will be the least complex (e.g. half white, half black).

Performance	Creativity & Aesthetics
Your grade will be based on the most complex of the 4 strips you can successfully read. If you do not show up to class, you will get an "F".	A+: Best of show A: Outstanding B: Good C: Okay D: Nothing special F: Divert your eyes!

Representative barcodes

A- barcode

B- barcode

C- barcode

D- barcode

F- barcode

Transition	Note
Black – White	A-note
White – Black	B-note
Black – Grey	C-note
Grey – Black	D-note
White – Grey	E-note
Grey – White	F-note

3.1.9   Round and Round (a.k.a. shaft encoder)

Challenge: Build a shaft encoder to measure the distance traveled by a LEGO® car. Display the total distance traveled on the LCD display.

Skill Badges: | Structures | AND | Containers | AND | Tasks |

Procedures:

Experimental Setup: This Challenge requires a tape measure and a flat surface.

Robot Design: Shaft encoders are commonly used to measure the rotation and velocity of an axle. The odometer in your car measures the total number of rotations of the wheels and the speedometer measures the angular velocity of the wheels. Encoders can be built from touch sensors that count the number of clicks or a light sensor that counts the number of light/dark transitions. In this Challenge you'll use the light sensor.

Build a LEGO® vehicle and either make an encoder like the one shown in the photo above or attach one of the black and white disks below to a wheel, axle, or gear (or you can create your own black and white disks using some paper and a black pen). Your car should be programmed to move a random amount of time, between 5-10 seconds, before stopping (your car must travel at least 3 feet in 5 seconds). Measure or calculate the distance traveled per black-white transition and use a little container math to convert the number of transitions into the distance traveled.

Program: The program will use at least 2 containers and 2 tasks. One task will turn on the motor for a random time (5-10 seconds) and then stop the car. The other task will be used to measure the distance traveled and display it on the LCD display. You will have to determine what light level corresponds to black and white for your light sensor. A basic encoder flowchart algorithm is shown on the next page. In the flowchart, we've used Container1 to keep track of the last light sensor reading (1 = white, 0 = black) and Container2 to keep a running total of the number of transitions (e.g. a counter).

Hints: The LEGO® light sensor is very sensitive to ambient light levels. You may want to consider shielding the light sensor from the room lights as in Figures 2.12 and 2.13 or even under some kind of shield.

Also think about how the speed of your vehicle might affect the accuracy of your measurements.

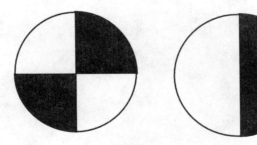

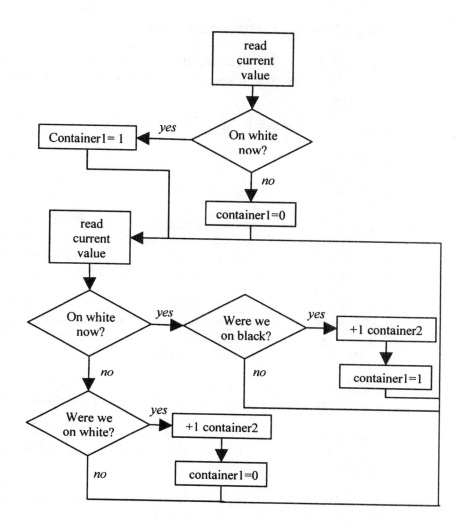

Grading:

Your grade will be based 75% on performance and 25% on creativity and aesthetics.

Performance	Creativity & Aesthetics
A: You're accurate to within 6 inches	A+: Best of show
B: You're accurate to within 12 inches	A: Outstanding
C: You're accurate to within 2 feet	B: Good
D: Your car runs, stops, and displays something to the LCD panel.	C: Okay
	D: Nothing special
F: You don't show up to class	F: Divert your eyes!

3.1.10   Two steps forward, one step back

Challenge: Build a non-motorized car. The instructor will push your car forwards and backwards. Your car should make a noise when the net forward distance traveled exceeds 4 feet.

Skill Badges: [Structures]   AND   [Containers]

Procedures:

Experimental Setup: A flat surface and a tape measure.

Robot Design: Shaft encoders are used in many devices (see Challenge 3.1.8). The problem with shaft encoders is that they cannot differentiate forwards from backwards rotation. However, it is possible to make an encoder that can tell which direction the shaft is turning as well as the position by using 3 colors instead of 2.

Build a LEGO® vehicle and attach one of the shaded disks below to a wheel, axle, or gear (or you can create your own disks using an Excel pie chart). Measure or calculate the distance traveled per black-white transition and use a little container math to convert the number of transitions into the distance traveled.

Program: The program will use at least 2 containers. One to keep track of the forward distance traveled and another to keep track of the last light sensor reading.

When the <u>net</u> forward distance traveled exceeds 4 feet, your car should beep (or make some other creative noise). For example, 2 feet forward and 1 foot backward is 1 net foot forward.

Hints: See Challenge 3.1.9 for tips building a shaft encoder. You may find it useful to display the current distance traveled to the LCD.

Grading:
Your grade will be based 75% on performance and 25% on creativity and aesthetics.

Performance	Creativity & Aesthetics
A: You're accurate to within 6 inches	A+: Best of show
B: You're accurate to within 12 inches	A: Outstanding
C: You're accurate to within 2 feet	B: Good
D: Your car runs, stops, and beeps.	C: Okay
F: You don't show up to class	D: Nothing special
	F: Divert your eyes!

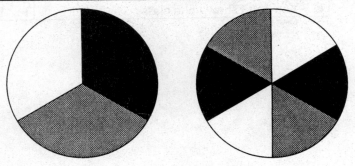

3.1.11 There and back again

Challenge: Build a LEGO® car that will drive forward until it bumps into something and then backs up and returns to the start line. The objective is to get as close to the start line as possible. The trick is you are not allowed to use a touch sensor! You are also forbidden from using the light sensor to detect the start line.

Skill Badges: | Structures | AND | Containers | AND | Tasks |

Since there are many ways to complete this Challenge, your instructor will decide which skill badges you earn after examining your program. The most common badges earned are Structures, Containers, and Tasks.

Procedures:

Experimental Setup: This Challenge only requires a flat surface and something to bump into (the instructor's foot works well).

Robot Design: Shaft encoders are used in many devices (see Challenge 3.1.8). By monitoring the rotation of a non-drive wheel, you can use an encoder to detect that you've bumped into something. If you're supplying power to the drive wheels and the non-drive wheel isn't turning, there's a good chance that you've bumped into something and aren't actually moving!

Build a LEGO® vehicle and attach one of the shaded disks below to a non-drive wheel. Your car should be programmed to drive forward until the drive wheel(s) start to slip. You should then stop, reverse the motor direction and drive backwards, stopping as close to the start line as possible. Thus, you also need to use the encoder on the non-drive wheel to monitor how far forward you traveled before stopping.

Program: The program will use at least 2 containers and one of the timers. You will have to monitor the time between black/white transitions and stop the motors if too much time elapses between transitions. You will also have to count the total number of transitions on the way out and then use the total on your journey back to the start line.

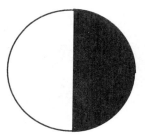

Hints: See Challenge 3.1.9 for tips building a shaft encoder.

Grading:

Your grade will be based 75% on performance and 25% on creativity and aesthetics.

Performance	Creativity & Aesthetics
A: You're accurate to within 6 inches	A+: Best of show
B: You're accurate to within 12 inches	A: Outstanding
C: You're accurate to within 2 feet	B: Good
D: Your car runs, stops, and backs up	C: Okay
F: You don't show up to class	D: Nothing special
	F: Divert your eyes!

3.1.12   Swinging with Gravity.

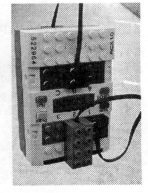

Challenge: Measure the Earth's Gravitational acceleration using Inventor.

Skill Badges: Basic Investigator

Procedures:

Experimental Setup: You need to swing the pendulum over some kind of light/dark transition. A piece of white paper on a dark table provides an excellent transition (resulting data is a square wave).

Robot Design: Build the LEGO® pendulum using some string (or lead wire), the RCX, and a light sensor. An example is shown above. Use a length of string that results in a period of oscillation of about 1 second.

Program: Using Investigator Program Level 1, 2 or 3, write a program to collect light sensor data every 0.05 seconds for at least 10 seconds.

Data Analysis: Upload the data to the computer. View the data and determine the gravitational acceleration on Earth. The period of oscillation of a pendulum is given by the equation:

$$T = 2\pi\sqrt{\frac{L}{g}}$$

where T is the period of oscillation (seconds), L is the length of the pendulum (meters), and g is the Earth's gravitational acceleration (m/s^2).

Thus, if you could measure both L and T of a pendulum, you could calculate the Earth's gravitational acceleration. In this exercise we will build a pendulum of known length (L) and measure the period of oscillation with the light sensor to get T.

Hints: Remember that the formula is only valid for small angles (less than 10 degrees). The length, L, is measured from the point of rotation to the center of gravity of the pendulum (the RCX in this case).

Grading:

Your grade will be based 90% on performance and 10% on creativity and aesthetics.

Performance	Creativity & Aesthetics
A: You get something close to 9.81 m/s^2	A: Outstanding
B: Graph looks normal	B: Good
C: You get a graph and estimate	C: Okay
D: You have data	D: Nothing special
F: You don't show up to class	F: Divert your eyes!

Submit both your graph and your calculations showing how you estimated g.

3.1.13 Going the Distance with Data Logging

Challenge: Like Challenge 2.1.1, the goal is to design, build, and calibrate a car that can travel a specified distance. This time, however, you will use Investigator 2 or higher.

Skill Badges: | Basic Investigator |

Procedures:

Experimental Setup: The instructor will need several lines (electrical or masking tape), a tape measure, and an area clear of obstacles to run the robots. The instructor will place several (3 or more) parallel lines on the ground (make sure the tape is a contrasting color from the flooring). The instructor will also supply computers with ROBOLAB installed to program the cars in class.

Robot Design: Design and build a motorized car using the RCX that can travel in a straight line and has at least one light sensor that can detect lines on the ground.

Program:
1. Program your robot to collect light sensor data while moving forward (program level 2 or higher). Run the program and collect data while moving over the lines your instructor has placed on the ground. Examine the data: and determine the time when your robot passed over the lines. You should pay careful attention to the sampling interval. If you do not sample often enough, it is quite possible to miss a line completely!
2. *Calibration* of velocity: By measuring the distance between the lines on the ground (*d*) with a tape measure and the corresponding time from the data colleted (*t*), calculate the average velocity of your robot ($v=d/t$). If the instructor has set up several parallel lines, then you should be able to generate several estimates of average velocity.
3. Class Competition
   - The in-class competition will be to see who can get the closest to the finish line without crossing it.
   - The distance to be traveled will not be revealed until the competition.
   - Your grade will depend on how close you get to the line.

Grading:

Your grade will be based 100% on accuracy.

Accuracy
A+: You get the closest
A: You get within 6 inches
B: You stop short by more than 6 inches
C: You go over the line
D: Your car runs when turned on
F: You don't show up to class

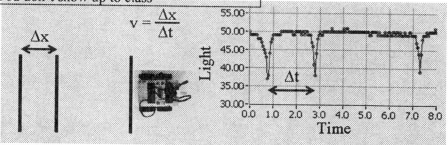

3.1.14   Tomb Raider

Challenge: Determine the path a burglar took around the room using multiple RCX's outfitted with light sensors. This is multi-team project, typically conducted with at least 6 teams.

Skill Badges: | Basic Investigator |

Procedures:

Experimental Setup: A relatively dark room, a flashlight, and a PC with ROBOLAB are required for this Challenge. The PC may be located in another room, but should be located near the "tomb" to save time.

Robot Design: This is a multi-team project. The goal of this Challenge is to determine, as a group, what path the burglar took around the room by collecting and analyzing light sensor data. The instructor will play the part of the burglar by walking around the room with a flashlight and "tagging" each RCX he/she passes.

Each team should program their RCX to record light sensor readings for 4 minutes. As a group, you will determine how often to take readings. Each team should position their RCX somewhere in the room. Make a map of the room and mark the position of all the RCX's (every RCX has serial number).

Everyone will need to start their programs running at the same time and then leave the room so the burglar can go to work. When the burglar is "finished," everyone will return to the room and upload the light readings their RCX collected.

Looking at the graph of light data, determine at what time(s) the burglar passed by your RCX. Mark that time on the map next to your RCX. Find out what time the burglar passed by the other RCX's and record those times as well. Finally, reconstruct the path you think the burglar took around the room.

Program: You must program your RCX to collect light sensor data for 4 minutes. The sampling period will be determined by the collective group.

Hints: Things to consider: how will you synchronize your data? How often should you sample? In the real world, there is usually a cost associated with data collection. Where will you place the RCX's?

Grading:
> Determine the correct path (A).
> Successfully collect data (B).
> Show up and have fun (C).
> Bicker and argue with others (D).
> Don't show up to class (F).

3.2 The Structures Badge [Structures]

The Structures badge will cover *jumps, loops*, and *forks*, which are the basic control structures in ROBOLAB. Up to now, your programs have been sequential and linear, meaning they basically read like a book; they start at the green light and without fail march step by step towards the red stop light. Introducing *jumps* and *loops* into your program will allow you to develop programs which skip some steps while repeating others. Using *forks* in your programs will allow your program to make decisions based on sensor inputs, which is the foundation for artificial intelligence. Combined, these functions will allow you to create programs to make your robots react to their environment in an autonomous fashion.

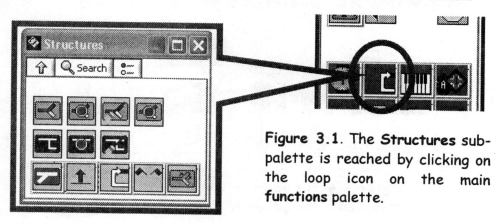

Figure 3.1. The **Structures** sub-palette is reached by clicking on the loop icon on the main **functions** palette.

3.2.1   Jumps

Getting a robot to repeat a set of commands is one of the most basic behaviors we can think of.

The *jumps* are equivalent to the *GoTo* commands in C and FORTRAN. When the program reaches an up arrow it "jumps" to the corresponding "land" down arrow. There are 5 color-coded jump/land and one generic jump/land pairs of arrows. *Jumps* are most commonly used for creating a simple loop, as shown below in Figure 3.3. However, it is usually better programming etiquette to use the *loop* functions rather than *jumps* because the jump command creates an infinite loop, meaning the program never ends (the stop light is never reached).

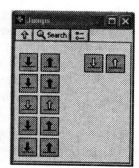

Figure 3.2. Jumps sub-palette

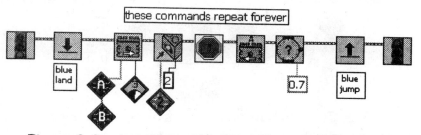

Figure 3.3.. An infinite loop using the blue jump/land.

By the way, since this book is printed in black and white, we suggest you get some colored pencils and color the jump/land arrows. This makes reading the programs much easier.

In addition to jumping backward in a program as in Figure 3.3, jumps can also be used to jump forward in a program, as shown in Figure 3.4. Here we've also used the generic jump function, which can be used to create up to 20 different jump/land pairs in case you want to use more than the 5 standard colored jumps. The jump number (#8 in this case) must be wired to both the jump and land functions. Note how we've also wired the constant (the number 8) to both the jump and the land. This is a good habit to get into as your programs become big. For example if you want to change this from jump #8 to jump #9 at some point in the future and you only have to change it one place.

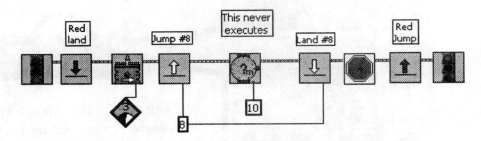

Figure 3.4. The wait for 10 minutes function is never executed in this program.

While *jumps* are most commonly used to create loops (which is better done with the *loop* function), the real power of the jump function comes when it is used in combination with *forks*. In the example below, the red jump/land is being used to ensure touch sensor 1 is not pressed before turning on Motor A. If touch sensor 1 is not pressed, then the upper portion of the fork executes. If the touch sensor is pressed, then Motor B is turned on until the touch sensor is released and then the program jumps from the lower fork to the upper fork. Here the *jump* is being used to perform a task that *loops* cannot. *Forks* will be covered in detail in section 3.2.3

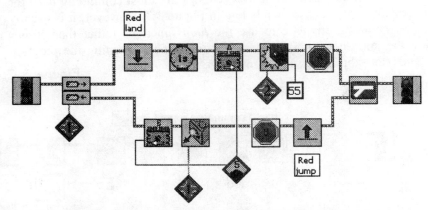

Figure 3.5. Jumping between forks is okay. Here the red jump is being used to make sure touch sensor 1 is not pressed.

While using *jumps* and *forks* together is highly encouraged, *YOU CANNOT JUMP FROM ONE TASK TO ANOTHER! Tasks* will be covered in section 3.5.

Another really useful trick is to use multiple jumps of the same color, which works as long as you have only one land. In the figure below, we created a simple controller that uses the touch sensor to determine which direction Motor A will spin.

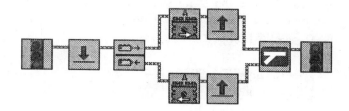

Figure 3.6.. Multiple jumps of the same color are okay, as long as you have only one land.

3.2.2   Loops

 Loops are conditionals which allow you to repeat specific sections of your program over and over. The **loop** sub-palette contains many types of *loops*. On the right side of the sub-palette is the *generic loop* function. On the left side of the sub-palette are over twenty *loops* that depend on sensor, container, timer, mail, clock, and camera values.

All the *loops* have the same basic form; loops are defined by one of the *start loop* commands and terminate with the *end loop* command. All of the functions that you want to repeat (loop) are bracketed by the *start* and *end loop* commands:

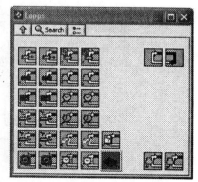

Figure 3.7.. Loops sub-palette.

 functions to be repeated go here

We saw the *generic loop* used in Figure 2.63 briefly. The *generic loop* is similar in function to a *jump* function, the exception being that you can specify the number of times the loop repeats. The number of repeats is wired to the *start loop* command.

 If no value is wired, the default is to loop only twice!

The figure below illustrates a simple loop that plays musical D-note 5 times before turning the RCX off.

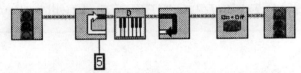

Figure 3.8.. A simple loop that repeats 5 times before turning the RCX off.

The next figure shows the same set of functions used in Figure 3.3 sandwiched between the *start* and *end loop* commands. Unlike the *jump*, the *loop* will repeat a random number of times before the program ends.

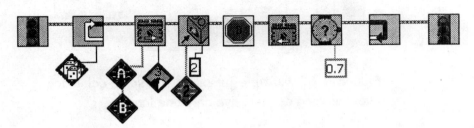

Figure 3.9. This program will loop (repeat) a random number times.

Unlike *jumps*, *loops* can be nested quite easily. Figure 3.10 shows an attempt to utilize nested jumps. Because the inner (blue) jump/land pair repeats indefinitely, the outer (red) jump is never reached. The program is "stuck" in the inner jump/land. This is why you shouldn't use *jumps* to do the work of a *loop*!

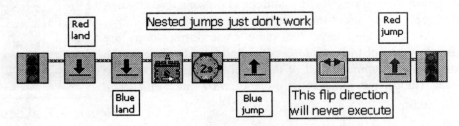

Figure 3.10. An unsuccessful attempt at nesting jumps.

In Figure 3.11 we have created a program that uses nested loops. The inner loop repeats twice, adding 5 to the red container each time. The outer loop repeats 5 times, subtracting 1 from the red container each time. The trick, however, is that the inner loops executes twice *each time* the outer loop is repeated. Thus, the inner loop repeats a total of 10 times.

If we were to keep track of the value of the red container it would look like this:

5, 10, 9, 14, 19, 18, 23, 28, 27, 32, 37, 36, 41, 46, and finally 45.

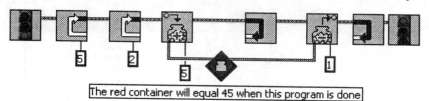

Figure 3.11. Example of nested loops.

In figure 3.12 we've created a program for a LEGO® cockroach. The bug will move around randomly as long as it's dark (light sensor value less than 40). When the lights are turned on, the bug will run away at full power. Since we've used a *jump*, our program will repeat forever (or at least until the batteries die).

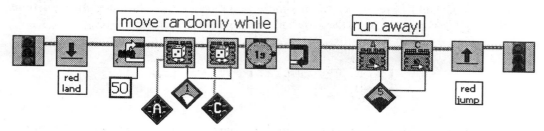

Figure 3.12. A program for a LEGO® cockroach.

The following is an example of a LEGO® alarm clock done with a pair of *loops*. The program begins by setting the RCX clock, which is displayed on the LCD panel in hours.minutes, equal to your computer's clock. The program then loops, checking the time every 0.5 minutes, until the clock exceeds 480 minutes, or 8:00. Then it plays sound #2 five times before ending. We could have used the *wait for clock* function instead of the clock loop. Can you modify this program to add a snooze for 10 minutes button? Give it a try!

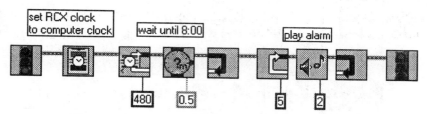

Figure 3.13. A LEGO® alarm clock set for 8:00.

Back in Chapter 1 we discussed stepper motors (see Figures 1.91 through 1.96). To get a stepper motor to work, you need to turn the motor on very briefly (0.1 seconds) and then pause to give the rubber band enough time to recenter the wheel. The next example shows a program to make the car in Figure 1.96 go exactly one wheel revolution. Notice we've used he *float* command. Using the *stop A* would prevent recentering because the stop function acts like an electric brake (see section 2.7.1).

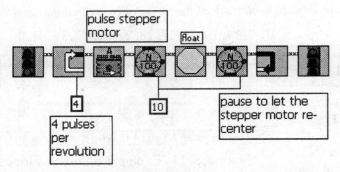

Figure 3.14. This program will make the car shown in Figure 1.96 move exactly one wheel revolutions (4 steps).

So far we've only used constants for the loop counter (the number of loops) but there's no reason why you can't use a container value (or mail value, timer value, etc). In the example below we've created a simple program that counts the number of times the touch sensor is pressed in 10 seconds and then beeps once for each press.

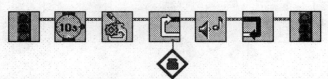

Figure 3.15. This program will beep however many times the touch sensor is pressed in 10 seconds.

In the next example we've taken it one step further and used the red container to control the loop threshold. Our program is meant to be a refrigerator alarm to keep dad from snacking in the middle of the night. The program takes an initial light sensor reading inside the fridge when the light is off (we've given ourselves 10 seconds to close the door). Whenever the light level exceeds this initial reading (because fridge light goes on), the RCX will beep continuously. Close the door and the RCX stops beeping. Of course, there is the little detail of the batteries running dead overnight (plus the low temperature slows down the chemical reaction in the batteries which makes them perform worse).

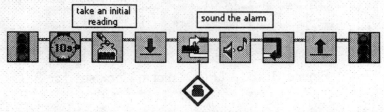

Figure 3.16. This refrigerator alarm works by taking an initial reading inside once the door is closed and then beeps whenever the fridge light goes on.

3.2.3   Forks

ROBOLAB *forks* are equivalent to the traditional *If-Then-Else* statements used in many programming languages and spreadsheets. When a fork is reached in the program, one of two "paths" will be taken. For example, in the figure below if the touch sensor is pressed Motor B will turn on. If the touch sensor is not pressed, Motor A will turn on. All *fork* commands require that a *merge fork* command (the green and white icon) be used later in the program. The merge fork command is equivalent to the *end if* command in many text-based programming languages.

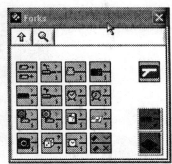

Figure 3.17. Forks sub-palette.

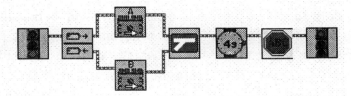

Figure 3.18. Sample program using a touch sensor *fork*.

When the program encounters a fork command, only one of the two fork paths will execute. However, you may jump between paths, as shown earlier in Figure 3.5.

All of the fork commands on the fork sub-palette use the greater-than/less-than condition to determine which path to execute. With the exceptions of the touch and the random forks, all fork commands require you to wire a threshold value, or decision level, to the command. For example, Figure 3.19 illustrates a light sensor fork with a threshold value of 43. If the light sensor value exceeds 43, then the upper path executes. Conversely, if the value is 43 or less, the lower path executes.

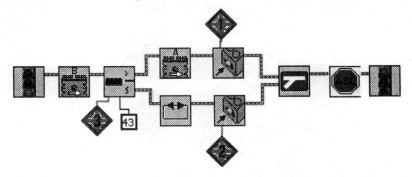

Figure 3.19. Example of a light sensor fork with threshold value of 43.

Unlike the other forks, neither the touch sensor nor the random fork commands require a threshold value to be used. In the next example the number 1, 2, or 3 will be displayed on the LCD panel of the RCX for 4 seconds depending on which path is taken.

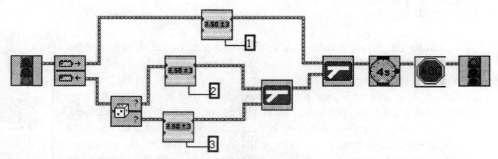

Figure 3.20. The touch and random forks do not require threshold values.

Displaying data to the LCD panel is a common way of debugging a program since it lets you see where you are in your program or what the container value is. In this example, you can determine which path was executed depending on which value is displayed. Playing a sound is another common debugging technique.

Notice we've used nested forks in Figure 3.20 to achieve 3 possible paths. There is no limit to the number of nested forks that can be used. In the program below, we've used nested forks to divide the light sensor value into 4 different levels. Also note that all the forks need to be merged before the end of the program.

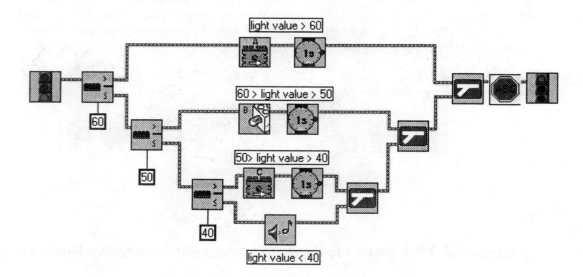

Figure 3.21. Example of nested light sensor forks.

Getting the fork merge paired up with the wrong fork is the most common mistake when first trying to use nested forks. Figure exemplifies this error. While there aren't any bad wires (dashed lines), if you try to download this program you will get an error warning (something about merging two different tasks not being allowed).

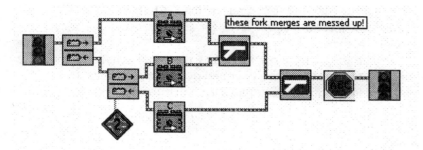

Figure 3.22. In this example, the fork merges are not paired up with the correct forks.

We mentioned back in Chapter 1 (section 1.6.6) that you can multiplex touch sensors. In this next example, we've connect two touch sensors to input port 1. We'll call these touch sensors 1a and 1b. Below is quick example of a 3-note musical instrument. Depending on which combination of touch sensors is pressed, it will play 1 of the 3 possible notes or no sound at all if neither is pressed. We've also used the red timer so that the program only runs 15 seconds (red is the default timer). Our instrument only uses one input port. What kind of musical instrument could you make using all 3 input ports? If you ever get a full piano (88 keys), let us know! [**Note: at the time of writing, ROBOLAB 2.5.4 had a bug in all of the sensor adapter forks which caused the greater than and less than branches to be reversed. The bug has since been reported and may be fixed on your version. If it hasn't, download the latest patch**].

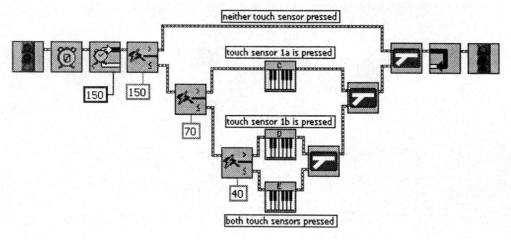

Figure 3.23. A quick example for multiplexing touch sensors (see Figure 1.87)

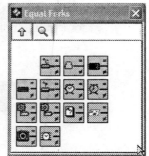

The **Equal Forks** sub-palette can be accessed by the icon on the far right of the **Forks** sub-palette. The *equal forks* are identical to the standard *forks* except that the conditional statement is "equal to/not equal to" instead of "greater than/less than." Like the standard *forks*, there are *equal forks* for all the sensors, container, timer, clock and mail.

The program below initializes the touch sensor counter and then waits a random time, over and over until the touch sensor is pressed at least once. Then it plays the default sound and ends.

Figure 3.24. Equal Forks sub-palette.

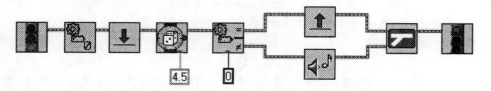

Figure 3.25. Example of a touch sensor equal fork.

In this next example, we've created a simple driving program that will run for 10.05 seconds. The equal fork is an example of an unpowered **sensor adaptor** fork (also see Figure 3.23), for using sensors like a CdS light sensor (see Table 1.2). If robot goes forward as long as the sensor value equals exactly 256. Otherwise it goes backwards. As a side note, we think the CdS sensors are nice because they typically return values from 0 to 1023, rather than the 0 to 100 of the LEGO® light sensor. The range of colors that the CdS sensor is sensitive to also matches the sensitivity of the human eye better than the LEGO® light sensor, which is very sensitive to infrared light.

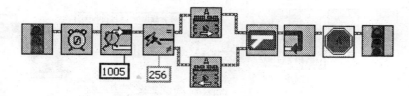

Figure 3.26. Unpowered sensors produce readings from 0 to 1023.

3.2.4 Looking Forward: Advanced Structures

In Figure 3.15 we used a container as the loop counter. In Chapter 5 we take this a step further and show you how to change the loop counter on the fly. We also get into two more very important aspects of computer programming, subroutines and subVI's, which allow you to re-use parts of your program over and over.

3.3 The Containers Badge [Containers]

Containers are what computer scientists call *variables*. They allow you create flexible programs that don't use fixed constants for the modifiers. Containers are ***Global Variables*** in ROBOLAB, meaning they can be used anywhere in the program (in all subroutines and tasks). The *containers* sub-palette is accessed by clicking on the container icon towards the bottom of the main **functions** palette. Next to the ***wait for*** functions, *containers* are one of the most commonly used commands in ROBOLAB. In this section you will learn how to use containers effectively.

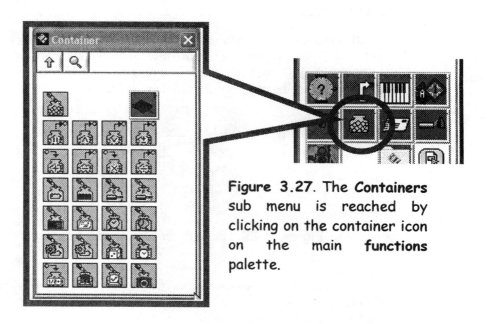

Figure 3.27. The **Containers** sub menu is reached by clicking on the container icon on the main **functions** palette.

3.3.1   Container Basics

There are 3 basic *containers* to use: red, blue and yellow. All of the ***container*** functions are found in the **Containers** sub-palette (Figure 3.27), but the containers themselves are found in the **Modifiers** sub-palette (Figure 2.51). Containers are used to store numbers. In ROBOLAB *all containers are integers*, which means that you cannot store floating point numbers; ROBOLAB will round down to the nearest integer (e.g. 1.9 becomes 1). In this example, all we are doing is setting the red container to 10.

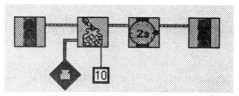

Figure 3.28. Set the red container to a value of 10.

Admittedly, this isn't very exciting. In order to do something useful, we have to introduce *container values*. Think of *containers* as the color of the jar (red, blue, yellow) and *container values* as the amount of stuff in the jar.

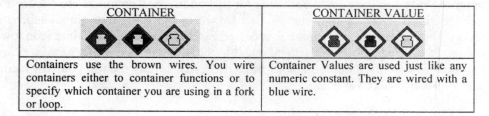

CONTAINER	CONTAINER VALUE
Containers use the brown wires. You wire containers either to container functions or to specify which container you are using in a fork or loop.	Container Values are used just like any numeric constant. They are wired with a blue wire.

In this example, we again set the red container to 10 and then we used the value of the container to make the program wait 10 seconds. Notice that *container values* are wired using a blue wire, just like a numeric constant, and *containers* are wired with a brown wire. Container values can be used anywhere a numeric constant is used.

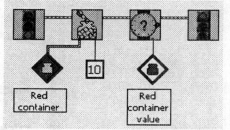

Figure 3.29. Using a container and a container value.

The purpose of the program in the next example is to take a light reading and then wait for the light to increase by a 5 units before playing some music. In order to accomplish this, we have used yet another modifier, the *port value*, to store the value of the light sensor on port 1 into the yellow *container*. We then add 5 to the yellow *container* and use this *container value* as the threshold for the *wait for light* function. When the light sensor value exceeds the value of the yellow container a quarter D-note is played.

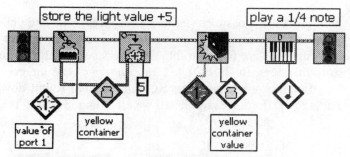

Figure 3.30. Using port values and container values.

Just like *container values*, *port values* can be used wherever a numeric constant is used. *Port values* return the value (integer) of the sensor attached to the corresponding port. For a light sensor, this would be the intensity of the light. For touch sensor, this is either 1 (pressed) or 0 (released).

As a side note, this type of program can be used to make an advanced line following robot. By starting with the light sensor over the black line and storing the sensor value to a container, the threshold value can be determined for almost any lighting condition. You don't have to re-program the threshold value for different ambient light conditions! This is commonly referred to as *calibration by demonstration*.

3.3.2 Container Sub-Palette

The **container** sub-palette (Figure 3.27) has all the container functions, which are functions that operate on containers. The upper portion of the sub-palette has arithmetic and logic container functions. The arithmetic functions are fairly straightforward. The most commonly used container functions are the *fill container* and *add to container* commands. The *fill container* command is good for initializing a container to a specific value, as we did in Figures 3.28 and 3.29. The *add to container* command is good for counting (the default is to add 1 to the red container) as we did in Figures 3.11 and 3.30.

The logic functions are equivalent to the AND and OR logic gates which you will probably learn about in an introduction to electronic circuits course.

The lower portion of the **containers** sub-palette has the all the container functions relating to sensors, timers, clock, etc. All of these functions basically fill the specified container with the value of the sensor, timer, clock, etc. In each case the container is wired with a brown wire and the value is wired with a blue wire.

The following program measures the time, in tenths of a second, between two touch sensor presses and then displays the time on the LCD display of the RCX for 4 seconds. The program utilizes both the blue *timer* and the *timer value*. Just like the *container value* and *port value*, the *timer value* is used just like a numeric constant and is wired with a blue wire.

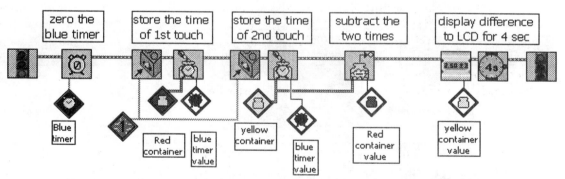

Figure 3.31. Measuring the time between touch sensor presses.

3.3.3 Container Wait For, Loop, and Fork functions

The *container wait for*, *container loop*, and *container fork* functions operate in the same fashion as the other *wait for*, *loop*, and *fork* functions described earlier. The *container wait for* causes the program to wait until the specified container is exactly equal to the integer value specified. The *container loop* will cause the loop to be repeated as long as the specified container is less than or greater than the specified value. The *container fork* is a conditional that will cause one of two program forks to be executed depending on whether the container is less than or greater than the specified value. For all the *container wait for*, *container loop*, and *container fork* functions, the container is specified by wiring one of the 3 colored containers (on the **modifiers** sub-palette) using a thick brown wire. The threshold value is specified by using a thin blue wire to connect a *numeric constant*, *port value*, *container value*, or *timer value* (all found on the **modifiers** sub-palette).

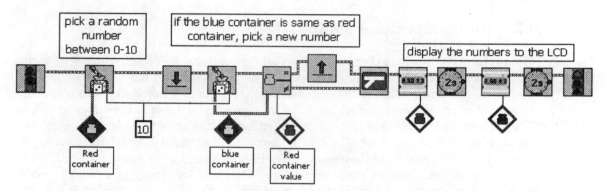

Figure 3.32. A program that selects two different random numbers.

In figure 3.32 we've created a program that will select two random numbers between 0 and 10. The first number is stored in the red container and the second is stored in the blue container. The container fork is used to ensure that the two numbers are not the same. If they are the same, the program jumps back and selects a new number for the blue container. Finally, both numbers are displayed to the LCD for 2 seconds each.

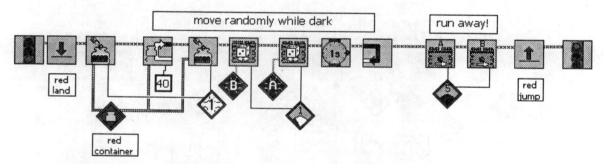

Figure 3.33. The LEGO® cockroach program done with a container loop.

Here we've redone the LEGO® cockroach program (see Figure 3.12) using a container loop instead of a light sensor loop. This also demonstrates a common phenomenon in programming: there are usually several ways to accomplish the same task using a different set of functions.

3.3.4   Integer Math

We keep stressing that the containers only work with integer values for a good reason. Realizing the consequences of integer math can save you a lot of headaches in the future. In integer math, all numbers are rounded down to the nearest integer. In integer math 1.99999 is treated the same as 1.00001, namely they are both equal to 1. In the example below, 3 divided by 2 equals 1 in integer math. Thus, the end result is that "2" is displayed on the LCD panel. In general you always want to do your multiplications first and divisions last.

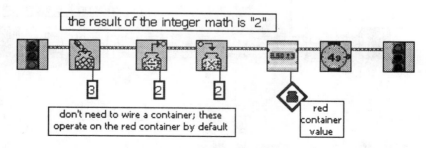

Figure 3.34. Integer math.

3.3.5   Generic Container

If you ever need to use more than 3 containers, you can use the ***generic container*** and ***generic container value***, which allows you to use up to 31 different containers. You specify the container number using the ***container.ctl*** modifier, which is a pull-down menu listing the 31 container options. Be careful, however, because containers 23-28 are used by Investigator to hold the current data point collected (pad value) and the total number of data points collected (pad size). See Chapter 5 for details on containers #23-47.

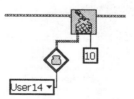

Figure 3.35. Example of filling container #14 with the integer 10.

3.3.6   Container Examples

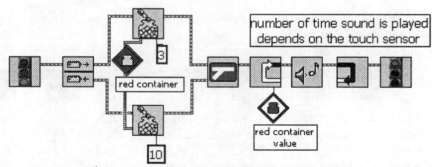

Figure 3.36. In this example we've used the red container to specify the number of times the loop is repeated depending on whether or not the touch sensor is pressed.

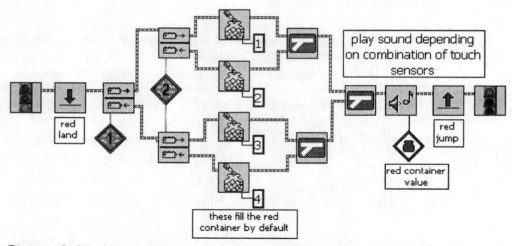

Figure 3.37. Here we've created a simple musical instrument. Depending on the combination of the two touch sensors, we will play one of 4 system sounds.

3.3.7   Looking Forward: Advanced Containers

Container math is useful, but doing long calculations using containers can get a bit cumbersome. In Chapter 5 we introduce the formula container, which allows you to do multiple math operations in one step. We also show you a neat trick to share containers among programs. Finally, we introduce the Container's Container, which a bit strange at first but very useful once you get the hang of it.

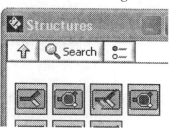

3.4   The Tasks Badge   [Tasks]

The RCX has the ability to multi-task, meaning it can run more than one program at a time. The way this is accomplished is with Tasks.

If you have ever surfed the Internet, you probably have encountered a web link which opens a whole new browser window when selected. You then have two browser windows open and closing one does not close both windows. ROBOLAB *Tasks* are similar. You can have your program spawn a new task, just like opening a new browser window, which will execute independently of the original task. *The program does not end until all the tasks have ended.* This means that every tasks must end with its own red stop light. You can have up to 8 tasks running at the same time.

3.4.1   Task Splits

To spawn a new task, the task split command is used. This command allows you to essentially run two different programs at the same time. This is very handy for monitoring two sensors at the same time. Figure 3.38 shows a program which utilizes a task split to *independently* control Motors A and B and monitor the touch sensor on input port 1 and the light sensor on input port 2. Notice that because the tasks are independent, even if one motor stops (its task ends), the other will keep running.

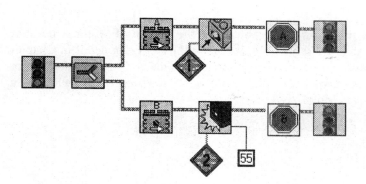

Figure 3.38. Task splits create independent programs that must both end with a stop light.

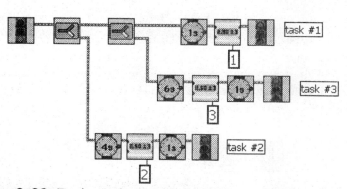

Figure 3.39. Task numbering. Task 1 starts at the green light, task 2 starts at the first task split, task 3 starts at the 2nd task split and so on.

3.4.2   Conflicts, Containers & Jumps

The ability to run independent programs is a double edged sword because the programs share the same hardware resources. If one task tells the Motor A to run forward and the other tells it to run in reverse at the same time, it's hard to predict what will happen. Conflict resolution will be covered in Chapter 5, but it is easy to avoid conflicting tasks by making sure tasks are not fighting over the same resource at the exactly the same time.

In the example below, the lower task will turn on Motor A in the forward direction. After 2 seconds the upper task will reverse the direction of the motor and end (even though the upper task has ended, the program will continue to run since the lower tasks is still active). Two seconds later (4 seconds into the program) the lower task will again reverse the motor direction (forward direction) and wait for 10 more seconds before stopping and ending the program. Since both tasks were controlling Motor A at different times, there was no conflict between tasks. The point is: make sure you are aware that hardware conflicts may occur with multi-tasking.

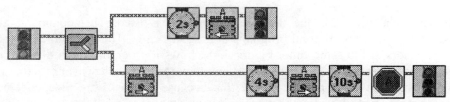

Figure 3.40. Watch out! Both tasks are trying to control motor A.

In this next example, the two tasks are fighting over the control of Motor A because they are both trying to control it <u>at the same time</u>. As we will describe in detail in Chapter 5, the upper task will win because it has a higher priority. Thus, the end result is that Motor A will run in the forward direction for 2 seconds. The lower task essentially does nothing since it lost out in the conflict over Motor A.

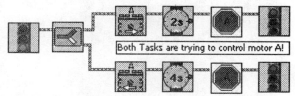

Figure 3.41. Task conflict over Motor A.

While controlling outputs may cause conflicts, tasks can share inputs without any problems. In the following program a single touch sensor is used to terminate both tasks. Both tasks are monitoring the same touch sensor at exactly the same time.

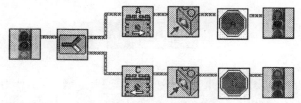

Figure 3.42. Two tasks monitoring the same sensor is not a problem.

In addition to the ability to access sensors at the same time, tasks can also access containers. In fact, containers are the only real mechanism available for sharing information between tasks. In the example below, we fill the container in task #1 and use the container value in task #2.

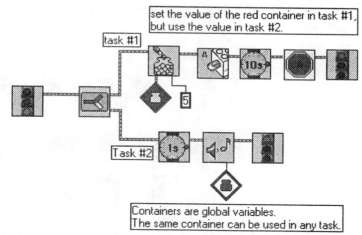

Figure 3.43. Tasks can also share container values. Containers are the only way to pass information between tasks.

A couple of quick reminders about tasks:

- <u>You cannot merge tasks.</u> You can only merge forks.
- A task split is basically the same thing as having another program running.
- If you use a task split, each separate program MUST have its own stoplight.
- Be aware of hardware conflicts when two tasks try to control a single output at the same time.
- You cannot use a *jump* to jump between tasks.
- **<u>NEVER</u>** use a *jump* to jump from one side of a task split to the other side.

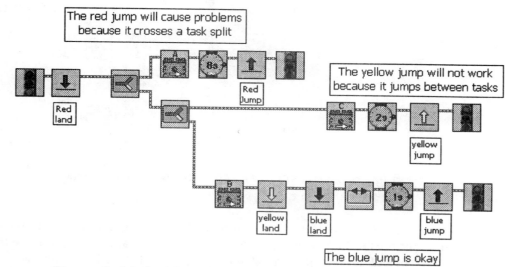

Figure 3.44. Bad (illegal) jumps used in combination with task splits.

3.4.3   Starting and Stopping Tasks

The *stop tasks* command will cause all the tasks to stop running. In the program below, both tasks are stopped after 10 seconds. The lower task may finish executing before 10 seconds has elapsed, but this does not affect the upper task. Note that the default sound is never played since the *stop tasks* command is executed first, which essentially ends the program.

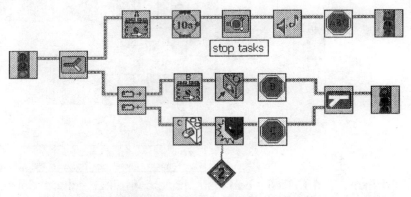

Figure 3.45. Both tasks will stop after 10 seconds.

Here's another example of stopping tasks. In this case, we've specified which task to stop, so rather than stopping all tasks, only task #2 is stopped. As always, the program will continue to run as long as any of the three tasks are still running. Each task is essentially an independent program.

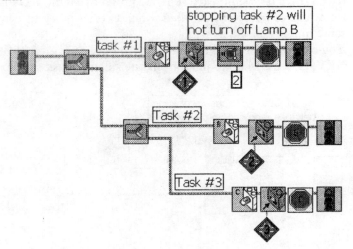

Figure 3.46. Only task #2 is stopped in this program.

In addition to stopping tasks, it is also possible to restart tasks using the ***start tasks*** command. In the next example the upper task will cause both tasks to stop if more than 10 seconds has elapsed. However, if the touch sensor is pressed before 10 seconds has elapsed, the lower task will stop Motor B, send the number 10 out as mail via the IR port, and then restart both tasks to from the original task split. The ***start tasks*** command essentially restarts the upper task (which happens to be task 1) from the task split. The program will "stay alive" as long as the touch sensor is pressed at least once every 10 seconds.

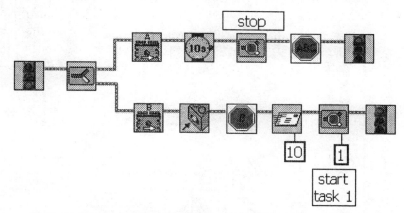

Figure 3.47. Tasks will restart from the tasks split.

Figure 3.48 shows one final example of tasks that puts it all together. The objective of this program is to avoid obstacles using the light sensor and both the left and right touch sensors (tasks 2 and 3). We've used the stop and start task functions to prevent conflicts over the control of the motors. Only one task at a time can have control because each task stops the others before controlling the motors.

3.4.4   Looking Forward: Advanced Tasks

There is only one new concept covered in Advanced Tasks in Chapter 5. Task Priorities are introduced as another way to avoid conflicts over the output ports. We will present an alternative to the program shown in Figure 3.48 that uses task priorities rather than stop and start tasks.

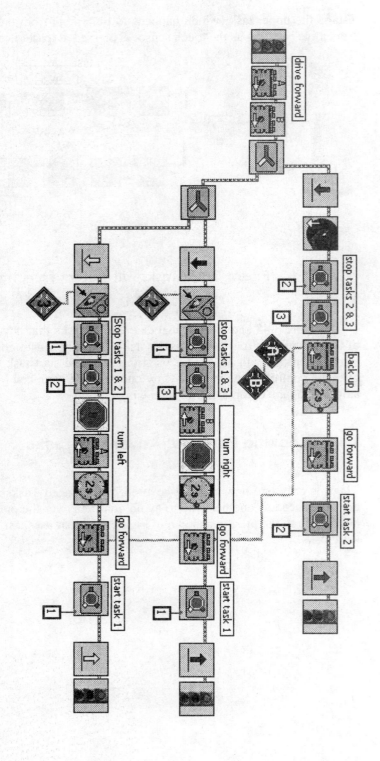

Figure 3.48. One final example of tasks. Each task controls a different function of the robot to help it avoid obstacles. The stop and start task functions are used to ensure no two tasks are attempting to control the motors at the same time.

3.5 Investigator Basics

Welcome to Investigator, the third and last programming mode in ROBOLAB. Investigator, in our opinion, takes advantage of the coolest feature of the RCX: data logging. In this section we'll cover some the basics of getting around.

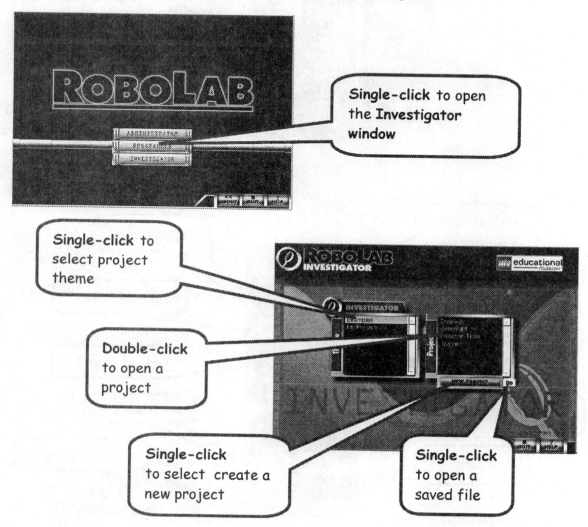

Single-click to open the **Investigator window**

Single-click to select project theme

Double-click to open a project

Single-click to select create a new project

Single-click to open a saved file

Figure 3.49. Getting started with investigator

The open saved file option is only available in ROBOLAB version 2.5.1 and higher.

When you open an investigator project, two windows open: the **Navigation window** (left) and the **Project Working Area** (right).

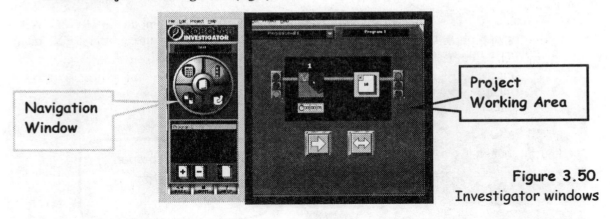

Navigation Window

Project Working Area

Figure 3.50.
Investigator windows

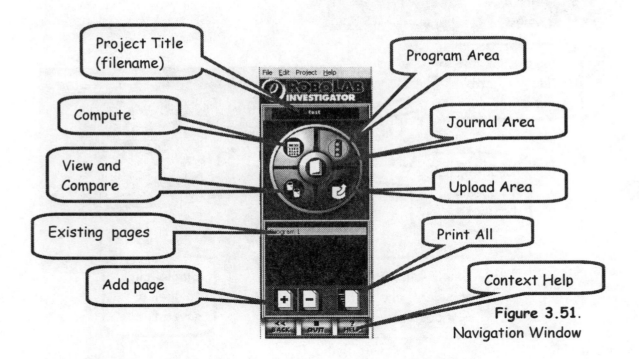

Project Title (filename)

Compute

View and Compare

Existing pages

Add page

Program Area

Journal Area

Upload Area

Print All

Context Help

Figure 3.51.
Navigation Window

Unlike Pilot and Inventor, Investigator has 5 different **project areas**, which are accessed using the **Navigation Window**. The **Navigator Window** always stays open. The **Project Working Area** will change as you move between the different project areas.

Program Area:
The Program Area is very similar to Pilot and Inventor modes. You write your ROBOLAB programs here. You also download your programs to the RCX in the Program Area. What's new in Investigator is the ability to collect sensor data using the RCX's built-in data acquisition system.

Upload Area:
Once you've collected some data using the RCX, you can upload the data back to the PC. Each data set must be uploaded to a new Page in the Upload Area.

 Compute Area:
The Compute Area is used to manipulate a data set. Computations can be simple manipulations such as addition and subtraction or more complex ones such as integration and differentiation. You can also write ROBOLAB code to process the data in almost any way imaginable.

 View and Compare Area:
The View and Compare Area is used to view data sets that have already been uploaded or manipulated. You can also get simple statistical information such as mean and standard deviations. You can also print your data from the View and Compare Area.

 Journal Area:
The last area, the Journal Area, is used to document your project. You can create simple reports or make notes for yourself. You can also import digital images to help you document your project.

3.6 The Basic Investigator Badge

Basic Investigator

In this section, we'll discuss basic data acquisition and analysis using the RCX. Using a Pilot mode type program, you'll learn the basics of data acquisition and analysis.

3.6.1 Program Area

The program area has 5 levels. Levels 1-3 are very similar to Pilot mode in that you don't have to wire anything together and all of your programs will compile and collect data. Program levels 4 and 5 are equivalent to Inventor in that you have to wire functions together, but you are not limited to the sequential Pilot-like programs of levels 1-3. For the Basic Investigator skill badge, we'll skip to Program Levels 3.

Program Level 3

Just as we did in Pilot mode, we're going to skip Program Levels 1 and 2. We have full confidence that you can handle Program Level 3 since you've already earned the Basic Pilot and Basic Inventor skill badges back in Chapter 2.

To change the Program Level, click on the pull-down menu at the top left of the Program Area window. Select Program Level 3 from the list. Program Level 3 is very similar to Pilot mode with the added benefit that you can collect sensor data while controlling the outputs. Figure 3.52 shows a typical program for Level 3.

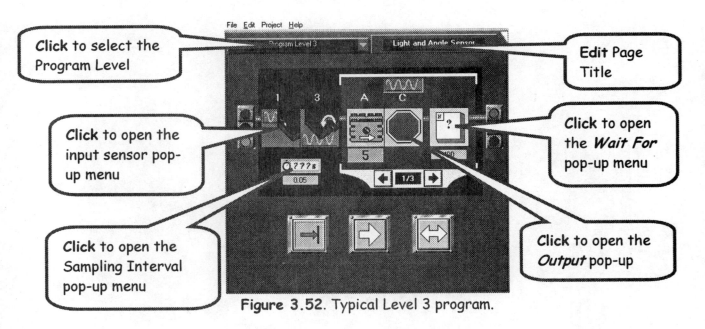

Figure 3.52. Typical Level 3 program.

The program starts by defining which 2 sensors will be used for data collection. While you cannot change the input ports (you have to use ports 1 and 3), you can change which sensors you want to use by clicking on the sensor's icon. The pop-up menus for input ports 1 and 3 are slightly different, as shown in Figure 3.53. On port 1 you can collect timer and camera data in addition to all the other sensors. On port 3 there is the option to not collect any data.

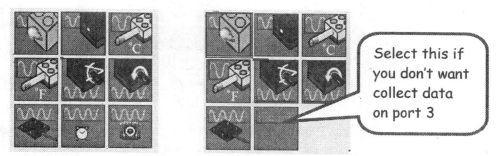

Figure 3.53. Sensor pop-up menus for input port 1 (left) and input port 3 (right).

Below the sensor icons is the **sampling interval** indicator. The **sampling interval** defines how often you want to collect data. Clicking on the indicator will open the **sampling interval** pop-up menu. The 5 **sampling interval** options are: 1 second, 1 minute, 1 hour, any time in seconds, or on touch sensor press. The last option will collect a data point for each of the sensors specified each time touch sensor 2 is pressed (this is why you can't collect data on port 2 – it's used for the touch sensor).

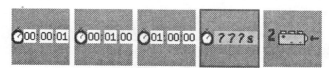

Figure 3.54. Sampling interval pop-up menu.

Just like in Pilot mode, you can have multiple steps. You can scroll forward and backward using the arrows on either side of the step number at the bottom of the frame.

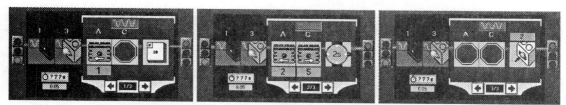

Figure 3.55. All Level 3 programs have 3 steps.

Unlike Pilot mode, however, you cannot add or subtract steps. **All Level 3 programs have 3 steps**. However, you can essentially remove a step by having the step do nothing for zero seconds as shown in Figure 3.56.

Click to open the *Data Log* pop-up menu

Figure 3.56. Skip a step by creating a step that does nothing.

Just as in Pilot mode, clicking on an output icon will open the **output** pop-up menu, from which you can select one of the 4 output options. You've probably noticed that the output ports cannot be modified. You are restricted to using **output ports** A and C for now.

Figure 3.57. Output pop-up menu.

Unlike Pilot mode, you have the unique option being able to set the Motor/Lamp power to be proportional to the sensor reading on input port 1. Clicking on the power level modifier just below the output functions opens the power level modifier pop-up menu as shown in Figure 3.58.

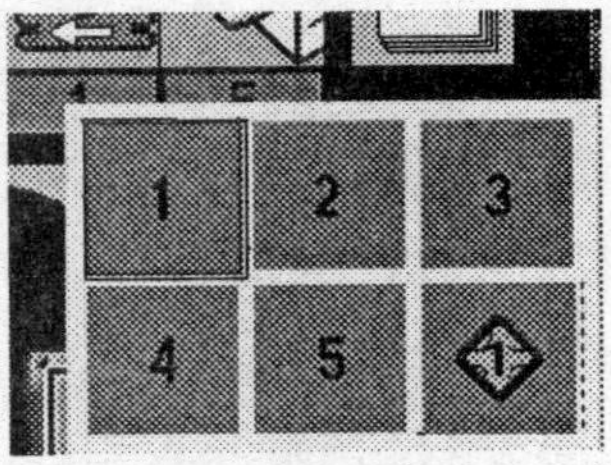

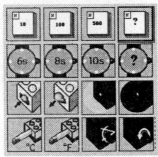

Figure 3.58. . Motor power can be set for levels 1-5 or based on sensor port 1.

The last function (far left) in each step is the familiar *wait for* function. We can wait for touch, light, temperature, angle, or rotation just as before, but now we can also wait for a specified number of data points (top row in Figure 3.59). Exactly how long this will take will depend on the **sampling interval** you selected.

Figure 3.59. Wait for pop-up menu.

Figure 3.60. The Data Log pop-up menu lets you select
either collect data (left) or don't collect data (right).

The yellow sine-wave icon above **output C** is the **data log** icon and it indicates whether or not you want to collect data during the current step. Clicking on the **data log** icon will allow you to turn on and off data logging for the current step.

Figure 3.61. Run mode.

The pink run-mode icon is also back from Pilot mode. Selecting *run continuously* will cause the program to repeat over and over indefinitely.

Figure 3.62. Run (left) and Direct Mode (right).

The large white **Run** arrow will download the program from the PC to the RCX. The double white arrow is used for running in **direct mode**. In **direct mode** the PC downloads the program to the RCX and immediately starts the program (no need to push the green run button). In **direct mode**, the RCX sends the data collected as fast as it can directly back to the PC via the IR port. The PC will display the data as it is received. In order for this to work, the RCX must remain within range of the IR tower at all times (a few feet typically). **Direct mode** can be very useful for debugging because you can see exactly what the data collected looks like. Note, this does not upload the data collected into a bucket; you must use the **Upload Area** to do that.

Finally, Investigator has the feature that you can create multiple *pages* in each area for a given project. You can think of pages as analogous to worksheets in Microsoft Excel. In the **Program Area**, you can write multiple programs, storing each one on its own page, without leaving the current project. You can add or delete pages using the "+" and "-" icons at the bottom of **Navigation window**.

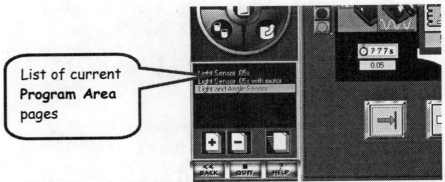

List of current **Program Area** pages

Figure 3.63. Pages allow you store multiple programs for a single project.

3.6.2 Upload Area

Once you have collected the data, it is stored in the RCX and must be uploaded to the PC in order for you to view, manipulate, and save the data. On the PC side, data is stored in one of 10 different colored buckets. Each page in the **upload area** can only have one bucket, so you are effectively limited to only 10 data sets.

While it may not be apparent, all the **upload area** pages share the same buckets so you should be careful not to use the same bucket for more than one page. You can change the name of a page by entering the name in the upper right hand corner, as shown in Figure 3.64.

Clicking on the large white arrow will upload the data from the RCX to your PC. The IR tower and IR port on the RCX must be facing each other and be in close proximity (just like when downloading a program). If you collected data for 2 sensors, the data for each sensor will be uploaded to a different page.

> **Note**
>
> The 5 **Investigator Areas** do not share pages. That is, **Program Area** pages are independent from the **Upload Area** pages.

Enter data set title

Click here to upload data from the RCX to the PC

Upload Area pages

Graph control tools

Figure 3.64. Upload Area.

All data is initially uploaded into the red data bucket. If you are going to upload more than one data set, you will need to change the bucket color by clicking on the bucket icon *after the data has been uploaded*. This will open the **bucket** pop-up menu (figure 3.65). You can also change the names of the data buckets by clicking on the title bar just below the bucket icon, which will open the **set titles** pop-up menu (figure 3.66).

Even thought you can store more than one data set in each data bucket, for the beginner it's best to store each data set in a separate color data bucket. Chapter 5 (section 5.5) goes into the details of data sets versus data buckets in more detail.

Figure 3.65. Bucket pop-up menu.

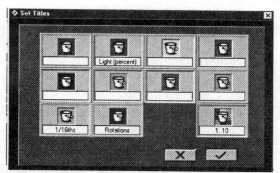

Figure 3.66. Set Titles pop-up menu.

The type of plot can also be controlled. Clicking on the icon just to the right of the bucket will open the **plot type** pop-up menu (figure 3.67). This menu has 4 plot types and a numerical value option. The numerical value option lets you see the raw data in 3 columns: data point number, time, and value (see Figure 3.68).

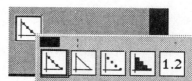

Figure 3.67. Plot Type pop-up menu.

	time (sec)	Light (per)				
0	0.0	5.0				
1	0.0	5.1				
2	0.0	5.2				
3	0.0	5.3				
4	0.0	5.4				
5	0.1	5.5				
6	0.1	5.6				
7	0.1	5.6				
8	0.1	5.7				
9	0.1	5.8				
10	0.1	5.8				
11	0.1	5.9				
12	0.1	5.9				

Figure 3.68. The Numerical value Plot Type option lets you view the raw data.

Once you've uploaded a data set, you can adjust the way the graph looks using the graph control tools.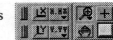

 Autoscale axis. This will adjust the X or Y axis ranges to fit the data to the screen.

 Lock autoscaling. Setting the switch to the right will lock the autoscale feature on.

 Format axis. This allows you to adjust the format of the axes.

 Zoom button. This allows you to adjust the zoom in several ways.

Pan button. This allows you to move the graph around.

 Enlarge button. This opens a full-screen version of the graph.

On the enlarged graph there are 2 cursors that can be moved around. The X and Y locations of the cursors are indicated at the bottom of the graph. You can also lock a cursor to the data set.

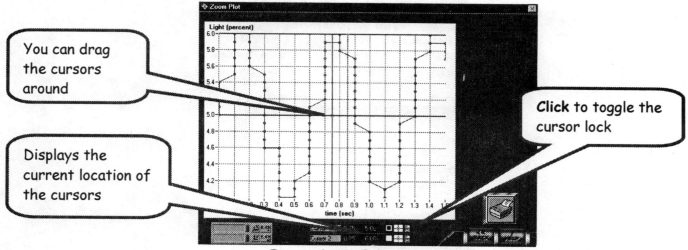

Figure 3.69. Enlarged graph.

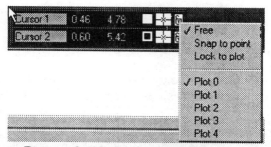

Figure 3.70. Lock Cursor pop-up menu.

Internet Upload

Internet upload allows you upload data over the Internet. The host computer (where you are getting the data from) must be set up as a ROBOLAB Internet Server (see section 4.6).

Exporting Data

If you prefer to process and/or graph the data in another program (e.g. Microsoft Excel), data collected can be exported to a file. To export data to file, select the **file** menu on the project window and scroll down to the Export: Page selection. A standard dialog box will open where you can type in the filename (typically with the .txt extension) and choose the location (folder) to save the file.

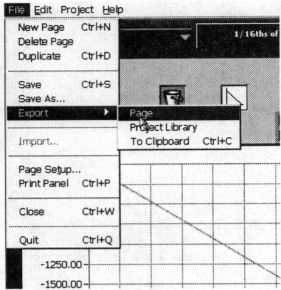

Figure 3.71. Use the File: Export: Page function to exporting data to a file.

3.6.3   View and Compare Area

The **View and Compare Area** is used to view, compare, measure, and print data sets. Each page in the View and Compare Area can be used to perform one of these four functions.

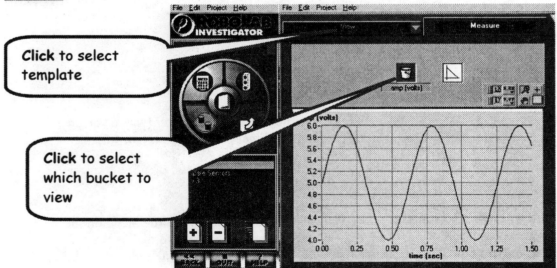

Figure 3.72. View and Compare Area.

The **view** template (figure 3.72) is used to view a single data set much like the Upload Area. You can select which bucket to view, the plot type and access the graph controls. In the **Upload Area**, the bucket icon defines which bucket the data will be stored in. In the **View and Compare Area**, the bucket indicates which data set is to be examined.

The **Compare** template is used to examine two data sets on the same graph. Just as before, you can control the plot type and access the graph control tools.

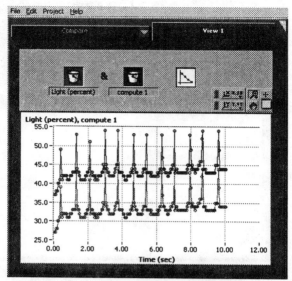

Figure 3.73. Comparing two data sets.

The **Measure** template (figure 3.74) can be used to perform basic statistical measurements on a single data set. You can determine minimum, maximum, mean, standard deviation, slope, and area under the curve.

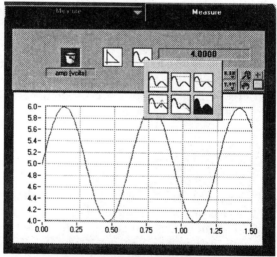

Figure 3.74. The measure template allows you to do simple statistics on data.

Finally, the **Print** template can be used to print one or more of the pages you've created in the View and Compare Area.

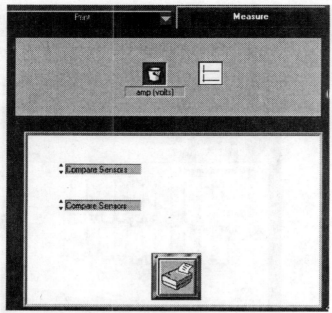

Figure 3.75. The Print template is used to print pages.

Exporting Data

Just as in the upload area, data can be exported to text file by selecting **Export: Page** from the **File** menu (see Figure 3.71). In the compare template, the exported text file will contain both sets of data.

3.6.4   Compute Area

The **Compute Area** is for manipulating data that has been uploaded into a bucket. For example, you may want to subtract the mean and then integrate a data set, which can be accomplished quite easily in ROBOLAB.

There are 5 different Compute Tool Levels. For the Basic Investigator skill badge, we'll only cover Compute Tools 1, 2, and 3 here (Compute Tools 4 and 5 will be covered in Chapter 5).

Compute Tools 1

Compute Tools 1 allows you to manipulate a single data set using basic algebraic operations. You can perform up to two sequential operations using up to three data sets or constants. If you want to do more than 2 math operations, you will have to spread it among multiple pages. The same buckets can be used in the calculations on different pages, but you should use a different results bucket for each page.

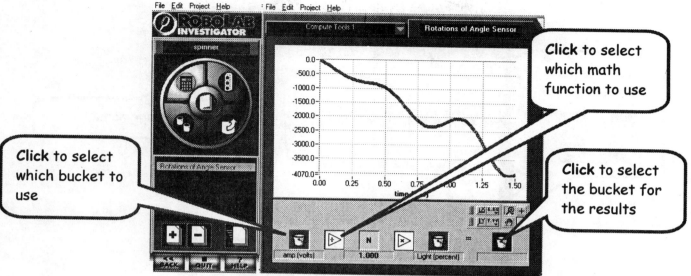

Click to select which bucket to use

Click to select which math function to use

Click to select the bucket for the results

Figure 3.76. Compute Tools 1 template.

All 10 buckets are available for use, along with a numeric (floating point) constant. There are 9 different algebraic operations available: add, subtract, multiply, divide, sine, cosine, tangent, exponential, and natural logarithm.

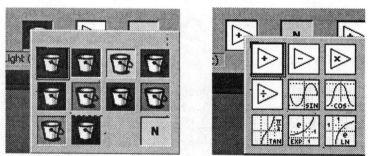

Figure 3.77. Compute Tools 1 Bucket and Math pop-up menus.

Compute Tools 2

Compute Tools 2 is used to plot one data set against another. Unlike **View and Compare Area,** here we can select which part of the each data set we want to use. Since each bucket actually contains 3 columns of data (data point number (**N**), time (**X**), and value (**Y**)), we have a choice of three values to choose from. In the figure below we've plotted **N** versus **Y** instead of the standard **X** versus **Y** (take a close look at the axes labels).

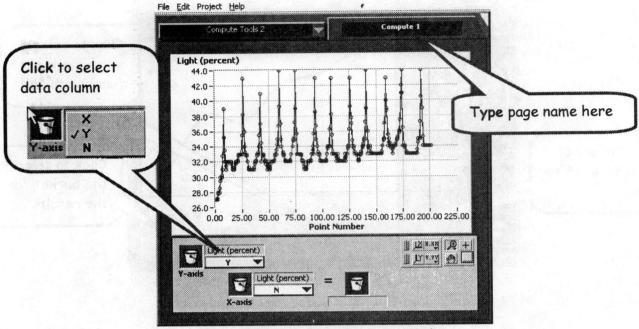

Figure 3.78. Compute Tools 2 template.

Compute Tools 3

Compute Tools 3 is used to manipulate a single data set with basic math functions. Two sequential operations can be performed on any of the 10 data buckets. As always, be sure to use a different bucket for your results for each Compute Tools page.

In figure 3.79, we've differentiated the light sensor data in the red bucket and stored this processed data in the light blue bucket.

Figure 3.79. Compute Tools 3 template.

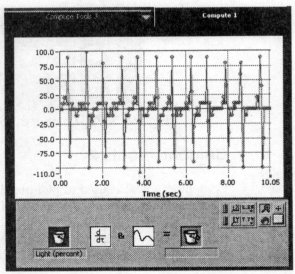

There are 11 different math functions available in Compute Tools 3: no change, minimum, maximum, mean, standard deviation, slope, area under the curve, derivative, integral, average lines, and linear curve fit.

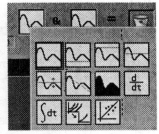

Figure 3.80. Compute Tools 3 functions pop-up menu.

Interesting from a numerical methods standpoint, integrating the light blue bucket does not result in the recovery of the original data, which was in the red bucket (compare Figures 3.78 and 3.81).

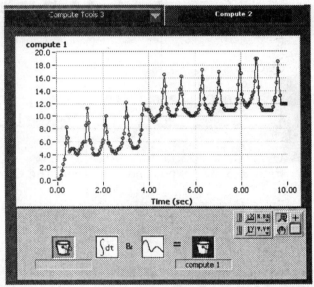

Figure 3.81. Integrating the differentiated data does not recover the original data set!

Exporting Data

After you've manipulated the data, it can be exported to a text file as shown in Figure 3.82.

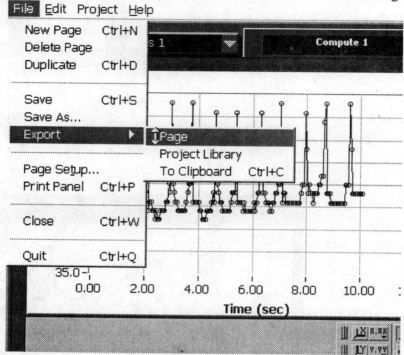

Figure 3.82. Exporting data from the Compute Area.

3.6.5   Journal Area

The journal area is used to document your project. You can include graphs, programs, and digital images to help you describe your project.

Figure 3.83. Journal Area

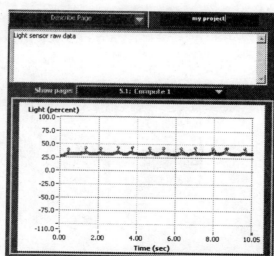

CHAPTER 4
BLACK LEVEL

Skill badges available in this Chapter

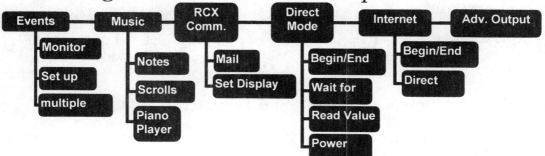

4.1 Black Challenges

All Black Level Design Challenges presume that you have already earned all the Green and White Level skill badges.

4.1.1 LEGO® Slot Machine

Challenge: We're from Nevada, so the one-armed-bandit was bound to make an appearance in this book sooner or later. The objective of this challenge is to make a LEGO® slot machine which randomly picks three numbers between 1 and 4 and if all three numbers match, do something spectacular.

Skill Badges: `Events`

Procedures:

Experimental Setup: Nothing special needed, except a gaming permit if any money changes hands.

Robot Design: Rather than use reels like actual slot machines, for this challenge we will use the LCD to display the numbers. Each random number selected will be displayed using one of the digits on the LCD. For example, if the numbers were 1, 4 and 2, then 142 would be displayed on the LCD. The user should see the numbers on the LCD changing randomly to simulate the spinning of the reels.

Your version of a slot machine should use a light or touch sensor to begin the "spinning" of the reels and then stop one number every 2 seconds (for a total of 6 seconds). Thus, after the spinning starts all three digits should be randomly changing. After 2 seconds, 1 digit is fixed and the other 2 are still randomly changing. After 4 seconds, 2 digits are fixed and the third is randomly changing. Finally, after 6 seconds all three digits should be fixed, and your program should check for a winner (such as 333) and do something creative if a winner is detected.

Program: To program the slot machine, you will need to use **containers**, **events** and the **set display** function. You actually could do this challenge without events, but we will insist that you use them for this challenge. Either a light or touch sensor should be used to start the reels spinning. To get the reels to stop spinning at 2 second intervals, _you must use a **timer event**_.

A flowchart for a sample algorithm is shown on the next page, but there are many possible programs that will satisfy this Challenge. The example shown does not use a task split, but your solution may.

Hints: Each task can have its own independent event start and land.

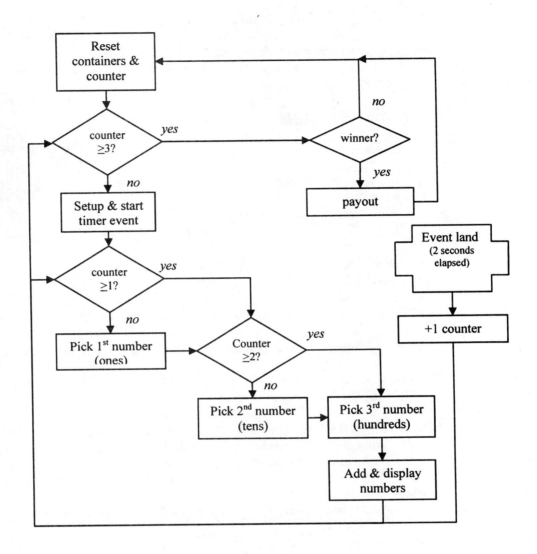

Grading:

Your grade will be based 50% on performance and 50% on creativity and aesthetics.

Performance	Creativity & Aesthetics
A: Your slot machine works perfectly	A+: Best of show
B: "Spins" and stops, but doesn't pay winners	A: Outstanding
C: The reels "spin" but don't stop	B: Good
D: The reels don't "spin"	C: Okay
F: You don't show up to class	D: Nothing special
	F: Divert your eyes!

4.1.2   The Sound of Music

Challenge: The band geeks finally get revenge! Your job is to make a musical instrument using LEGO® bricks. You should try to emulate the real instrument's look and sound as best as possible.

Skill Badges: `Music`

Procedures:

Experimental Setup: No special setup is required for this Challenge.

Robot Design: Since you have a limited number of sensors (2 touch and 1 light), you'll have to improvise a bit. Here are some things to consider:
- What does the real instrument look like?
- What does the real instrument sound like?
- How many different sound combinations can you get with 3 sensors?
- How are you going to control the duration of the notes?

You might want to visit your local musical instrument store to get ideas.

Program: Your program must play each note individually. You are not allowed to use the music scrolls for this Challenge.

Hints: Don't overlook the light sensor. It turns out that a light sensor also makes a good proximity sensor. As shown in the photo above, sliding the white beam in an out of the black "tunnel" results in light sensor values ranging from 30 to 60.

Grading:

Your grade will be based 50% on performance and 50% on creativity and aesthetics.

Performance	Creativity & Aesthetics
A+: You play a duet with another team	A+: Looks like the real thing
A: We can recognize the song	A: Outstanding
B: Looks like an instrument & plays sounds	B: Good
C: Makes noises	C: Okay
D: Looks like an instrument	D: Nothing special
F: You don't show up to class	F: Divert your eyes!

4.1.3   Bionic Bat

Challenge: The objective of this challenge is to make a proximity detector using the light sensor and the RCX infrared communications port. You detector should play ascending notes as it gets closer to an object.

Skill Badges: RCX Comm.   AND   Music

Procedures:

Experimental Setup: Nothing special is needed for this challenge. However, a fairly dark room with no external windows (which can act as significant IR sources) is helpful.

Robot Design: The physical appearance of the robot will count towards creativity. However, in terms of functionality only the RCX and a light sensor are required (as shown in the photo). See section 4.4.3 to get started on investigating the behavior of an IR proximity detector.

Program: The ***send mail*** function will be used to activate the IR emitter on the RCX. Since the IR signal is not continuous (it's actually a series of short pulses), you will have to develop a way of filtering the light sensor readings. You might consider either averaging the readings or using the maximum value during a short time interval.

Your "bat" should emit a tone at all times (to help it navigate of course). The pitch should be inversely proportional to the distance from the object. That is, as you get closer, the pitch should increase.

Hints: You should make sure the IR power on the RCX is set to high. This is done via the Administrator tab on the introductory ROBOLAB window. Also, the maximum frequency at which you can repeatedly send mail will depend on the total size of your program, so try to be conservative with your code (especially task splits).

Grading:
Your grade will be based 75% on performance and 25% on creativity and aesthetics.

Performance	Creativity & Aesthetics
A: You can navigate with your eyes closed	A+: Best of show
B: Your bat works most of the time, only occasionally bumping into walls	A: Outstanding
	B: Good
C: Your bat detects walls, but not reliably	C: Okay
D: Your bat makes noise	D: Nothing special
F: You don't show up to class	F: Divert your eyes!

4.1.4   Speed Walking (revisited)

Challenge: This is an advanced version of the Challenge described in section 2.1.7. Design and build the fastest walking robot you can. Just to make things interesting, you will be racing over a pebble surface. The "start gun" will be in the form of RCX mail.

Skill Badges: [RCX Comm.]

Procedures:

Experimental Setup: This challenge is typically run over a pebble course in a single elimination format with the winner of each race advancing to the next round. The instructor will also need to have an RCX ready to send out the mail values (be sure to set IR power to high). The program should send out several "false" signals to keep things interesting.

Robot Design: For this exercise you need to design and construct a robot that can walk (crawling may also be permitted) over a mildly uneven surface.

Most running races begin with the famous phrase, "On your mark, get set, go!" In this challenge, we will simulate this phrase with a series of 3 mail values: 11, 12, and 13. Thus, your robot should react to each mail value but not begin racing until the last number (13) is received. For the first 2 mail values (11 and 12) you should think of something creative to do without starting the race (i.e. without moving forward).

The only restriction is that you cannot intentionally trip another robot.

Program: You must program your robot to react to the 3 different mail values (11, 12 and 13). Your robot should not react to any other mail values or repeated mail values.

Grading:

Your grade will be based 25% on performance and 75% on creativity and aesthetics. Creativity will be based on your "on your mark" and "get set" actions in addition to the walking/crawling mechanism employed.

Performance	Creativity & Aesthetics
A+: You are the fastest walker	A+: Best of show
A: You walk, react, and win at least once	A: Outstanding
B: You walk and react to mail correctly	B: Good
C: You walk, but react to the wrong mail	C: Okay
D: You walk, but don't react to mail	D: Nothing special
F: You don't show up to class	F: Divert your eyes!

4.1.5   Simon Says

Challenge: You know the rules of the game. Now we want you to make a robot that plays it as well as you do. Your instructor will build a robot that acts as "Simon," and your robot has to do is exactly what we say or suffer the consequences. The last robot standing wins in this battle of wits and deception.

Skill Badges:

> RCX
> Comm.

Procedures:

Experimental Setup: The instructor will have an RCX programmed to send out mail values ranging from 0-255 (it should send the value 4 times in a row in rapid succession). The RCX should be programmed to display the mail value sent to the LCD panel so everyone knows what value was just sent. Typically, up to 10 student robots can participate simultaneously.

Robot Design: Since the RCX can't decipher voice commands (yet) Simon will be "talking" to your robots over the IR port. You can read and write to the IR port by using the Mail commands in ROBOLAB.

Everybody lines up their robots with the IR transmitter/receiver facing Simon. Your robot must perform a specific action based on the number Simon sends to you via the IR port. We will send the number four times consecutively so nobody misses the signal. For this reason, do not check the IR port while you are performing the requested action (i.e. don't do the action 4 times in a row). Simon will wait long enough for everybody to complete the action before sending out another signal.

Program: If Simon sends out a:
"1," your robot must turn to the clockwise 90 degrees (approximately) and turn back to face Simon.
"2," your robot must turn counterclockwise 90 degrees and turn back to face Simon
"3," your robot must drive forward for 6 inches, play a tune for 5 seconds, then return to its original spot.
"4," your robot must drive back 6 inches, do a full 360 and drive forward to its original spot
If Simon sends any other number, you should do nothing.

The Goal - don't get knocked out: if your robot performs the wrong task or moves when it shouldn't, it's going to be obvious since it will stand out from the competition like a sore thumb.

Hints: Try to make your motions as precise as possible since having your IR port in view of Simon's is essential to lasting the whole round. In order to make two motors behave the same (to drive straight forward without curving, for instance), you may need to run them at different power levels. Experiment.

Grading:

Your grade will be based 75% on performance and 25% on creativity and aesthetics.

Performance	Creativity & Aesthetics
A+: You're the last one standing	A+: Best of show
A: Your robot performs admirably, performing all the correct functions	A: Outstanding
B: Your robot gets dumped early on due to very imprecise movements or incorrect actions	B: Good
C: Your robot does the wrong move the first round	C: Okay
D: Your robot is left at the line, wondering what happened	D: Nothing special
F: You don't show up to class	F: Divert your eyes!

4.1.6   The Almost Demolition Derby

<u>**Challenge:**</u> This Challenge requires cooperation between two teams. The objective is to build two LEGO® cars that race straight towards each other and then stop, narrowly avoiding a head-on collision.

<u>**Skill Badges:**</u>

<u>**Procedures:**</u>

Experimental Setup: All that is required is a flat surface with two lines 4 feet apart that indicate the start location of each vehicle.

Robot Design: Your two LEGO® vehicles will start facing each other 4 feet apart. You accomplish this daredevil feat by constantly communicating, via the IR port, the distance your car has traveled to your partner. By knowing how far you and your partner have traveled, each of you should be able to calculate the remaining distance between your vehicles and determine when to stop.

One obvious solution is for only one of the cars to actually move, which is okay except that you will get a D grade if you take this approach (both teams get the same grade in this Challenge). Neither car can stop moving for more than 2 seconds if you want to earn a C or better grade.

Finally, to stress the point that engineering is a conservative profession, if your cars crash into each other (or pass each other if your aim is poor), then you will get a C. It is much better to stop way short than to go too far.

Program: The IR port cannot send and receive data simultaneously, so it won't help if you are both sending data at the same time. Thus, you will have to work out a *handshaking* protocol that defines when you will send and when you will receive data. To measure how far you've gone, you can either go by time or build an encoder (see chapter 3.1.9).

Hints: You many want to set the IR power level to high (see chapter 1.5.1)

<u>**Grading:**</u>

Your grade will be based 75% on performance and 25% on creativity and aesthetics (more creativity points will be given if you cars are very different).

Performance	Creativity & Aesthetics
A+: Fastest pair to within 9 inches	A+: Best of show
A: You stop within 9 inches of each other	A: Outstanding
B: You run, communicate, and stop without crashing into each other.	B: Good
	C: Okay
C: You crash into each other - be conservative!	D: Nothing special
D: One of the cars stops for more than 2 seconds	F: Divert your eyes!
F: You don't show up to class	

4.1.7   Marching Band

Challenge: This challenge requires the cooperation of all teams in your class. The teams will each contribute to the creation of a multi-robot marching band that interacts with each other and puts on an entertaining "show."

Skill Badges: **Music** AND **RCX Comm.**

You have to earn the Music Skill Badge. You most likely will use RCX Communication in this project. Your instructor will determine which skill badges you get based on an examination of your programs.

Procedures:

Experimental Setup: The event will be held in the hallway (on the linoleum floor).

Robot Design: You may use only LEGO® components, and at most, only <u>one</u> RCX may function as a remote control (i.e., human-controlled). All other members of the band must operate without direct human involvement. The marching band should be moving/translating (this is after all a "marching" band).

Program: Your program will most likely include communication and music features.

Hints: You may wish to consider the following aspects of this problem...
- How is your group (the whole class) going to arrive at a basic design?
- Do you want to have a "conductor" or "Band Leader"?
- How do you handle communications between so many robots?
- Perform once or loop?
- Will you feature different or identical robots in terms of both the mechanical aspects and the music being played?

Grading:

Your grade will be based 50% on performance and 50% on creativity and aesthetics.

Performance	Creativity and Aesthetics
A: Lots of translation across the floor, very effective communication & the instructors can recognize the song.	A: "Worth the ticket price". A well-choreographed and executed show.
B: Some translation of robots, in-place motion and music. Minimal collisions and timing problems.	B: Suitably ambitious and good execution.
C: Collisions and out-of-time music prevail. Many members of band are not "with the program".	C: Not a very ambitious show, but it was executed fairly well.
D: Only one member of the band seems to be doing something.	D: The crowd either fell asleep or fell off their chairs laughing during your show.
F: You don't show up to class.	F: You don't show up to class.

4.1.8   Animal Behavior

Challenge: This is civilized head-to-head sumo wrestling battle. Just like real sumo wrestling, the objective is to push your opponent out of the ring. However, your robots must display some *animal behavior* at the start and end of the battle to make things interesting.

Skill Badges: [Events] AND [RCX Comm.]

Procedures:

Experimental Setup: The competition arena is a white circular area 3 feet in diameter. The outer edge of the competition arena is lined with silver (mirror-like) tape. Approximately 6 inches inward is a concentric ring colored black. The competition can be autonomous or tethered (the instructor will inform you). Your instructor may also place a limit on the size of your robots.

The instructor will also have an RCX or two on hand that can send and receive the 3 mail commands just in case things go awry. Typically, most problems occur while trying to receive the surrender mail signal.

Robot Design: In the Animal Kingdom, animals fight all the time over territory, mating rights, food, etc. A typical encounter (typically between two males) starts with *posturing* (grunting, beating chest, or stomping feet). Then the actual battle commences. However, animals rarely fight to the death. One animal, the loser, *submits* (runs away, puts it's tail between its legs, or rolls over belly up). The winner then often performs some kind of *victory* behavior just to rub salt into the wounds.

In this competition your robot will have to be able perform three kinds of behaviors:
   Posturing – try to intimidate your opponent.
   Submission – "I give up!"
   Victory- "Yeah, and don't come 'round here anymore!"

The rules of the game are simple. Start by taking turns performing your posturing behaviors. If you get pushed out of the competition ring (i.e. reach the outer silver tape) you lose and must submit to your opponent. If you win, you must perform a victory behavior.

Program: Since you won't know until the battle whether you go first or second, you should have 2 programs that are nearly identical. If you go first, you should perform your posturing behavior and then send mail (value = 10) to your opponent. You should then wait until you receive a mail value of 20 from your opponent before commencing to seek and destroy.

If you go second, you should wait patiently until you receive mail with a value of 10. Once this happens, it's your turn to display your posturing behavior. When you are done showing off, you should send mail with a value of 20 and begin fighting!

Both robots **_must use an Event_** to monitor the outer edge of the ring (the silver tape). If you cross the outer edge, you robot should perform its submission behavior and start continuously sending out mail with a value of 30.

If you detect mail with value of 30 at anytime, this is a clear indication that your opponent has given up (submits to your overwhelming dominance) and your robot should perform its victory behavior.

Your robot should not react to any mail values other than 10, 20 and 30. The instructor may have an RCX on hand that will send out "false signals" just to be diabolical.

Hints: Be creative with your behaviors. Your light sensor should point downwards to detect when you are getting close to the edge (the black line) and when you've lost (the silver line). If you reach the black line, you may want to perform some kind of "evasive" maneuver. Finally, don't block the IR port or you won't be able to send/receive mail.

It is also important to end up facing your opponent after posturing or you won't be able to send or receive mail effectively.

Grading:

Your grade will be based 30% on performance and 70% on creativity and aesthetics. The 3 behaviors will obviously play an important role in evaluating the creativity of your design.

Performance	Creativity & Aesthetics
A+: Undefeated champion	A+: Best of show
A: You win more than once	A: Outstanding
B: You battle and display the posturing and submit/victory behaviors on cue	B: Good
	C: Okay
C: You posture and start battling on cue	D: Nothing special
D: You have something that moves	F: Divert your eyes!
F: You don't show up to class	

4.1.9   Feeding Frenzy

Challenge: Build a robot that wanders around randomly looking for food, stops and plays music when it finds food and is smart enough to call for help if it hasn't found any food in the past 15 seconds.

Skill Badges: Events   and   Music   and   Adv. Output

Procedures:

Experimental Setup: All you need is a large enough area to let all robots wander around and some contrasting colored tape as food to put on the floor.

Robot Design: All you need is robot that can wander around (on legs or wheels) that has a light sensor facing down to detect the food on the floor.

Program: You'll have to use some of the advanced output functions to drive around randomly. The more often you change direction, the smaller the area your robot will search for food. Try to compose or chose music that represents the mood of your robot when it finds food or is going hungry. Finally, our only requirement is that you **must** use an **event** to determine when the 15 seconds has elapsed.

Grading:
   Your grade will be based 50% on performance and 50% on creativity and aesthetics.

Performance	Creativity & Aesthetics
A: Your robot can find food and cries for help	A+: Best of show
B: Your robot can find food	A: Looks like the real thing
C: Your animal moves and makes noise	B: Looks like an animal
D: You animal moves	C: Something moves around
F: You don't show up to class	D: Looks like it was once alive
	F: Put it out of its misery!

This challenge is based on an assignment described by Gage and Murphy in "Principles and experiences using LEGOs to teach behavioral robotics" proceedings of the 33rd ASEE/IEEE Frontiers in Education Conference, Session F4E, Boulder, CO, November 2003.

4.1.10   Can you hear me now?

<u>Challenge:</u> The objective is to send a short coded message over the Internet.

<u>Skill Badges:</u>   Internet

<u>Procedures:</u>

Experimental Setup: Two computers with Internet access are required for this challenge. Ideally, the computers are located in different rooms. The instructor will configure the ROBOLAB Internet Server software on the host computer.

Each team must have at least one person to program and one person to receive the message. During class, the instructor will specify to the programmers a short message (3 or 4 letters). The programmers must then write a ROBOLAB program and send it via the internet to their partners, who must execute the program on their robot and decode the message.

Robot Design: Your team will have to determine how to decode a message. There are lots of ways: Morse code, flashing lights, alphabet wheel, LCD display, Braille, etc. Creativity will be largely based on the method you choose to decode the message.

Program: The program will depend on the method your team selected to decode messages. You can practice without using the Internet, but be sure you know how to send and receive using ROBOLAB Internet Server before class.

Hints: You may want to include some kind of error checking scheme in your program.

<u>Grading</u>:

Your grade will be based 50% on performance and 50% on creativity and aesthetics.

Performance	Creativity & Aesthetics
A: You successfully decode the message	A+: Best of show
B: Your program is received and runs	A: Outstanding
C: You send the program somewhere	B: Good
D: You show up to class with something	C: Okay
F: You don't show up to class	D: Nothing special
	F: Divert your eyes!

4.1.11   CodeMaster

Challenge: The objective is to decode a short message based on container values. The trick is that the container values will be set using **direct mode** while your decoder program is running.

Skill Badges:

Procedures:

Experimental Setup: Computers with ROBOLAB and IR towers are required for this challenge.

Robot Design: In his book, *Creative Projects With LEGO Mindstorms*, Ben Erwin describes the CodeMaster developed for sending secret messages. This is a similar design task in that you must somehow translate a container value into letter. There are lots of ways of communicating text: Morse code, flashing lights, alphabet wheel (see next page), LCD display, Braille, etc. Creativity will be largely based on the method you choose to decode the message. Displaying a number to the LCD and then looking up the corresponding letter will not earn you very many creativity points.

Program: The exact program will depend on the method your team selected to decode messages. However, all programs must use containers #3 through #6 to store the 4 numbers. Each number will correspond to the letter's place in the alphabet. That is, 1=A, 2=B, and so on through 26=Z. Once the first non-zero container value is detected by your decoder program, it should start decoding the 4 letter message.

During class, the instructor will tell you the message that must be decoded by your robot. With your decoder program already running, you must use **direct mode** and write a program that fills each of the containers (#3 through #6) with the appropriate number.

Hints: Typically, the faster your decoder moves (if it moves at all), the more prone to error it will be.

Grading:

Your grade will be based 75% on performance and 25% on creativity and aesthetics.

Performance	Creativity & Aesthetics
A: You successfully decode the message	A+: Best of show
B: Message received but decoded wrong	A: Outstanding
C: Direct mode program works	B: Good
D: Your decoder program runs	C: Okay
F: You don't show up to class	D: Nothing special
	F: Divert your eyes!

4.1.12 Reverse Engineering

Challenge: The objective of this challenge is to reverse engineer another team's program that is sent to you over the Internet.

Skill Badges: Internet

Procedures:

Experimental Setup: Two computers with Internet access are required for this challenge. The computers do not need to be located in different rooms. The instructor will configure the ROBOLAB Internet Server software on the host computer.

Robot Design: Your team should build a robot and write a program to download to it over the Internet. In class, you should give your robot to another team and then send your program over the Internet. The other team (the one with your robot) will then play with your robot and try to determine what your program looked like. Your robot must utilize at least 2 sensors and one motor.

While they are busy trying to reverse engineering your code, you will be busy reverse engineering another team's code.

Program: Unless you derive pleasure from watching your classmates sweat, you should create a program with only moderate complexity. To make things fair, your program cannot contain any mail functions and must contain at least one fork and one loop/jump.

Hints: In order to reverse engineer code, you will probably have to run the program and test the reaction to the sensors many times.

Grading:

You should submit both your original program and the other team's reverse engineered program. Be sure to clearly label which team reversed engineered your program. Your grade will be based 70% on how well you reverse engineered the other team's program and 30% on how well your program was reverse engineered by them.

Performance
A: You essentially reverse engineer the entire code
B: You get most of the main program features
C: You reverse engineer some of the code
D: You get a program over the Internet
F: You don't show up to class

4.1.13   Virtual Spring

<u>**Challenge:**</u> The objective of this Challenge is to investigate the basics of feedback control by building a robot that tries to stay in one place when pushed.

<u>**Skill Badges:**</u>   **Adv. Output**

<u>**Procedures:**</u>

Experimental Setup: All robots will need to use a rotation sensor, which are not part of the standard ROBOLAB Team Challenge Kit. No other special setup is required.

Robot Design: All you need for this design challenge is a robot that has at least one motor and a rotation sensor. The robot should try to return to its original position when pushed. That is, if you push it forward the robot should return to the original position by backing up. Likewise, if you push it backwards, the robot should drive forward. Like a spring, the further you push it, the faster it should return.

The ***error*** is defined as the difference between the actual and desired number of rotations. Since the desired number of rotations is zero for our case, the error will be equal to the actual reading from the rotation sensor. In order to simulate a spring, you need to set the motor power to be proportional to the error (thus the term, ***proportional control***). That is, large errors should cause high motor power to be used.

In terms of robot construction, any LEGO® car will do. We have found that cars that are so underpowered that they do not move at power level 1 seem to work well. Play with various gear ratios and wheel diameters to find a combination that works. We also recommend using an AC adapter, as stalling a motor drains the batteries very quickly.

Program: You will use Proportional control (a.k.a. P-control) to make the robot return to its original position. You will need to use one container for the P-gain and, unless you use the ***Motor Forward-Back*** function, you will need one more container for the motor power (an integer from 0 to 7). Note, the ***Motor Forward-Back*** function stops the motor when the error is zero. You may want to use a ***float*** instead (see section 2.7.4 to learn how to see the source code of a function).

Try lots of different P-gain settings to investigate the different responses. In general the lower the P-gain, the longer it will take for the robot to "settle down". But increasing the P-gain can cause some strange behaviors! Can you get both stable and unstable behaviors using the same program but different P-gains?

<u>**Grading:**</u>

Your grade will be based 80% on performance and 20% on creativity and aesthetics.

Performance	Creativity & Aesthetics
A: You demonstrate 2 different responses	A: Outstanding
B: You demonstrate 1 response	B: Good
C: It works only in one direction	C: Okay
D: One show up to class with a robot	D: Nothing special
F: You don't show up to class	F: Divert your eyes!

4.1.14   Stay Away From the Light

<u>**Challenge:**</u> The objective of this Challenge is to investigate the basics of feedback control by building a robot that adjusts the motor power level according the light level.

<u>**Skill Badges:**</u>   **Adv. Output**

<u>**Procedures:**</u>

Experimental Setup: All that is required is a flat surface and a flashlight.

Robot Design: This project is an advanced version of the light following project (see 3.1.5). Instead of simply heading for the light, this time you need to build a robot that will home in on a specific light intensity (specified by the instructor). When the intensity is too low, the robot should drive forward. When the intensity is too high, the robot should back up. Thus, the robot should go towards the light, but not get too close.

The *error* is defined as the difference between the actual and desired light intensities. In this challenge, you need to set the motor power to be proportional to the error (thus the term, *proportional control*). If the error is positive (desired intensity is less than actual intensity) the robot should back up. The larger the error, the faster (more power) it backs up. If the error is negative, the robot should move forward (towards the light), again with the motor power proportional to the magnitude of the error.

In terms of robot construction, any LEGO® car will do. The only caveat is that the car should not move at power level 1. That is, at power level 1, the motors should stall. Play with various gear ratios and wheel diameters to find a combination that works. We also recommend using an AC adapter, as stalling a motor drains the batteries fast.

Program: You will use Proportional control (a.k.a. P-control) to make the robot return to its original position. You will need to use one container for the P-gain and, unless you use the *Motor Forward-Back* function, you will need one more container for the motor power (an integer from 0 to 7). Note, the *Motor Forward-Back* function stops the motor when the error is zero. You may want to use a *float* instead (see section 2.7.4 to learn how to see the source code of a function).

Try lots of different P-gain settings to investigate the different responses. In general the lower the P-gain, the longer it will take for the robot to "settle down". But increasing the P-gain can cause some strange behaviors! Can you get both stable and unstable behaviors using the same program but different P-gains? In-class you must demonstrate at least 3 different P-gain settings.

<u>**Grading:**</u>

Your grade will be based 80% on performance and 20% on creativity and aesthetics.

Performance	Creativity & Aesthetics
A: You demonstrate 2 different responses	A: Outstanding
B: You demonstrate 1 response	B: Good
C: It works only in one direction	C: Okay
D: One show up to class with a robot	D: Nothing special
F: You don't show up to class	F: Divert your eyes!

4.2 The Events Badge `Events`

The Events badge covers the basic concepts of an event: what an event is, how you program an event, and the rules about multiple events. The more advanced event concepts (e.g. hysteresis) will be covered in Chapter 6.

Figure 4.1. The **events** sub-palette is located at the bottom of the **Structures** sub-palette.

4.2.1 What's an event?

An *event* is like a special combination of a *wait for* and a *jump* that runs in the background. When the specified *event* occurs, the program jumps to the *event landing* location.

The program below is an example of using an *event* to jump out of an infinite loop created with a *jump/land* pair. The program sets up a *red event* that is triggered when touch sensor 1 is pressed, *starts monitoring* for the *red event* and then enters an infinite loop that turns on *Motor A*. When the *red event* occurs (i.e. touch sensor 1 is pressed), the program jumps out of the infinite loop and lands at the *event landing* and then stops *Motor A* before ending.

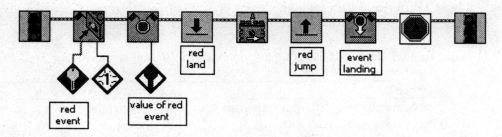

Figure 4.2. The red event is used to jump out of the infinite loop.

4.2.2   How to program an event

All events follow the same basic format:

1. *Set up the event* – define what condition you want to wait for
2. *Start monitoring event* – tell the RCX to start checking for the event(s)
3. *Event landing* – this specifies the location in the program that ALL the events will jump to.

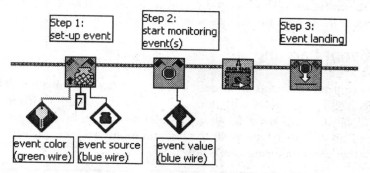

Figure 4.3. The 3 basic steps in using an event and the 3 basic event modifiers required to setup and monitor an event.

 ## Step 1: Setting up an Event

Setting up an *event* is very similar to using the familiar *wait for* command. Figure 4.4 shows the most common types of events that we will use (for now, we'll ignore the rest). The most common types of *events* range from a *touch event* to a *light event* to a *timer event*.

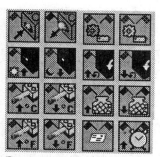

Figure 4.4. The 16 common types of events to set up.

In addition to defining what you want to monitor (Figure 4.4), you also have to define the *event source*, and which *event* (red, blue, or yellow) you are setting up. The *event source* is *sensor port value, container value, mail value,* or *timer value,* depending on the type of event. There are 3 basic event keys (red, blue, and yellow) and a generic event key in case you want to monitor more than 3 events.

Figure 4.5. Red, blue, and yellow events.

 ## Step 2: Monitoring an event

After you set up the event, nothing actually happens until you start monitoring for the event. This is done using the green *start event monitoring* command and wiring the *value of event* to it (see figure 4.3). If you want to monitor more than 1 event, you should wire all the event values to a single *start event monitoring* command (see section 4.2.4 below)

 ## Step 3: Event Landing

The final step in using events is to define the *event landing* location. The *event landing* defines where ALL the events will land. Even if you've set up 3 different colored events, they will all land at the same location. By definition, the event landing also stops the monitoring of all events. If you wish to continue monitoring events after the landing, you need to restart event monitoring (see below).

 TIP

All events share a single event landing

The number one problem students have is getting used to the fact that events can occur at any time during the program. Motors will keep running, timers keep going, etc. For example, in the program below, once the event occurs a sound is played and the program ends. We forgot to turn off the motors!

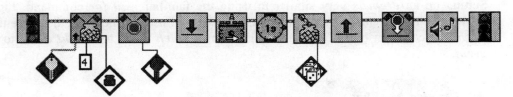

Figure 4.6. This program turns on Motor A until the red container is greater than 4. But we've forgotten to turn the motor off!

4.2.3   Stopping and re-starting event monitoring

We can also stop monitoring and then re-start event monitoring in case you have a part of your program you don't want interrupted for any reason. In the example below, we have stopped the event monitoring while we perform some container math and then re-started the event monitoring after we're done (interrupting us in the midst of doing a calculation could be very bad). In short, if touch senor 3 is pressed while we're doing the math, the event will be ignored because we temporarily stopped monitoring it.

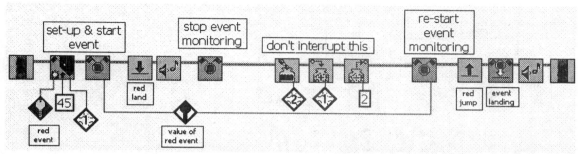

Figure 4.7. Stopping and re-starting event monitoring.

We can also re-start *event monitoring* after the *event landing*, as shown in Figure 4.8. In this example, if the touch sensor is not pressed, the motor will run for a total of 22 seconds. Pressing touch sensor 3 will terminate the loop early and then wait 2 seconds before turning the motor off. However, since we've re-started *event monitoring* after the *event landing*, pressing touch sensor 3 a second time will cause the program to jump backwards (to the event landing). As long as the touch sensor is pressed at least once every 2 seconds, the program will keep jumping backwards from the *wait for 2s* to the *event landing* and the motor will stay on.

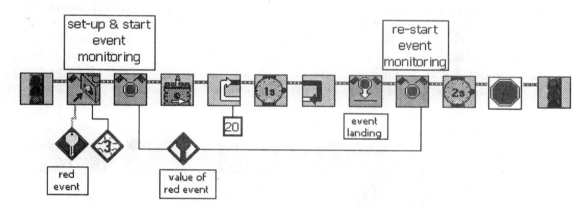

Figure 4.8. Jumping backwards in a program by re-starting event monitoring.

4.2.4 Multiple events

You can monitor up to 15 different events in ROBOLAB using, of course, the generic event because there aren't enough standard event colors (the red event is event #0, blue is event #1, and yellow is event #2). In the example below, we've setup both the blue event and generic event #4. In this case, we can jump out of the infinite loop by either pressing touch sensor 3 or by exposing the light sensor to a bright light. Notice that only one *start monitoring event* command and one *event landing* command are used.

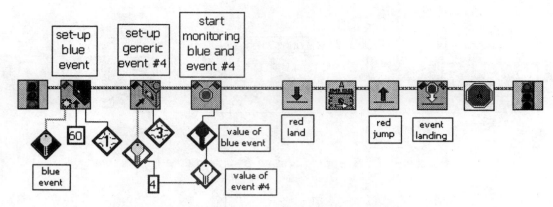

Figure 4.9. You can monitor multiple events, but all events land at the same location.

4.2.5   Events and tasks

It gets a bit complicated when events are used in conjunction with tasks. The basic rule is that you cannot start monitoring an event in one task and have the *event landing* in a different task. This is because each task is essentially an independent program.

However, you can take advantage this independence because you can have one *event landing* per task. Figure 4.10 shows a program that utilizes events in both tasks. Pressing touch sensor 3 will stop motor A and exposing light sensor 1 to a bright light will stop motor C. The program won't end until both tasks have ended.

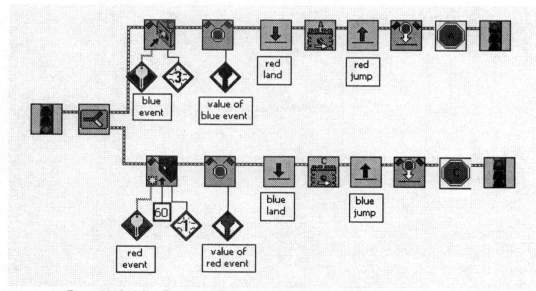

Figure 4.10. Events cannot cross tasks, but you can have one *event landing* per task.

4.2.6   Event Examples

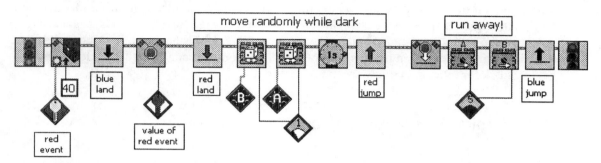

Figure 4.11. An attempt at the LEGO® cockroach program done using events, which doesn't quite work correctly!

You may find it strange to give an example that doesn't work as intended, but we find it very educational so here we go. In Figure 4.11, we've tried to make the LEGO® cockroach program again, this time using events (see Figures 3.12 and 3.33). Unfortunately, it doesn't quite work correctly. Here's why: the event is actually defined as occurring when the light value transitions from below 40 to above 40 (this is called a *leading edge trigger* in electronics lingo). If the light value is already above 40 when we start monitoring for the event, then, by definition, the event has not occurred yet (i.e. it must start below 40 for this to work).

The same will hold true for the other events examples. In Figure 4.10, if the light sensor value starts off greater than 60 at the start, then motor C will not stop until the light value drops below and then rises above 60. Likewise, if the touch sensor is already pressed when the program starts, then it must first be released and then pressed again before Motor A will stop; a very subtle but important point to understand when using events. To learn how to get around this little problem, skip ahead to Chapter 6.

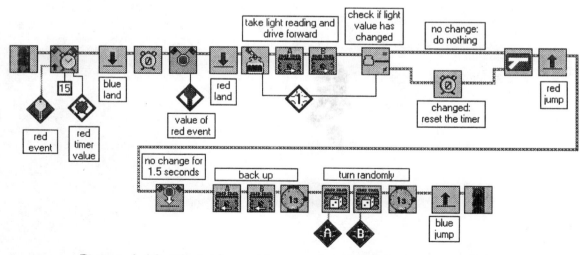

Figure 4.12. Obstacle avoidance using the light sensor and timer event.

Figure 4.12 shows a complex, but very effective, method of obstacle avoidance using a combination of the light sensor and the timer event. The basic idea is to drive forward as long as the light sensor value is changing. If there is no change for 1.5 seconds, chances are you have run into something and are not actually moving. If this happens, back up and then turn randomly. A car running this program will randomly roam around the floor, never getting stuck for more than a few seconds. Try it out!

4.2.7   Looking forward: Advanced Events

Now that you've got a taste for how events work, you may want to know more. In the Advanced Events section of Chapter 6, we show you how to use event forks and containers to determine whether or not an event has occurred or, in the case of multiple events, which event(s) occurred. We also go on to show you how you can control the event triggers more carefully and how to make your program think the event has occurred, even if it has not.

4.3 The Music Badge   [Music]

The Music skill badge emphasizes, not surprisingly, music. There are two main ways to program music in ROBOLAB: the **music sub-palette** and the **piano player**.

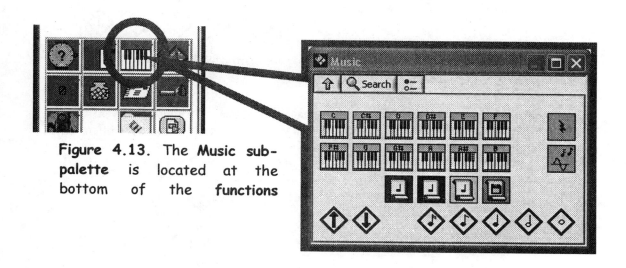

Figure 4.13. The **Music** sub-palette is located at the bottom of the functions

4.3.1   Basic Notes

Using music is fairly easy; in fact you may have already used it in one of the White Level Challenges (Chapter 3).

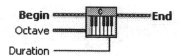

Figure 4.14. Wire terminals for a single note.

All the notes have the same set of wire terminals. If no modifiers are wired, the default is to play a quarter-note on the standard scale. To specify a different duration, the *duration modifiers* are used. When multiple *duration modifiers* are wired together, the durations add. To raise or lower and the octave, the *octave modifiers* are used. By stringing more than one *octave modifier* together, you can raise or lower the note by multiple octaves.

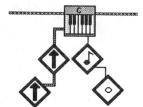

Figure 4.15. Example of raising two octaves and increasing the duration to 1 1/8 counts.

As an example of using both the duration and octave modifiers, we've programmed the first few bars of "On Top of Old Smokey" in the figure below.

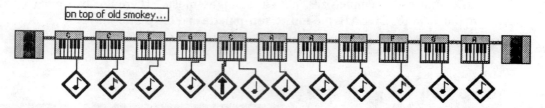

Figure 4.16. First few bars of "On Top of Old Smokey."

This next example demonstrates the major drawback of trying to play a song by wiring together individual notes. Obviously, you wouldn't want to do this very often. There has got to be a better way!

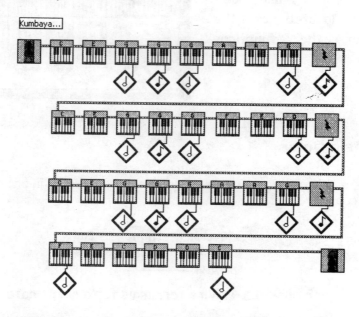

Figure 4.17. There has got to be a simpler way to write music!

4.3.2   Piano Player

Rather than enter all those notes individually, we could make use of the ROBOLAB *music scrolls*. The program in Figure 4.17 can then be simplified to the one shown in Figure 4.18 below once we have saved the song to the *red music scroll*.

Figure 4.18. Making music with the *red music scroll* function.

By default the red, blue and yellow music scrolls have "Frere Jacques," "Row, Row Your Boat," and "Twinkle Little Star" recorded to them. If you want to use any of these three standard songs, then you can simply wire them as shown in Figure 4.18.

To get a custom song, like "On Top of Old Smokey," onto the *red music scroll*, we must utilize the **piano player**. From the **Projects** menu (or **Tools** menu if you are using ROBOLAB version 2.5.2 or earlier), select **Piano Player** as shown in Figure 4.19.

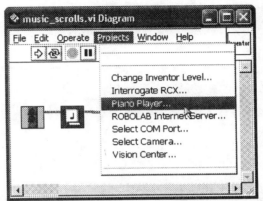

Figure 4.19. The **Piano Player** is accessed via the **Projects** Menu.

The **piano player** actually allows you to do a lot of things, but we're only going to cover the basics here. Recording a song to a *music scroll* is as simple as playing the song on the keyboard and then selecting which music scroll to save it to. If you have the record button on (red = on, gray = off), the notes will appear on the sheet music as you play them. You can select individual notes to change their duration or delete them. When you are satisfied with your creation, you can save your song to one of the three colored scrolls or to a generic file.

In the lower right corner there is one icon of a computer and another of an RCX. Clicking on one of these will determine where your song is played as you compose it. To open a song from a file, either use the File menu or simply click on the title bar (Bach-Inventions shown in the figure below).

Figure 4.20. Left: click on the title-bar to open a new song file. **Right:** click on either the PC or RCX icon to select the output device for the piano player.

Figure 4.21. The **Piano Player** window.

 When the program encounters a music scroll, it will play the song in its entirety before progressing onto the next function.

You can think of a music scroll as a "wait for song to end" function. And because a song can take a long time to play, it is best to put scrolls in a separate task from the rest of the program, as shown in Figure 4.22.

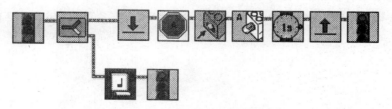

Figure 4.22. The **Piano Player** window.

4.4   The RCX Communication Badge

The front of the RCX houses the IR (infrared) communications port. So far you've used the IR port to download programs from your PC to the RCX and to upload data collected from the RCX to your PC. The RCX Communication skill badge focuses on using the IR port to send messages (mail) between two or more RCX's.

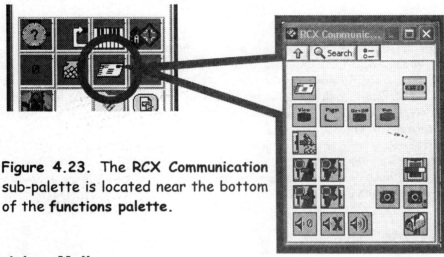

Figure 4.23. The **RCX Communication** sub-palette is located near the bottom of the **functions palette**.

4.4.1   Mail

In ROBOLAB, **mail** is any integer between 0 and 255. Mail is sent and received over the IR port. It is important to note that you cannot send and receive mail at the same time. In real life we're all used to the fact the postman will deliver our mail even if we're not home (and it's not a Sunday or a holiday). A similar feature exists in LEGO® life; *you don't have to wait for mail in order to receive it*. And just like junk mail in real life, in LEGO® life you don't have the choice to decline mail that another RCX sends – you always accept mail in your mailbox automatically (replacing any existing mail in the process).

To send mail to another RCX you use the ***send mail*** function. You can also send yourself mail by filling your own mailbox, just in case you can't wait for someone else to send you mail. Both the ***send mail*** and ***fill mailbox*** functions are located on the **RCX Communication** sub-palette (Figure 4.23)

If you would rather wait for the mail to be delivered, you can use the ***wait for mail*** function, which is located on the **wait for** sub-palette. The ***wait for mail*** function zeros the mailbox and then waits for the specified mail value to arrive before proceeding to the next function in the program. It's like sitting at home next to your mailbox and waiting for the postman to arrive with an important letter.

Once you've received mail, it's stored in your mailbox. Unfortunately, in ROBOLAB your mailbox is very small and can only hold one piece of mail (i.e. a single integer from 0 to 255). However, there are lots of things you can do with your one piece of mail. There are ***mail forks***, ***mail loops***, ***mail containers***, and ***mail events***. You can also use the ***value of the mail*** anywhere an integer **numerical constant** can be used.

Figure 4.24. Some of the various mail functions.

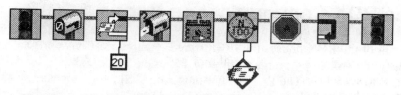

Figure 4.25. An example using the mail wait for, loop, and value.

Figure 4.25 is a program illustrating a few of the mail functions. The program starts by *emptying the mailbox* (sets the mail equal to zero) and then begins looping. Inside the loop, the program *waits for mail* and then turns on **Motor A** for a length of time governed by the *value of the mail*. As long as the mail received is less than 20, the loop will repeat. If mail with a value greater than 20 is received, the program will turn on the motor one last time for that length of time and then end.

Note that in this program, the value of the mailbox may change if another RCX sends mail between the *wait for mail* and the *end of loop* functions. To get around this problem, it is best to use a *mail container* rather than the value of the mail. Figure 4.26 shows the same program done with containers.

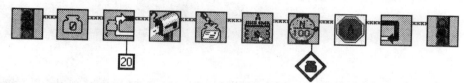

Figure 4.26. Since you can receive mail at any time, it's best to use a container to store mail values.

Of course, mail is most commonly used for multiple team projects (of which there are many in this book) when two or more robots need to communicate with each other. Since the IR port cannot send and receive data simultaneously, some kind of *handshaking* protocol needs to be worked out so that each robot knows when to "listen" and when to "talk." For example, in Figure 4.27 we've written a program that sends mail ("talks") for 0-1 seconds and then waits for mail ("listens") for up to one second. If mail is received, it plays a sound, if no mail is received by the end of one second, it jumps back to the start and "talks" again. Try it out with 2 RCX's and you should hear them beeping away at each other, indicating they are holding a conversation successfully.

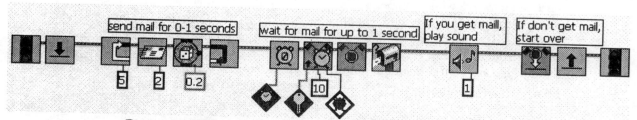

Figure 4.27. This program that spends roughly equal time listening and talking.

To make the program in Figure 4.27 useful, you would want to replace the number sent via mail to something meaningful (e.g. a container value) and the replace the sound with some other action (e.g. several mail forks).

A common mistake students make is to *send mail* in one task and *wait for mail* in another task. This never works because the *send mail* function always takes priority over the *wait for mail* function (the IR port cannot do both at once). Thus, you never end up listening. To get around this, you need to include a *wait for time* immediately after the *send mail* function. This ensures there is some time for listening.

4.4.2 Set Display

 The *Set Display* function is also included in the **RCX Communication** skill badge simply because it's located on the same sub-palette, not because it involves inter-RCX communication (it can, however, be thought of as *intra*-RCX communication).

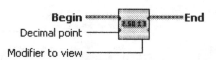

Figure 4.28. The wire terminals for the Set Display function.

The *set display* function requires 2 modifiers, one for the number to display and a second for the location of the decimal point. Any integer up to 4 digits can be displayed to the LCD. There is also a sign placeholder, which doesn't count as one of the 4 digits. This means that numbers ranging from -9999 to 9999 can be displayed. The decimal point specifies the location of the decimal point. Valid values for the decimal point modifier are from 0-3. The program below would display the sequence of numbers, 1001, 100.1, 10.01, and 1.001.

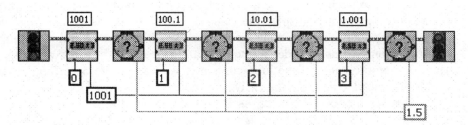

Figure 4.29. This program will display 1001, 100.1, 10.01, and 1.001.

The program in Figure 4.30 *waits for mail* and then displays the *value of the mail* to the RCX for 4 seconds. Note that we cannot wire the *value of the mail* to the *wait for seconds* function because it requires a floating point number (orange). The only type of integer it will accept is the integer *numerical constant* (blue). This also holds true for other functions that require floating point modifiers (e.g. *wait for temperature*).

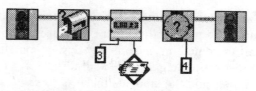

Figure 4.30. Displaying the value of the mail to the LCD.

ROBOLAB is a bit quirky (in case you haven't figured it out yet). There are some things you can't display directly to the LCD, despite the fact that they utilize the standard blue (integer) wire. The most common ones that students want to display but can't are the *value of the loop container* and the *value of local variables* (both local variables and the loop container are covered in Chapter 5). In fact, ROBOLAB can only display the value of containers #0 through #22. As shown in Figure 4.31, the program can be written and it will download to the RCX without any errors. However, when run, the program will not display anything to the LCD other than the standard clock.

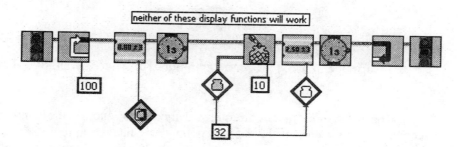

Figure 4.31. You cannot display the value of the loop container or the local variables to the LCD.

If you do want to display a value that cannot normally be displayed, you can use a container to "indirectly" display the value. Figure 4.32 shows us using the red container to display the value of the loop container. Of course, this is not a good use of the red container and should only be done to debug the program. Once you know it's working, you shouldn't need to view the value of the loop container. As a side note, when the program in Figure 4.32 is downloaded and run, the LCD will count down from 99 to 0, not from 100 to 1.

The same process can be used to view the value of any of the local variables (containers #32-47). Please note, as will be discussed in Chapter 5, the local containers are dangerous to use since they are often used by ROBOLAB (see Table 5.1).

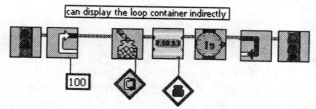

Figure 4.32. Containers can be used to indirectly display the value of the loop container or the local variables.

4.4.3 RCX Communication Examples

In this first example, we've created a simple remote control for a car that uses one RCX as the remote control and another for the car. Figure 4.33 shows the sending program (remote controller) while Figure 4.34 shows the receiving program (the car). The remote controller basically sends one of two commands: back up (mail = 11) or turn off (mail = 255). The car's program basically says to drive forward unless instructed to do otherwise.

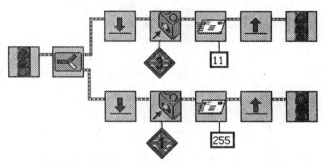

Figure 4.33. The sending program for a simple remote control.

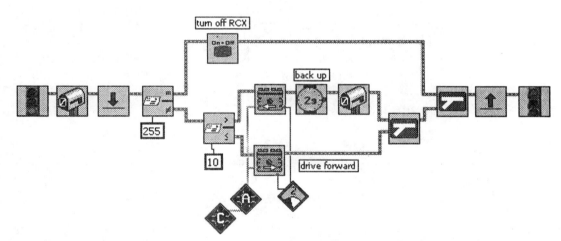

Figure 4.34. The receiving program for a simple remote control.

While not strictly a communications example, this next example is fun to do. The LEGO® light sensor is very sensitive to infrared (IR) light along with the visible range of light. In fact, this is often the source of much frustration for our students. IR light sources are everywhere, we just can't see them!

Rather than get mad about the light sensor's overly sensitive behavior, we can try to exploit it instead. Try this: download the following program to your RCX, mount the light sensor facing forward so the IR bean the red LED on the light sensor are sending out light in the same direction, then hold your RCX about 6 inches from a wall. If you view the light sensor readings on the LCD with and without the program running, you will see that indeed, there is a lot of IR light being reflected off the wall. The first function in this program basically sets the IR power to high (which you could also have done via the Administrator area as described in Chapter 2).

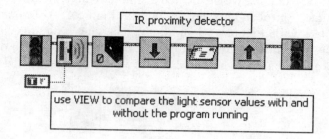

Figure 4.35. Simple program that uses the IR port as a proximity detector.

4.4.4   Looking forward: Advanced RCX Communication

The number one trick students always want to know after learning about basic RCX communication is how to be malicious by either reprogramming another team's RCX or turning it off completely! Interested? Flip forward to Chapter 6 (Advanced RCX Communication) to learn how. If you've been the victim of one of these malicious attacks, you'll also be interested to know that we also show how best to defend against these sorts of pranks.

4.5 The Direct Mode Badge

Direct mode is a unique way of running programs on the RCX. Rather than downloading an entire program to the RCX as you normally do, in **direct mode** each function is sent one at a time, one after the other.

So why would you want to run in **direct mode**? The real power will be unlocked later in Chapters 5 and 6 where you will learn basic LabVIEW G-code. Then you can use your PC to perform operations too complex for the RCX. Essentially you will write programs part of which run on the RCX and part of which run on your PC. But, alas, we are not ready for that yet!

The main disadvantage of **direct mode** is that <u>you cannot use any control structures such as loops, jumps, and task splits</u>. If you try, you will generate an error message that indicates you can only use them in "**remote mode**" (the normal way of programming).

So why would you want to run in **direct mode** if you don't know G-code and you can't use any control structures? The answer is a bit surprising: *<u>you can run direct mode programs on top of programs that are already running!</u>*

With that said, many of the **direct mode** functions output either True or False (Boolean), which you can't really utilize unless you know some real G-code. So for now, we'll restrict ourselves to just about half of the functions: ***Begin Direct Mode, End Direct Mode, Wait for RCX to be in View, Read Value, Read and Display Value***, and ***RCX Battery Power***.

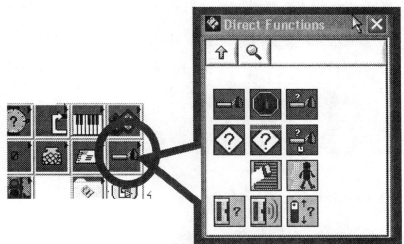

Figure 4.36. The Direct Mode sub-palette is accessed on the bottom right of the main **functions palette**.

4.5.1 Begin and End Direct Mode

Creating programs that run in **direct mode** is accomplished simply by replacing the standard green and red traffic lights with the ***Begin Direct Mode*** and ***End Direct Mode*** functions as shown in Figure 4.37. Just be sure to keep in mind that you cannot use any control structures (loops, forks, jumps, or task splits).

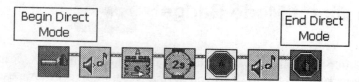

Figure 4.37. The *Begin Direct Mode* and *End Direct Mode* functions are used in place of the green and red traffic lights. **Direct mode** commands execute as soon as they are received by the RCX.

In order for **direct mode** programs to work correctly, the RCX must remain in view of the IR tower for the duration of the program. Since functions are sent one at a time, if you move the RCX before the entire program is completed, you will get a communication error. However, you can "recover" by moving the RCX back into view of the IR tower and then clicking the "try again" button on the error dialog box.

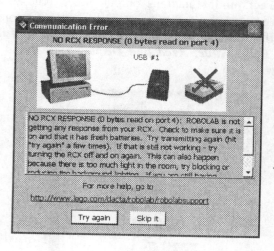

Figure 4.38. If you move the RCX before the program is complete, you'll get the dreaded "Communication Error" dialog box. To recover from this, simply move the RCX back and hit "try again."

4.5.2   Wait for RCX to be In View

You'll get the Communications Error message if you don't have the RCX in view at the start of the program too. To avoid this, you can use the *Wait for RCX to be in View* function. Just like any other *wait for* function, it will wait for the IR link to be established before proceeding. Since it doesn't hurt, most **direct mode** programs will start with this function, as shown in Figure 4.39.

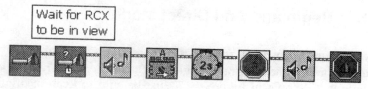

Figure 4.39. The *Wait for RCX to be in view* function is very useful. **Direct mode** programs won't execute until the RCX is in view of the IR tower.

4.5.3   Read Value

The ***read value*** function outputs any value (sensor, container, mail, timer, etc.) as a real number. In the upper program in Figure 4.32, the read value function is used to output the value of sensor port 1 to the LCD. It may seen a bit strange to have a function that does this, when you could just wire the sensor port value to the LCD directly as shown in the bottom program in Figure 4.40. However, there are many cases where a "middle man" is needed, and the ***read value*** function serves as this middle man.

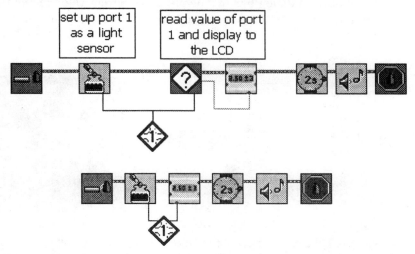

Figure 4.40. Both programs shown have the same end result. The ***read value*** function in the top program is used to access the values of sensor ports, container values, and mail value.

For example, in Figure 4.41 the ***value of port*** 1 is being used to define how long to wait (in seconds). You can't wire the ***value of port 1*** directly to the ***wait for seconds*** function because it only accepts floating point numbers (orange wire) and the port value only provides integers (blue wire). Try it out.

Additionally, as we will see in the next section, when we want to share sensor values with another RCX we have to use the ***read value*** function as a middle man. There is no way around it.

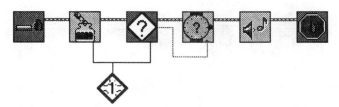

Figure 4.41. Example of a program that needs to use the ***read value*** function as a "middle man."

Finally, you may be wondering why we started each of the programs in Figures 4.40 and 4.41 with the *light container* function when we don't ever use containers in any of those programs. The RCX needs to know what type of sensor is connected to port 1 and by using ANY light sensor function we essentially let the RCX know that port 1 has a light sensor attached to it. Thus, we could have used any light sensor function; we just chose the *light container* function arbitrarily.

The *read and display value* function is not used as much as *read value* function but is similar in function. Rather than outputting the value as a real number that can be used in the program, it opens a dialog box that displays the current value in real time. The program will wait until you click on the green check mark before continuing to the next function in the program.

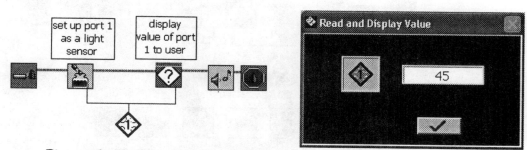

Figure 4.42. The *read and display* function allows you to see the value of a port in real time in a new window (right)

4.5.4 RCX Battery Power

The *RCX Battery Power* function returns the current battery voltage as a real number, which can be used anywhere a numeric constant is used. In the example below, we first display the battery level to the LCD (note: this is rounded down since the *Set Display* function uses an integer numeric constant) for one second. We then go on to use the battery level to control both the power level and duration of Motor A (see Advanced Output in section 4.7 for more information on controlling power levels). As the batteries wear down, the motor will run slower and for a shorter length of time (a simple kind of self-preservation).

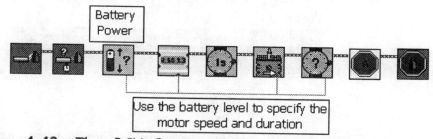

Figure 4.43. The *RCX Battery Power* functions outputs the battery voltage as a real number (0-9).

4.5.5   No Mail in Direct Mode

Since **direct mode** uses the IR communications port, it shouldn't be too surprising that you cannot use any of the mail functions in **direct mode**. If you try to run a program like the one in Figure 4.44, you will generate an error message.

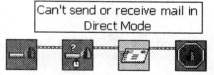

Figure 4.44. This program will generate an error message.

4.5.6   Running Direct Mode on top of Remote Mode

Finally, we get to the real power of **direct mode**. As mentioned previously, the best feature of **direct mode** is the ability to run **direct mode** programs on top of **remote mode** programs. For example, downloading and running the top program in Figure 4.45 will turn on Motor A in the forward direction every 4 seconds. Running the **direct mode** program shown in bottom of Figure 4.45 would stop Motor A. But since the **remote mode** program is still running (it has an infinite loop), Motor A will start again in a few seconds.

When we covered *task splits* in Chapter 3, you learned that the RCX can mulit-task and essentially run several programs simultaneously. This works exactly the same way, except that you get to "interject" a new task via **direct mode** whenever you want.

Can you think of any instances when it would have been nice to run two programs at the same time? Now you can!

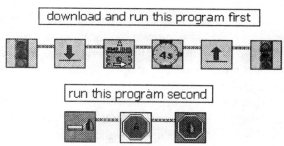

Figure 4.45. You can run two programs at the same time if one of them is a **direct mode** program.

4.5.7   Looking forward: Advanced Direct Mode

At first it would seem that we've pretty much described all the icons on the **Direct Mode** sub-palette. Yes and no. There are a couple of functions we haven't described yet. Plus, it turns out once you've learned some basic G-code (Chapter 5), then you can also use some of the **direct mode** functions we've already described here for some additional neat tricks. In other words, we'll both introduce a few new functions and revisit some of these **direct mode** functions, like the read display, in Chapter 6.

4.6 The Internet Badge   `Internet`

As the name implies, the Internet skill badge covers how to program the RCX over the Internet. The computer that receives the programs over the Internet is designated as the host computer. ROBOLAB programs are sent to the host computer via the Internet from the remote computer. Only the host computer needs to have an IR tower connected to it. The only requirement for all this magic to work is that the host computer must be running a special ROBOLAB program called ROBOLAB Internet Server.

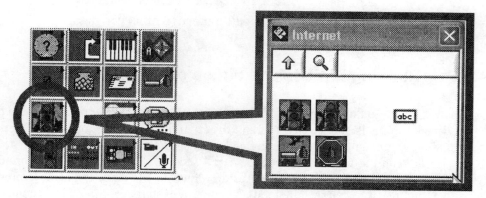

Figure 4.46. The **Internet** sub-palette is located at the bottom left of the **functions palette**.

4.6.1   Nomenclature: Remote, Direct, Internet, and Local

We have to be a bit careful with the nomenclature before getting started. We will use the terms "Internet" and "local" to denote the location of the RCX. The "local" RCX is the one right in front of your computer. The "Internet" RCX is the one at some other location which you will program over the Internet. It may be someplace very distant or simply on the next computer over.

The confusion lies in the programming *modes*: **direct mode** and **remote mode**. **Direct mode** programming is where code is downloaded to the RCX one line at a time and was covered in section 4.5. **Remote mode** is the normal way of programming where the entire program is downloaded to the RCX at once. Thus, there are 4 possible types of programs: local **remote mode** (this is the one you're most familiar with), local **direct mode**, Internet **remote mode**, and Internet **direct mode**. Got it?

4.6.2   Configuring the ROBOLAB Internet Server

The ROBOLAB Internet Server is a special ROBOLAB program that the host computer must run. The ROBOLAB Internet Server can be started by selecting it on the **project** menu as shown in Figure 4.47.

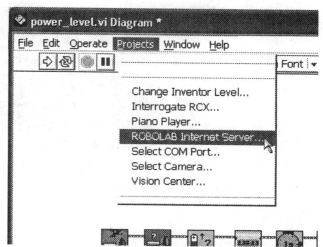

Figure 4.47. The ROBOLAB Internet Server program is located on the **Projects** menu.

To start The ROBOLAB Internet Server, simply select it from the **Project** menu (Figure 4.47) and the ROBOLAB Internet Server program window will open as shown in Figure 4.48. In the main Server window there are two panes showing the **Machine Access** list and the **Exported VI** list. At the bottom of the window the host computer's IP address is displayed.

The **machine access** lists controls which computers are allowed to send ROBOLAB programs to the host computer. The default list includes the *localdomain* and an asterisk (*). The *localdomain* allows all computers on the local network access. The asterisk (*) allows all computers access (easy to setup, but very unsafe from a network security standpoint). You can change the list of computers by simply entering either the computer's name or IP address as shown in Figure 4.49. In the example shown, only the 2 computers specified would be allowed to send ROBOLAB programs to the Host computer.

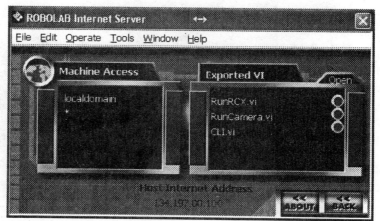

Figure 4.48. The host computer needs to be running the ROBOLAB Internet Server program .

Figure 4.49. ROBOLAB Internet Server with the **Machine Access** limited to two specific computers.

In case you haven't noticed it by now, all your Inventor mode programs have the *.vi* filename extension and your Investigator programs have the *.llb* filename extension. A library (*.llb*) is simply a collection of *.vi* files (the *vi* stands for Virtual Instrument). With this in mind, the Exported VI list, shown in the right hand pane of Figure 4.48, should make some sense. The list simply specifies which Virtual Instruments (VI's) can be run over Roboserver. The *RunRCX.vi* is used to run standard ROBOLAB programs. The *RunCamera.vi* is used to run Vision Center programs. Finally, the *CLI.vi* is used to run a Control Lab Interface (CLI) program (see Chapter 6 for more information on the CLI). You can add your own list of VI's to this list, **BUT WE DON'T RECOMMEND EDITING THE LIST OF VI's**! If you are interested, you can click on the green circle and open the corresponding VI and examine it. You will see that they were written in LabVIEW G-Code, not ROBOLAB. For more about LabVIEW, we highly recommend getting a book such as *LabVIEW for Everyone* or the *Learning with LabVIEW Express 7*, both available from Prentice-Hall.

When a program is submitted over the Internet, the **Exported VI** list will briefly highlight the VI being executed. For 99% of the time, this will be the *RunRCX.vi* as shown in Figure 4.50.

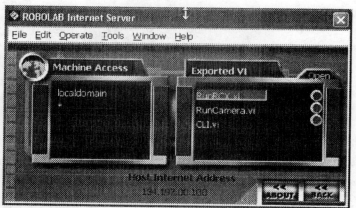

Figure 4.50. *RunRCX.vi* will be highlighted in red in the ROBOLAB Internet Server window as the program is received on the host computer.

Note that in ROBOLAB versions 2.5.0 and earlier, the Internet Server window appears slightly different (as shown below). It does not show the Host computer's IP address. This means that you will have to determine the IP address by examining the network properties or asking your local friendly Systems Administrator.

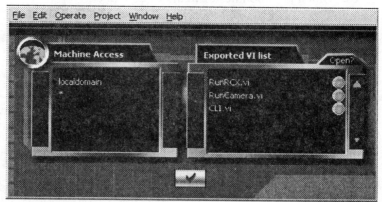

Figure 4.51. In ROBOLAB version 2.5.0 and earlier, the ROBOLAB Internet Server window does not show the Host IP address. Clicking the green check mark closes the Internet Server window.

4.6.3 Internet Begin and End

Submitting programs over the Internet is not much different than writing a normal ROBOLAB program (which you have ample experience with by now). The only differences are that the *Internet Begin* and *Internet End* functions are used in place of the normal *Begin* and *End* traffic lights as shown in Figure 4.52. The host computer's IP address must be wired to the Internet Begin function using the pink ***string constant*** (Figure 4.46). The host computer's IP address is always shown at the bottom of the ROBOLAB Internet Server window (Figure 4.48). Note that we've made up a fictitious IP address for these examples, so don't try using it!

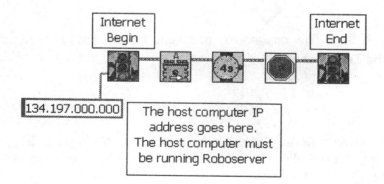

Figure 4.52. *Internet Begin* and **Internet End** functions replace the usual *Begin* and *End* traffic lights. The host computer IP address must also be wired to the Internet Begin function

For many local networks, using the host computer's Network ID (a.k.a. the computer name) will also suffice, as shown in Figure 4.53. This is often more convenient than using the IP address, which is sometimes difficult to remember.

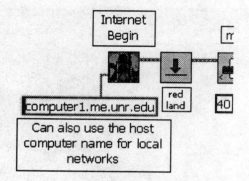

Figure 4.53. The computer name can be used in place of the IP address on most local networks.

Figure 4.54 shows the infamous LEGO® cockroach from Chapter 3, this time redone as an Internet program. Clicking the white run arrow would send this program over the internet to the host computer specified. Now you can create infestations anywhere on the planet!

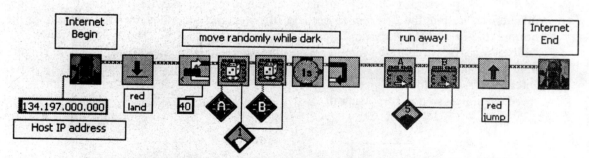

Figure 4.54. The cockroach program from Chapter 3, redone using the Internet.

As soon as you "run" an Internet program, the *ShowNet.vi* status window will open on the local computer (usually <u>very</u> briefly, depending on the connection speed) as shown in Figure 4.55.

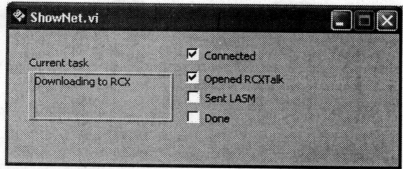

Figure 4.55. The status window will indicate progress on the remote computer.

4.6.4 Internet Direct Mode

Internet direct mode combines both **Internet mode** and **direct mode** and allows you to directly run programs over the Internet on a remote RCX. Just as before, the Internet RCX must be in IR communication with a computer running ROBOLAB Internet Server.

In the figure below, we've taken the **direct mode** program from Figure 4.43 and redone it using **Internet direct mode**. In **Internet direct mode**, you have the same programming limitations as **direct mode**; you cannot use many functions including control structures (loops, jumps, and forks) and some *wait for* function (e.g. *wait for container*).

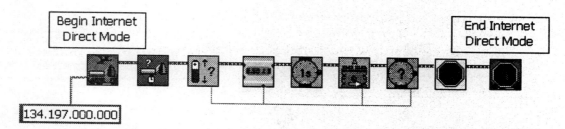

Figure 4.56. Using *Internet Direct Mode* you can run programs in **direct mode** over the Internet.

4.6.5 Controlling Two RCX's Simultaneously

One of the neatest tricks that we've stumbled upon is the ability to run two **remote mode** programs at the same time! This works as long as one of the programs is an Internet program. In Figure 4.57, we've created two programs, each with their own green and red traffic lights. Normally, this wouldn't work (only one program would be downloaded to the RCX). However, since the upper program is being sent to an Internet RCX and the lower program is being downloaded to the local RCX, it all works!

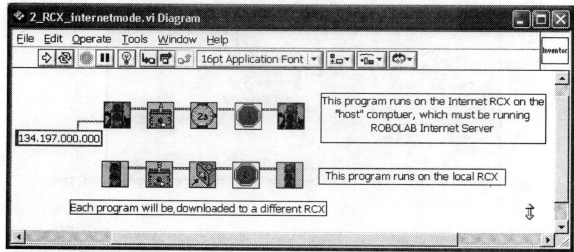

Figure 4.57. Using *Internet direct mode* you can run programs in **direct mode** over the Internet.

Okay, this is pretty cool trick, but it gets more interesting. We also have the ability to share data (sensor, container, or mail) between RCX's if we run one of the RCX's in **direct mode** rather than **remote mode.** Then the other RCX can access its data as shown in Figure 4.58. Here the local RCX's program uses the value of the Internet RCX's light sensor.

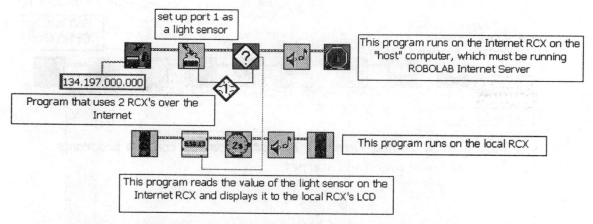

Figure 4.58. Using **Internet direct mode** you can share sensor data over the Internet.

The quirky nature of the *read value* function was mentioned previously in section 4.5.3. In Figure 4.59, we didn't use the *read value* function, so the local red container is filled with the local value of input port 1, which is not what we intended. Looking at Figure 4.59 and thinking from your computer's perspective, it isn't at all obvious which RCX the *value of port 1* function refers to; the local RCX or the Internet RCX. To avoid this ambiguity, the *read value* function was created to act as a "middle man." In Figure 4.58 it is clear which RCX's port value is being displayed.

The only other tricky point to the program in Figure 4.58 is that the sensor data from the Internet RCX will only be read once, when the local RCX's program is downloaded. In the example shown, running the local RCX's program over again will not reflect any changes in the light sensor values.

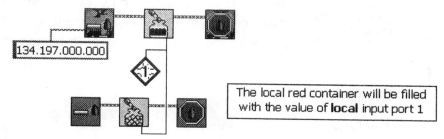

Figure 4.59. This does not produce the same result as Figure 4.58. The local container is filled with the local sensor port value. You need to use the *read value* function to share data.

In Figure 4.58 we could have just as easily switched the roles of the local and Internet RCX's with the Internet RCX using the local RCX's data, but that would still lead to the sensor data only being shared when the Internet program is downloaded.

To get around this limitation, we can run both RCX's *continuously* in **direct mode**. Then the data sharing can go both ways in real time. Running the program shown in Figure 4.60 will put the light sensor data of the Internet RCX into the red container of the local RCX. As mentioned back in section 2.6 (see Figure 2.23), selecting **Run Continuously** (the double white arrow) instead of the normal **Run**, will cause the program to be downloaded over and over. To stop the downloading, press either the red stop sign or the pause button (see Figure 4.61).

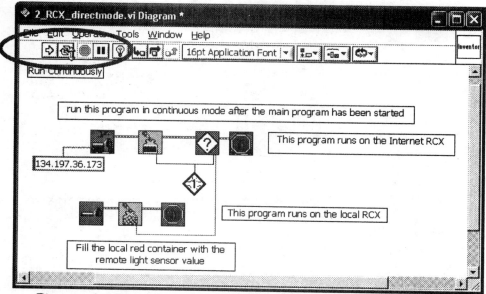

Figure 4.60. Using **direct mode** for both RCX's lets you can share data between RCX's in real time. Running Continuously will cause the program to repeat.

Figure 4.61. While Running Continuously, the icons will change. To abort the repeated downloading of the programs, click on the red stop sign. To simply pause the execution, click on the pause button.

So now we know how to pass data back and forth between RCX's. But what good is it if you can't use any control structures? Recall, that **direct mode** programs can be run on top of **remote mode** (normal) programs. Thus, we can first download and run a program like the one shown in Figure 4.62. The program is a generic program for steering a car using two containers. Each motor will run either in the forward or reverse direction, depending on the value in the blue and red containers.

By running the two **direct mode** programs, shown in Figure 4.63, on top of the other program (which should be in program slot #3), your buddy can drive your car over the Internet using his/her touch sensors. Touch sensor 1 will control the direction of Motor A and touch sensor 2 will control Motor B. Of course, realistically the delay caused by the Internet will make it hard to do any precision driving. To maintain constant communication between the RCX and IR tower, we've often directly mounted the IR tower on the RCX as shown in Figure 4.64.

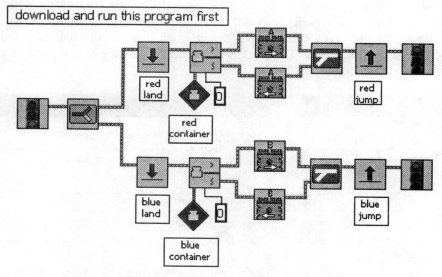

Figure 4.62. A simple program to steer a car. Download this to program slot #3.

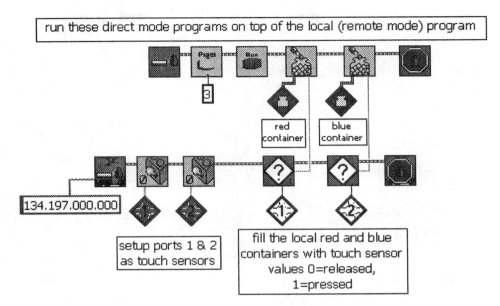

run these direct mode programs on top of the local (remote mode) program

red container

blue container

134.197.000.000

setup ports 1 & 2 as touch sensors

fill the local red and blue containers with touch sensor values 0=released, 1=pressed

Figure 4.63. Run these two **direct mode** programs continuously and your buddy can drive your car using 2 touch sensors.

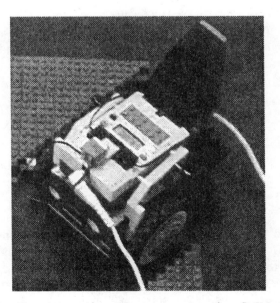

Figure 4.64. Mounting the IR tower to the RCX ensures the **direct mode** programs won't be interrupted.

4.7 The Advanced Output Badge

By now, you've gotten pretty used to using the LEGO® motors. The Advanced Output skill badge will provide you with a few more tools to help you both refine motor control and speed up the execution of your programs.

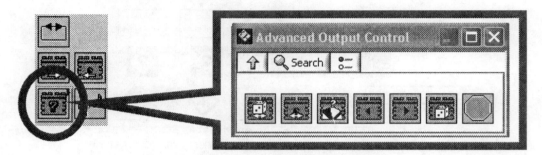

Figure 4.65. The **Advanced Output Control** sub-palette is located near the middle of the **functions palette.**

4.7.1 Advanced Output sub-palette

Through the Advanced Output sub-palette we have access to some motor controls we didn't have before. For Example, we can now set the direction randomly if we so desire. Recall out LEGO® cockroach from Figure 3.12? It was made possible using the ***Motor Random*** function.

It turns out the simple turn ***Motor A forward*** function is actually a combination of three individual functions, each of which can be accessed via the Advanced Output Control sub-palette. To turn Motor A on in the forward direction we actually ***set the direction*** to forward, set the ***motor power level*** to full, and then ***turn the motor on.***

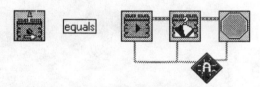

Figure 4.66. The ***Motor A forward*** is actually c combination of 3 basic commands.

Why would you ever want to use the individual functions rather than the ***Motor A forward*** function? The short answer is: to make faster executing programs. Why execute three commands to change the motor direction when you can accomplish it with a single command? Figure 4.67 shows a simple program that makes motor A reverse while the touch sensor is pressed. As shown this program will execute faster because we used the ***forward*** and ***reverse*** functions, rather than the ***Motor A forward*** and ***Motor A Reverse*** functions (2 functions instead of 6).

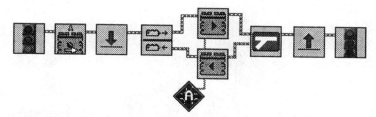

Figure 4.67. Using the *forward* and *reverse* functions make this execute faster.

We can make him faster, stronger, better than before. Below we show the next generation cockroach, from Figure 3.12, that takes advantage of some advanced output functions. Notice that the motors are only turned on once at the start of the program. Plus, the motor power is set to level 1 outside of the loop. All this makes our cockroach think just a little bit faster. Hey, every bit helps when there's someone trying to step on you!

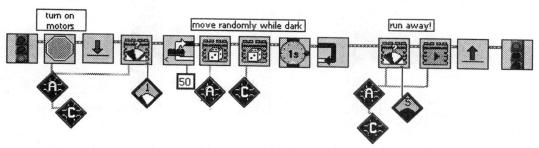

Figure 4.68. Our cockroach from Chapter 3 is now just a little bit faster!

4.7.2   Pulse Width Modulation

The RCX varies the motor power using a technique called **Pulse Width Modulation** (PWM). To turn the motor on at full power we simply apply 9 Volts to the motor continuously. To turn the motor on at 50% power, we quickly switch the Voltage on and off. Figure 4.69 shows a series of pulses being sent to the motor that represents a 50% duty cycle, meaning the Voltage is only on for 50% of the time. Since we are supplying Voltage to the motor only 50% of the time, the motor runs at half power. We can further decrease the motor power by decreasing the width of the pulses (thus, the term pulse width modulation). Figure 4.70 shows a 25% duty cycle.

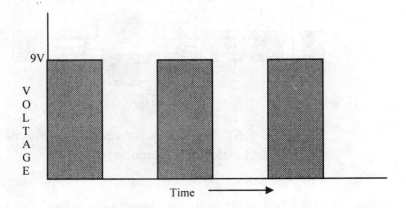

Figure 4.69. Pulse Width Modulation with 50% duty cycle.

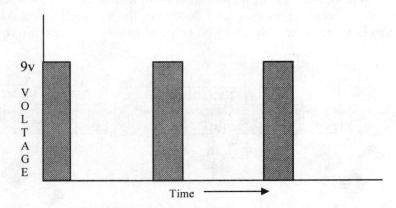

Figure 4.70. Pulse Width Modulation with 25% duty cycle.

4.7.3 Controlling Motor Power

Okay, so now you know how the RCX controls the motor power with pulse width modulation. Up to this point we've controlled the power level of the motors by simply using one of the 5 power level modifiers. However, the LEGO® motors actually can be run at 8 different power levels with each level corresponding to roughly 12.5% increments in duty cycle.

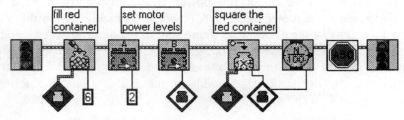

Figure 4.71. Setting the motor power using integers and container values. The motors will run for a total of 0.36 seconds in this program.

Table 4.1 Motor Power Levels		
RCX Power Level	Power Level Modifier	Integer Value
1		0
2		1
3	none	2
4		3
5	none	4
6		5
7	none	6
8		7

4.7.4   Power versus Speed

It's easy to confuse power and speed. We usually want to control motor speed to make a LEGO® car go faster or slower, but we actually are controlling the motor power. The missing links between power and speed are **mass** and **gear ratio**.

A very heavy vehicle will take lots of power to get moving. Thus, a low power level will appear to produce a low motor speed. Likewise, if we use a big gear ratio (a big gear driving a little gear) then controlling motor power will also appear to control motor speed. This is because a big gear ratio makes the vehicle appear to have a lot of inertia. Think of trying to get your car moving in from a dead stop using 4th gear or trying to pedal a bicycle while using a big gear ratio – it's hard! In these cases, varying motor power will seem to control motor speed.

The confusion arises when you have either a very light vehicle (which is pretty typical for LEGO® vehicles) or a low gear ratio (small gear on the motor turning a big gear on the wheel). In these two cases, the motor has more than enough power to get the vehicle moving. Even at the lowest power level the vehicle will take off at top speed. Changing power levels will appear to have no affect on the vehicle speed!

Thus, the bottom line is to remember that you are actually controlling motor power (using pulse width modulation), not speed. However, by varying the vehicle mass and/or gear ratio, you can use power to affect speed.

4.7.5   Motor Forward or Back

The remaining functions are pretty self explanatory, except for the ***Motor Forward or Back*** function (which is new for ROBOLAB 2.5.2 and higher). The context help is generally a good place to get information, but in this case, it's a bit confusing. Basically this function uses the sign (e.g. positive or negative) of the power level modifier to determine the direction of the motor. A positive value results in forward, a negative value results in reverse, and a zero results in a stop. One look at the sub-VI makes it clear.

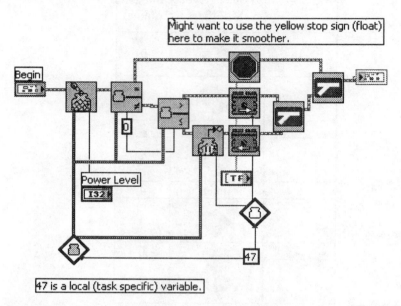

Figure 4.72. Block diagram for the *Motor forward or back* function.

The Motor Forward or Back function was added to ROBOLAB to make investigating feedback control easier. Recall back to Chapter 2, Figure 2.61 to be more specific, where we first introduced the concept of feedback control to turn a fan on and off based on temperature. This is basically what the thermostat does in your house. Now imagine we wanted to be a little more sophisticated and build a temperature control system which would blow air (*motor A forward*) if it were too hot or suck air (*motor A reverse*) if it were too cold.

In Figure 4.73 below, we have subtracted the desired temperature (75° F) from the current temperature. If the result is positive (actual temperature is greater than 75° F) then the motor will blow air. Not only does it blow air, but the motor power is proportional to the difference between actual and desired temperatures. That is, if the actual temperature is 77° F then the motor runs forward at RCX power level 3 (see Table 4.1 above).

On the other hand, if the temperature is only 71° F then, the motor will suck air at RCX power level 5. If the temperature is exactly 75° F then the motor stops completely (see figure 4.67). Engineers refer to a system like this, where the output is proportional to the input, as proportional control, or P-control for short.

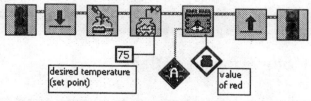

Figure 4.73. Example of proportional feedback control to control the temperature of a room.

CHAPTER 5
BLUE LEVEL

Skill badges available in this Chapter

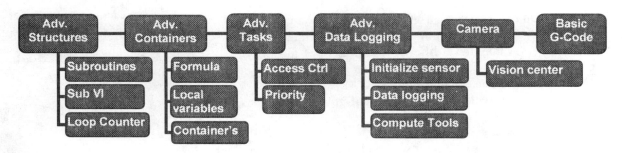

5.1 Blue Challenges

Quite honestly, creating design challenges that require you to use certain skills gets to be difficult when dealing with the advanced skill badges. The problem is that the challenges become very contrived (i.e. not fun anymore). Thus, for this chapter and Chapter 6, you won't find as many design challenges as in previous chapters. It is our hope that the advanced skills will most likely be used for major robot battles (that your instructor devises) or for those students who are trying to complete one of the earlier design challenges by using a few advanced tricks.

5.1.1   How Fast is That (revisited)?

Challenge: Design and build a robot to measure the torque versus RPM of a LEGO® motor using the light sensor.

Skill Badges: and

Procedures:

Experimental Setup: Back in Chapter 2 we introduced this Challenge using the rotation sensor. Now we want you to do it with a light sensor and a black and white disk. The instructor will supply calibrated weights for you to use.

Robot Design: For this exercise you need to design and construct a robot that can wind up a string with a weight on the end. Using the light sensor and a black and white disk you can data log the light sensor and then perform an FFT (Fast Fourier Transform) on the data to determine the RPM (revolutions per minute) of the LEGO® motor. Note: you cannot attach the black and white disk directly to the motor (it spins to fast).

By varying the weight on the string and/or the diameter of the hub you wind the string on, you can vary the torque applied to the LEGO® motor. You should acquire approximately 15-20 data points.

Program: Data log the light sensor. You'll have to use program level 4 or 5 to get a short sampling interval. Use Compute Tools 4 or 5 to run an FFT on the data to determine the RPM of the motor.

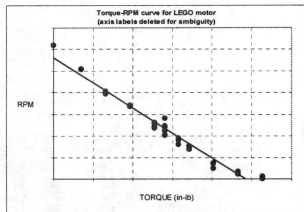

Bonus (extra half-grade): Most electric motors exhibit **asymmetry**, meaning they have different characteristics in the forward and reverse directions. Measure the torque-RPM in both directions for an extra half-grade.

Grading:

Your instructor will evaluate the accuracy of your Torque-RPM curve.

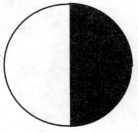

5.1.2   Feeding Frenzy (revisited)

Challenge: Build a robot that "hums" while wandering around randomly looking for food, stops and plays music when it finds food, and is smart enough to call for help if it hasn't found any food in the past 15 seconds.

Skill Badges:

Procedures:

Experimental Setup: All you need is a large enough area to let all robots wander around and some contrasting colored tape as food to put on the floor.

Robot Design: Your robot should resemble some kind of animal (after it is looking for food). Your robot must be able to wander around (on legs or wheels) and have a light sensor facing down to detect the food on the floor.

Program: You'll probably be using multiple tasks, several of which are probably going to be vying for access to the motors and speaker. You should use the task priority functions to avoid resource conflicts.

Grading:

Your grade will be based 50% on performance and 50% on creativity and aesthetics.

Performance	Creativity & Aesthetics
A: Your animal can find food and cries for help	A+: Best of show
B: Your animal can find food	A: Looks like the real thing
C: Your animal moves and makes noise	B: Looks like an animal
D: Your animal moves	C: Something moves around
F: You don't show up to class	D: Looks like it was once alive
	F: Put it out of its misery!

This challenge is based on an assignment described by Gage and Murphy in "Principles and experiences using LEGOs to teach behavioral robotics" proceedings of the 33rd ASEE/IEEE Frontiers in Education Conference, Session F4E, Boulder, CO, November 2003.

5.1.3　Bullseye

Challenge: Design, build and program a machine that uses a camera to find a target and then fire a "missile" at it.

Skill Badges:　　Camera

Procedures:

Experimental Setup: The only items required for this Challenge is a big red wall with a single blue brick somewhere in it. The blue brick is the target.

Robot Design: You will need to build some kind of platform that can rotate the camera on two different axes (horizontal and vertical). The motion of the platform must be controlled by the RCX (no human intervention). You'll also need a missile launcher that fires at the blue brick when it is found.

Program: You'll have to use the Vision Center to use the camera as a sensor.

Hints: The camera can be very sensitive to ambient light levels. Also pay special attention to the background (i.e. what's behind the wall when the camera looks at it).

Grading:

Your grade will be based 75% on performance and 25% on creativity and aesthetics.

Performance	Creativity & Aesthetics
A: Hit the target	A+: Best of show
B: Hits within 6 inches of the target	A: Outstanding
C: Your robot locates the target and shoots	B: Good
D: Your robot shoots something	C: Okay
F: You don't show up to class	D: Nothing special
	F: Divert your eyes!

5.1.4   Brick Recycler (revisited)

Challenge: Design, build and program a machine that uses a camera to sort LEGO® bricks based on color.

Skill Badges: Camera

Procedures:

Experimental Setup: The only items required for this Challenge are a few LEGO® 2x4 bricks: 4 black, 4 white, and 2 blue. The blue bricks are the "challenge" bricks – the hard ones to sort.

Robot Design: The operator (the instructor) will place the bricks into your machine in a random order. Your machine should move the bricks in front the camera and then sort them into one of three bins based on color. More creativity points will be given to designs that do not require the operator to load or orient the bricks in a special way.

You will use the camera and one or more motors for this Challenge. You may also consider using a touch sensor.

Program: You'll have to use the Vision Center to use the camera as a sensor.

Hints: The camera can be very sensitive to ambient light levels. Also pay special attention to the background (i.e. what's behind the brick when the camera looks at it).

Grading:

Your grade will be based 75% on performance and 25% on creativity and aesthetics.

Performance	Creativity & Aesthetics
A+: Sort the most bricks correctly the fastest	A+: Best of show
A: Sort 9 bricks correctly	A: Outstanding
B: Sort 6 bricks correctly	B: Good
C: Sort 4 bricks correctly	C: Okay
D: Move the bricks around	D: Nothing special
F: You don't show up to class	F: Divert your eyes!

5.1.5   Brick Recycler #3

<u>**Challenge:**</u> Design, build and program a machine that uses a camera to sort LEGO® bricks based on <u>size</u>.

<u>**Skill Badges:**</u>   Camera

<u>**Procedures:**</u>

Experimental Setup: The only items required for this Challenge are a few LEGO® bricks (any color) with the following sizes: 4 2x2, 4 2x4, and 2 2x3. The 2x3 bricks are the "challenge" bricks – the hard ones to sort.

Robot Design: The operator (the instructor) will place the bricks into your machine in a random order. Your machine should move the bricks in front the camera and then sort them into one of three bins based on size. More creativity points will be given to designs that do not require the operator to load or orient the bricks in a special way (i.e. if the instructor can just pour the bricks into a hopper).

You will use the camera and one or more motors for this Challenge. You may also consider using a touch sensor.

Program: You'll have to use the Vision Center to use the camera as a sensor.

Hints: The camera can be very sensitive to ambient light levels. Also pay special attention to the background (i.e. what's behind the bricks when the camera looks at them).

<u>**Grading:**</u>
Your grade will be based 75% on performance and 25% on creativity and aesthetics.

Performance	Creativity & Aesthetics
A+: Sort the most bricks correctly the fastest	A+: Best of show
A: Sort 9 bricks correctly	A: Outstanding
B: Sort 6 bricks correctly	B: Good
C: Sort 4 bricks correctly	C: Okay
D: Move the bricks around	D: Nothing special
F: You don't show up to class	F: Divert your eyes!

5.1.6   Dice Jukebox

Challenge: Design, build and program a machine that can toss a standard 6-sided die. Then use the camera to determine what number was rolled and play a song that corresponds to that number

Skill Badges: Camera   and   Adv. Structures

Procedures:

Experimental Setup: All you need is a die, a camera, and some music.

Robot Design: Your robot needs to be able to flip (roll) the die in a repeatable manner. Since the camera will be used to examine the die, you need to figure out how to catch the die so that it is oriented correctly in front of the camera every time. Repeatability is the key to getting this to work.

Program: You'll have to use the Vision Center to use the camera as a sensor. The six songs <u>must</u> be stored in separate subroutines, which are played when the corresponding number is identified on the die.

Hints: The camera can be very sensitive to ambient light levels. Also pay special attention to the background (i.e. what's behind the die when the camera looks at them).

Grading:
Your grade will be based 60% on performance and 40% on creativity and aesthetics.

Performance	Creativity & Aesthetics
A: Accurately and reliably able to roll the die, identify the number, and play the song	A+: Best of show
	A: Outstanding
B: Can correctly identify 5 out of the 6 numbers and play the correct songs	B: Good
	C: Okay
C: Can correctly identify 3 out of the 6 numbers and play the correct songs	D: Nothing special
	F: Divert your eyes!
D: Robot rolls the die but can't identify the number	
F: You don't show up to class	

This challenge is based on a robot that was built at Tufts University. You can find pictures (and perhaps a movie) on the Internet if you want to see one solution to this challenge.

5.1.7   Dice Checker

__Challenge:__ Design, build and program a machine that can toss a standard 6-sided die. Then use the camera to determine what number was rolled. Data log the number and repeat many times to determine if the die is "fair."

__Skill Badges:__ | Camera | and | Adv. Data Logging | and | Basic G-Code |

__Procedures:__

Experimental Setup: All you need is a die, a camera, and a whole lot of time.

Robot Design: This Challenge is very similar to the previous one except you need to data log and perform statistics too. Your robot needs to be able to flip (roll) the die in a repeatable manner. Since the camera will be used to examine the die, you need to figure out how to catch the die so that it is oriented correctly in front of the camera every time. Repeatability is the key to getting this to work.

Program: You'll have to use the Vision Center to use the camera as a sensor. You'll also have to data log the container(s) used by the camera and then do some statistics using G-code to determine if the die is fair (i.e. there isn't a probability of any one number showing up more often than any other).

Hints: The camera can be very sensitive to ambient light levels. Also pay special attention to the background (i.e. what's behind the die when the camera looks at them).

Grading:

Your grade will be based on *two performance categories* this time: 75% on the program and 25% on the robot.

Program	Robot
A: It works! (All three items accomplished) B: Can do any two items listed below C: Can do any one of the following: - identify the number of pips (dots) - data log the camera data - perform the statistics on the data D: Controls motors to flip the die F: You don't show up to class	A: Die lands oriented correctly in front of the camera every time B: Needs occasional human help to orient die C: Die lands in front of the camera D: Die is rolled/flipped F: You don't show up to class

This challenge is based on a robot that was built at Tufts University. You can find pictures (and perhaps a movie) on the Internet if you want to see one solution to this challenge.

5.2 The Advanced Structures Badge

Advanced structures introduces the loop counter and the concepts of subroutines and subVI's, both of which are used to organize and optimize large programs.

5.2.1 Loop Counter

We'll tackle the loop counter first, simply because it's the easiest. By now you are probably quite familiar with basic structures (loops, jumps, forks, etc.) because you've used them a lot. The loop counter is a special container that is used to keep track of how many loops are left (see Table 5.1). With each loop, 1 is subtracted from the loop container. The only nuance is that the loop container counts down from N-1 to zero. Thus, when you specify 5 loops, the loop counter container starts at 4 and counts down to zero.

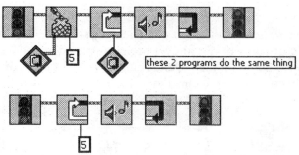

Figure 5.1. The loop counter container holds the remaining number of loops in it.

The next example shows a quick way to take 20 light sensor readings, storing each reading in a different container when the touch sensor is pressed. Instead of using the *container.cntl* modifier (see Figure 3.35) for the *generic container*, we've used the *loop counter value*. Recall that container #0 is the red, #1 is the blue, #2 is the yellow and so forth. We've taken advantage of the fact that the *loop counter container* changes each time through the loop (i.e. it is reduced by one). Thus, we start by filling container #19 with the light sensor reading after the touch sensor is pressed. The next time through the loop we will fill container #18 because the *loop counter container* has been decremented by one. This continues until we reach container #0 (the red container) and the program stops looping.

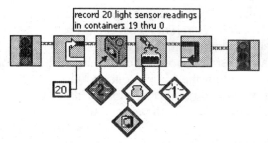

Figure 5.2. A quick little routine to fill 20 containers with a light sensor reading each time the touch sensor is pressed. Container zero is the red container.

We not only have the ability to use the *loop container value,* but we can also change it. Normally the *loop counter container* decrements by one each loop. In the figure below, we've subtracted an additional 4 from the *loop counter container* with each loop for a total of five. The end result is a program which counts down from 95 to 0 by 5's. Note, as mentioned in Chapter 4 (Figure 4.32), you cannot display the *loop container value* to the LCD directly.

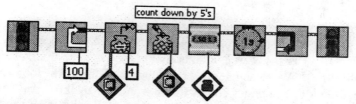

Figure 5.3. This program counts down from 95 to 0 by 5's.

We can also add to the loop container. Despite the fact that we only specified one loop, the next program will run forever because we add one to the loop container each loop. Why would you want to do this? Quite frankly we can't think of any reasons (yet). But this knowledge may come in handy one day.

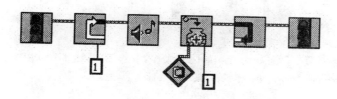

Figure 5.4. This program will run forever since we keep adding to the loop container.

5.2.2   Creating and Using Subroutines

A subroutine is basically a special set of functions that can be used over and over within a program. Creating a subroutine looks much like using a *task split*, as shown in Figure 5.5. However, unlike a task split, the functions in the subroutine don't run immediately. Instead the functions within the subroutine aren't executed until the subroutine is "run" or "called" using the *run subroutine function*. For each program slot, you can have up to 8 subroutines in memory, numbered 0 through 7.

Subroutines are most commonly used when you have a piece of code that you want to reuse several times within the same program. The neat thing about subroutines is that they can be used an unlimited number of times within a program. A subroutine can be run or "called" from *any task* within the program. Subroutines are local to the program, meaning subroutine #1 in program slot 2 is different than subroutine #1 in program slot 4. We'll discuss this in more detail in Section 5.2.4.

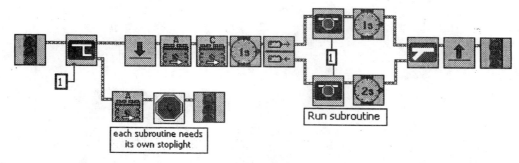

Figure 5.5. A subroutine allows you to use code over and over.

In Figure 5.6, we've created a subroutine for reversing and turning (we've only showed the subroutine to save room). The basic idea we were trying to accomplish was to have a single subroutine that would make our robot back up and then turn either left or right before proceeding to go forwards again. The value of the yellow container is used to specify how long to back up and turn before going forward again. The subroutine starts with a container fork to decide whether to make a left or right turn.

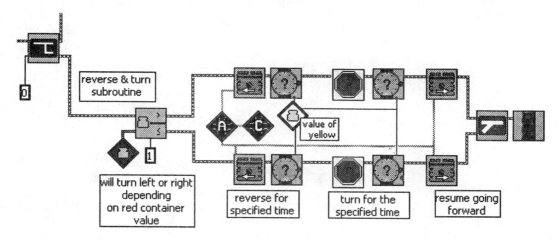

Figure 5.6. A subroutine allows you to use code over and over.

The part of the program that might call the subroutine in Figure 5.6 is shown in Figure 5.7. Here the program uses the red container to specify whether the turn should be left or right and the yellow container specifies the reversing and turning duration. So if touch sensor 1 is pressed, the robot backs up for 2 seconds and then turns right for 2 seconds. If touch sensor 3 is pressed, the robot backs up for 4 seconds and turns left for 4 seconds.

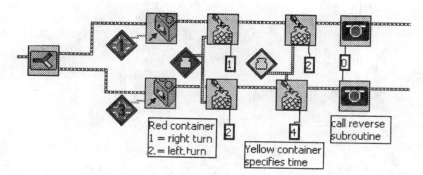

Figure 5.7. The part of the program that would call the subroutine in Figure 5.6.

In case you are wondering (because it's common to do it in other text-based programming languages like C), a subroutine cannot call another subroutine. You can, however, have one subroutine create another subroutine as shown in Figure 5.8. What students often forget is that the subroutine is not executed until it is run. Thus, in the program below, the two beeps are never played because subroutine 0 is never called. The only thing that happens is Motor A runs for 1 second.

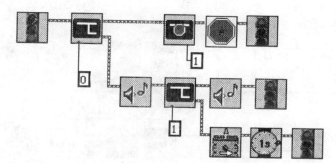

Figure 5.8. It is possible for one subroutine to create another subroutine. Note, the two sounds never play in this program.

As will be discussed later, subroutines stay in the RCX's memory even if you download a new program to the RCX. The upside of this is that you can use subroutines over and over, in any program at any time. The downside of this is that you have to explicitly delete subroutines from memory using the ***delete subroutine command***. Either that or reload the firmware. As we will show in section 6.4, the ***delete subroutine command*** can only be used in **direct mode**.

5.2.3   Creating and Using SubVI's

Recall that programs in ROBOLAB are called Virtual Instruments or VI's. A subVI is a program that is called by another program. In actuality all the functions you've used so far in ROBOLAB are subVI's. Remember way back in Chapter 2 (section 2.7.4) where we showed you how to get to the source code for each function? Then in Chapter 4 (section 4.7.1), we showed you that the *Motor A Forward* function is actually a combination of 3 other functions (that are on the **advanced output** sub-palette). Not only is getting at the source code easy in ROBOLAB, but it turns out that creating our own subVI's is also super easy. In fact, it'll only take 2 steps to show you how!

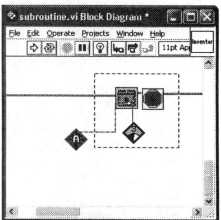

Figure 5.9. <u>Step 1</u>: Select the functions you want in your subVI by drawing a selection box around them. We've selected two functions and one modifier for this example. Any wires that cross your selection box will become wire terminals for your subVI. In this case, the output port will be a terminal but the power level will not.

Figure 5.10. <u>Step 2</u>: Select "Create SubVI" from the edit menu.

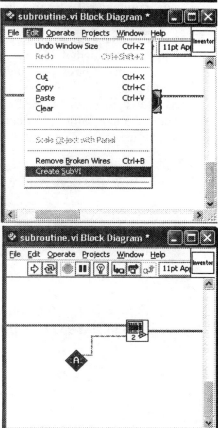

Figure 5.11. You've now got your very own subVI that can be used over and over again in any program (after you save it).

You can look at the block diagram of your subVI just like examining the source code for any other function. In our example, the block diagram is shown in Figure 5.12. The two functions we originally selected along with the power level modifier are all there. You'll also notice that the three wires we crossed with our selection box all show up with their respective terminals.

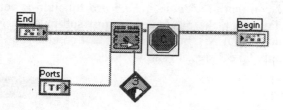

Figure 5.12. The block diagram of our new subVI.

As a side note, if you are *really* perceptive you may have noticed that our subVI has the pink "begin" and "end" terminals opposite of the normal ROBOLAB functions (compare Figure 5.12 to 2.57 and you'll see the begin and end labels are reversed). When our selection box crosses any wires (e.g. Figure 5.9), by default ROBOLAB assigns labels based on what they are wired to. In this case, the green wire was wired to the "ports" terminal on the *output A* modifier, the pink wire on the left was wired to the "end" terminal on the previous command, and the pink wire on the right was wired to the "begin" of the next command. To fix this discrepancy, simply rename the labels with the text tool on both the **block diagram** and the **front panel** (see section 5.7 for more on the **front panel**). You can also change the name by right-clicking on the pink "cluster" and selecting **properties**. Then rename both the Label and Caption on the Appearance tab.

Want to have your own icon? That's easy too. Just double click on the icon in the upper right corner of either the front panel or block diagram and the icon editor will appear as shown in Figure 5.13. From here it's just a matter of drawing up whatever you want using the icon editor. The end result is a subVI that you can use in any program (after you save it using the file menu) in the future.

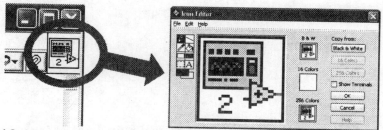

Figure 5.13. You can even create your own icon by double clicking on the icon in the upper right corner of the window.

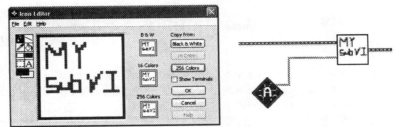

Figure 5.14. Viola! A custom subVI complete with your own icon.

Note that our subVI has one modifier terminal for the output port. Recall that we included the power level in the subVI when we selected the icons. That is, only the two pink begin/end wires and the port wire crossed our original selection box.

In case you're wondering, pretty much every function in ROBOLAB is a subVI. They were all created in exactly the same way we described above.

5.2.4   Subroutine versus SubVI

SubVI's make your program look very clean because it reduces the number of icons in the program. Subroutines, on the other hand, often seem to make the program messier.

The most important difference between the subroutine and the subVI is the way they are handled by the RCX. Subroutines are loaded into a separate section of memory on the RCX. One neat side effect of this is:

> Subroutines can be accessed by any task in a program

Since subroutines are loaded into memory only once, they make for more efficient code. SubVI's make your programs look simpler (i.e. fewer icons), but they don't reduce the amount of memory your program uses on the RCX. For example, if you use the same subVI ten times in one program, the subVI is loaded into the RCX memory ten times. Contrast that to a subroutine, which are loaded only once and can be called as many times as you want. Thus, subroutines will tend to be more efficient in terms of the amount of memory used. If you write big programs and are in need of memory, subroutines will help. If you just want to clean up your program or use a specific set of code in another program, then a subVI is the best bet.

5.3 The Advanced Containers Badge

This section covers the formula container, local variables and the *container's container*. Even though the *event container* is located on the **Container** sub-palette, we'll discuss it in Advanced Events (Chapter 6) because it really pertains to Events.

5.3.1 Formula Container

The *formula container* can be extremely useful for doing container math. Formulas are written using a *string constant*, which was introduced in Chapter 4 for the Internet Skill Badge. The context help describes how to write formulas very well. The help file indicates "c" stands for container, "s" stands for sensor, "m" for mail, "t" for timer and so forth. For example, the red container (which is container #0) is "c0," the blue container is "c1," sensor port 1 is "s1," and the yellow timer is "t2."

The only real drawback is that parentheses are not allowed, so you can't do simple formulas like (c1+c2)/2 which would be the (blue container + yellow container)/2. Instead you have to do c1/2+c2/2, which can generate an entirely different result thanks to integer math! Figure 5.15 shows the implementation of this exact formula using both the formula container and standard math containers (recall that if you don't specify any container, the default is to use the red container). It's pretty obvious that the formula container can save quite a bit of space.

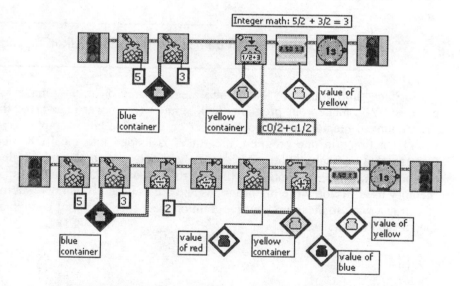

Figure 5.15. The formula container is used to reduce the number of functions required to do container math. These two programs do the same thing.

5.3.2   Local and Global Variables

Before we introduce the concept of local variables, let's first examine what a global variable is. In case you didn't already discover it on your own, container values are actually stored, even after the program ends. This means that you can access the container values at some other time in the future (in computer science lingo, this is called a *persistent variable*). Not only that but it turns out you can access most containers with any task, running in any of the 5 program slots. In other words, most containers are *global variables* (strictly speaking they are persistent global variables, but since all the containers in ROBOLAB are persistent, we'll drop that adjective in this discussion). Please note, that we have been careful to say "most" containers since, as you will see shortly, some variables can't be shared among programs.

A simple example will clarify the concept of a global variable. Let's imagine that you want to program a simple line following robot. Being experienced, you realize that the best line followers know what light levels correspond to "black" and "white." Wouldn't it be nice to be able run program 1 to store the value of black in the red container, then run program 2 to store the value of white in the blue container, and then finally run program 3, the actual line follower program? Sounds bizarre, but it's actually that simple.

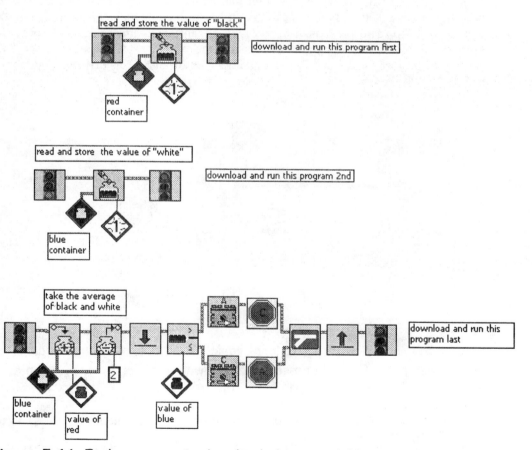

Figure 5.16. Each program is downloaded into a different program slot, but the containers are shared among the three programs.

The top program in Figure 5.16 is downloaded into program slot 1 (assuming you've unlocked that program slot). The middle program is downloaded into program slot 2. The bottom program is downloaded into program slot 3. Now you're set to show off. Simply place your robot over the black line and run program 1. Move your robot to the white and run program 2. Your robot now has the values of black and white stored as (persistent) *global variables*. Running program 3 makes use of this fact by using the average of the light readings as the threshold for the fork. Viola! A line follower that can be calibrated for varying lighting conditions.

Notice how the last program never assigned any values to the red and blue containers. It simply used whatever was put there by the other programs.

> Global variables (containers) can be used by any task within any program

This may seem pretty cool, but sometimes you don't want to share containers among programs. This is especially true if you are using a lot of containers or want to be sure that another task or program is not over-writing your container value. Containers that are not shared among programs and tasks are called *local variables*. In Figure 5.17 task #1 (the uppermost task) fills container #32 with the number 4 and then a split second later fills it with the number 100 and ends. Task 2 simply waits for container #32 to equal 100 before playing a beep. The beep is never played because container #32 is a local container, meaning that task 2's container #32 is not the same as task 1's container #32. A bit confusing isn't it? You can think of containers 32 through 47 as private containers for each task.

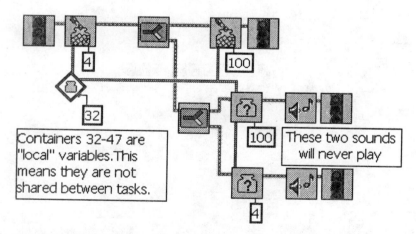

Figure 5.17. Container 32 is local variable, so only the upper task (task #1) has access to it. The other two tasks will wait forever in this example.

When you start adding up the total number of containers (variables) available in ROBOLAB, it's pretty staggering:

(16 local variables per task) x (8 tasks) = 128 local variables

Add to this the 32 global variables, and that gives you a grand total of <u>160</u> variables available for use in ROBOLAB! Before you get too excited about all those variables (containers) available, you need to know that several of both the local and global variables are commonly used by ROBOLAB for internal purposes. For example, global containers #23 through #28 are used by the data logging functions. If you aren't using any data logging then this isn't an issue. However, if you are doing data logging, then you will really wreak havoc by using any of these 6 containers. Local variables #32 though #47 are often used by other functions (see Table 5.1). For example, the *wait for brighter* function uses container #47 to calculate the threshold for the *wait for light* function.

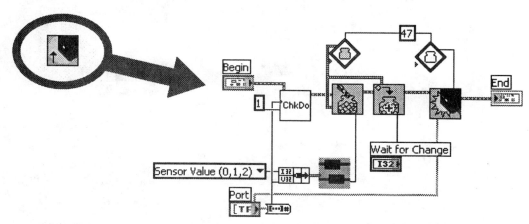

Figure 5.18. Container #47 is used by the *wait for brighter* function.

Our recommendation is that you should only use containers #0 through #22 unless you absolutely need the extra variables. And when you use those extra 138 variables available, be very careful. To use an old saying, you've been given enough rope to hang yourself!

Table 5.1: Description of the ROBOLAB containers.

Container #	Type	Description
0	Global	Red container
1	Global	Blue container
2	Global	Yellow container
3-22	Global	Generic containers
23-25	Global	Data pad values (red, blue, and yellow) Last value data logged for the respective data sets.
26-28	Global	Data pad counts (red, blue, and yellow) Number of data points acquired in the respective data sets
29-31	Global	Generic containers
32	Local	Unused?
33-47	Local	Used for loop iterations (accessible through the loop counter container)
46-47	Local	Used for wait for angle
47	Local	Used for wait for brighter or darker
47	Local	Used to play system sounds

5.3.3 The Container's Container

The *Container's Container* is one of the most confusing functions in ROBOLAB. But it's also very useful in the special situations that you need it. The example below demonstrates the fundamental difference between a *generic container* and the *container's container*. The program first fills container zero with the number 9. Here the number zero is used to specify which container to fill. Next, the program fills container #9 with the number 99. In this case the number zero is used to specify which container holds the address (container number) of the container we want to fill. Since container zero (red container) has the number 9 in it, container #9 is filled with 99. We told you it was confusing!

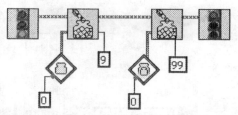

Figure 5.19. The *Container's Container* specifies which container value to use, not which container to use. Here, container #9 will be filled with 99.

When using the *container's container* you aren't specifying which container to use, instead you are specifying which container has the value you want to use.

Here's another way to think about the *Container's Container*. In the example below, neither function fills the red container. Instead, both functions use the value stored in the red container to determine which container to fill with 99. The red container stores the address (container number) of the container to be filled.

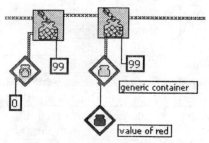

Figure 5.20. These two functions accomplish the same task. Neither fills the red container. Instead, the red container is used to specify which container to fill with 99.

In Figure 5.21 we have created a program that records 20 light sensor readings (just like in Figure 5.2) and then determines which reading was the brightest. The loop in the center of the program starts by comparing the value of container #19 to the value of container #0 (since container #22 has the number zero in the first time around). If the value of container #19 is larger than the value of container #0, then the number 19 is stored in container #22. This process is repeated over and over until all 20 containers have been compared.

Here we've used container #22 to store the address (container value) of the container that has the largest value. The largest value is never stored separately. Instead, we merely keep track of which container has the largest value.

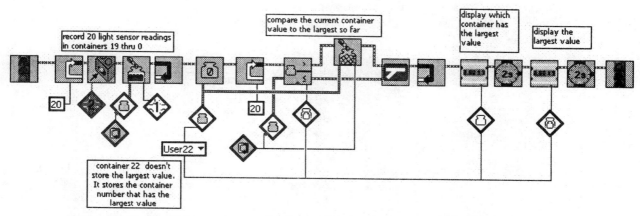

Figure 5.21. This program takes 20 light sensor readings and then finds which reading was the largest. Container #22 holds the address (container number) of the largest value.

5.4 The Advanced Tasks Badge

The advanced tasks section demonstrates how to precisely control the issue of resource conflicts that arise when more than one task is trying to control the same output port or sound. Let's imagine that you want a robot to go forward until the light sensor detects something dark, in which case it backs up for 2 seconds. It also has some bumpers so that if it bumps into something it turns either left or right, depending on which touch sensor is pressed. Your program might look something like the one shown in Figure 5.22. Of course we know this isn't a good program because each task is trying to control both motors and resource conflicts are inevitable. So how do we remedy the situation? Read on and we'll show you.

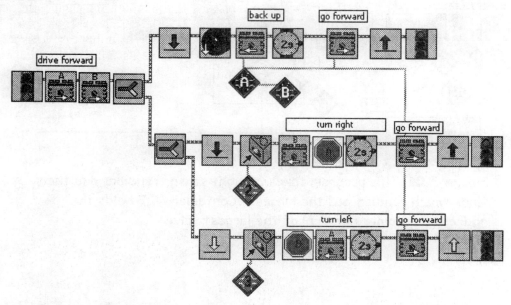

Figure 5.22. A simple 3 task program to back up, turn left, or turn right. Resource conflicts will occur since all 3 tasks are controlling the motors.

The Task priority sub-palette gives us a few new commands to control which task has priority over the motors and sounds when a conflict arises. There are three steps in using task priorities (why do all things ROBOLAB come in triplets?). First we have to define the priority, or ranking, of the task using the *task priority* function. The lower the number, the higher the priority. Second, we have to indicate when we want to start monitoring for resource conflicts using the *Start Monitoring for Output Access Control* function. Finally, we have to tell ROBOLAB where to go when a conflict occurs with the *Access Control Landing* function. Optionally, we can also tell ROBOLAB when to stop monitoring for resource conflicts using the *Stop Access Control Monitoring* function.

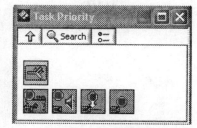

Figure 5.23. Task Priority sub-palette.

So how do the task priority functions work? When task priorities are used, resource conflicts are only monitored between the *Monitoring for Output Access Control* and the *Access Control Landing* functions. When a conflict does occur, the task with the lower priority will relinquish command of the motors and jump to the ***Access Control Landing*** point, much like an event.

Time for an example: Figure 5.24 shows a simple 2 task program in which both tasks are trying to turn on and off Motor A. There are three possible scenarios depending on which touch sensor is pushed first:

1) No conflict occurs because enough time elapses between touch sensor pushes that the first task is allowed to run its course before the second task starts.

2) Touch sensor 1 is pushed just prior to touch sensor 2. In this case task #1 starts first and turns on Motor A in the forward direction. When touch sensor 2 is pushed, task #1 relinquishes control of the motor because task #2 has a higher priority (lower number). When it gives up control, task #1 also jumps to the ***Access Control Landing*** point and plays the beep before ending. In the meantime, task #2 reverses the direction of the motor and then turns it off 4 seconds later.

3) Touch sensor 2 is pushed just prior to touch sensor 1. In this case Task #2 turns on the motor in the reverse direction. When touch sensor 1 is pushed, the conflict immediately causes task #1 to jump to the ***Access Control Landing*** point, play the beep, and end.

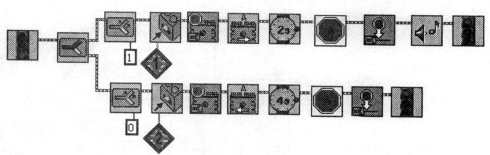

Figure 5.24. The task priority functions dictate how the conflict over motor A is handled. The bottom task (task #2) has a higher priority in this case.

Figure 5.25 shows a slight variation to the last example. In this case, the two tasks are simply trying to run the motor in opposite directions. If you push touch sensor 1, the Motor A goes forward and you hear the beep. If you then pushed touch sensor 2, you would hear the beep again while the motor direction is reversed. Since task #1 is waiting for touch sensor 1 to be pressed, it's not trying to control the motor. So why does it beep?

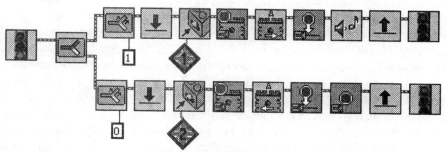

Figure 5.25. Task #2 must be forced to give up control of the motors with the ***Stop Access Control Monitoring*** function.

The subtle fact is that task #1 still had control of the output ports and was forced to give it up and, thus, the beep played after the landing. Task #1 doesn't have a ***Stop Access Control Monitoring*** function in it, so it retains control of the output ports until it is forced to relinquish control to a task with a higher priority.

When touch sensor 2 is pressed, task #2 takes control of the output ports. If we didn't include the ***Stop Access Control Monitoring*** function in task #2, then it would never relinquish control of the output ports. Since task #1 has a lower priority, it would never regain control. Fortunately, this isn't the case and we used the ***Stop Access Control Monitoring*** function to force task #2 to give up control.

> *Note*
>
> A task does not give up control of the outputs ports until it is either forced to by a task with a higher priority or until told to give up control with the ***Stop Access Control Monitoring*** function.

One final variation on this program. Here we've specified only port B to be monitored for conflicts in task #1. Since there is never a conflict over port B, all the task priority functions in task #1 have no effect. Conflicts over Motor A are handled just as if we weren't using task priorities (see Chapter 3).

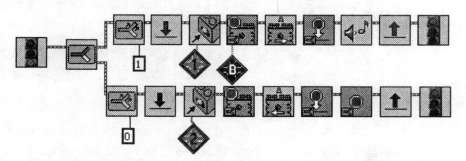

Figure 5.26. Task priorities don't work in this example because task #1 monitors only port B, but controls Motor A.

So now we're finally ready to fix that program shown in Figure 5.22 by using the task priority functions to handle the resource conflicts when they arise. In Figure 5.27 we've specified the task #1 (back up) as having the highest priority, task #3 (left turn) as the next highest, and task #2 (right turn) as the lowest. Tasks #1 and #3 each have the ***Stop Access Control Monitoring*** function so that they are forced to give up control to lower priority tasks once they are done with the motors. We could have included the ***Stop Access Control Monitoring*** function in task #2 also, but we don't have to since it's the lowest priority task and will always give up control when asked to do so by another task.

If you review Figure 3.48 in Chapter 3, you'll see that the programs in Figures 3.45 and 5.27 have nearly identical functions. They both prevent conflicts over the motors, but they do it in different ways. There is, however, one very significant difference between them. The program in Figure 5.27 allows the higher priority tasks to *interrupt* the lower priority ones. Contrast that to the program in Figure 3.48, where each maneuver (back up, turn left, or turn right) has to finish before the next one can begin. In Figure 3.48 all three tasks have essentially the same priority.

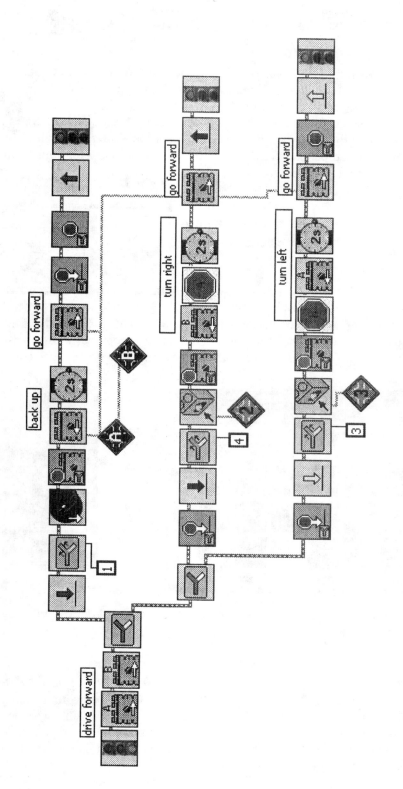

Figure 5.27. This program backs up, turns left, or turns right without any problems now. All the resource conflicts are handled with the task priority function.

5.5 The Advanced Data Logging Badge

Back in Chapter 3 we introduced one of the best features of the RCX, data logging. Investigator Program Levels 1, 2, and 3 are essentially Pilot-type programs. This section will cover Investigator Program Levels 4 and 5.

When you first start to program in levels 4 and 5 you'll notice that there is a new **Functions Palette**. Actually, there is a new palette *above* the **Functions Palette** you are used to seeing. The four sub-palettes from left to right are: **Data Logging and Motors**, **G Code**, **Multimedia**, and **Select a VI**.

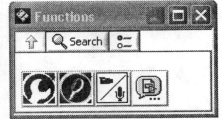

Figure 5.28. The new Functions Palette.

The **Data Logging and Motors** sub-palette is almost identical to the **Functions Palette** you are used to, except that it now has a sub-palette specifically for investigator. There are also several new functions in other sub-palettes, but we'll get to those later.

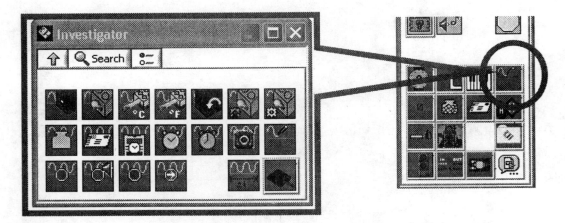

Figure 5.29. There is a new **Investigator** sub-palette available on the **Data Logging & Motors** sub-palette.

Like many things in ROBOLAB, there are three basic steps to perform data logging:
1. *Initialize the sensor* – tell ROBOLAB what type of sensor you are using, which port it is connected to and which data set you will be using.
2. *Start data logging* - define the sampling interval and begin data logging.
3. *Stop data logging* – stop data logging

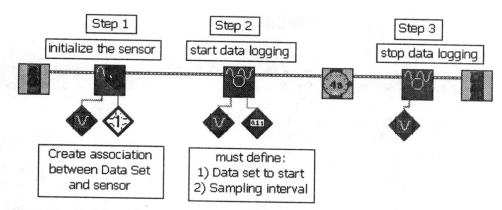

Figure 5.30. The three basic steps to data logging with Investigator Levels 4 and 5.

5.5.1   Step 1: Initializing the Sensor

Nearly all of the first two rows in the Investigator sub-palette are for initializing the sensor (note, we use the term "sensor" loosely because you can actually data log a couple of other things like containers, mail, and timers). There is also one sub-palette for initializing other, non-LEGO® sensors.

As shown in Figure 5.30, all you need to do in order to initialize the sensor is to wire both the data set and source (port value, container value, etc). Like everything else in ROBOLAB, there are three data sets available: red, blue, and yellow.

5.5.2   Step 2: Start Data Logging

To start data logging, you need to specify which data set you are going to log and the sampling interval. To specify the data set, you use one of the new data set icons on the **modifiers** sub-palette. To specify the sampling interval (the time between

samples) you can either use one of the new interval modifiers (as in Figure 5.30) or you can use a numeric constant (as in Figure 5.31).

In Investigator Levels 1 through 3, the minimum sampling interval was 0.05 seconds. In Investigator 4 and 5 we can have a considerably smaller interval, down to 0.01 seconds.

We can also *data log with clicks*, which basically means that each time a data point is logged, you will hear a short beep. Playing the beep takes time, so this considerably slows things down. You can't have a really small sampling interval, but that's often not important if you are using the RCX as a data logging device rather than a robot (e.g. for a science class). In these cases, getting audible feedback that the data was logged is useful.

5.5.3   Step 3: Stop Data Logging

Once you've initialized the sensor and started data logging you have to stop data logging at some point. If you don't explicitly stop data logging, data logging will automatically stop when the program ends. But it's much better to use the ***Stop Logging*** function. Just as with the ***Start Data Logging***, you have to specify which data set you want to stop.

One neat feature of ROBOLAB is that you can both start and stop data logging each of the data sets at different times. In fact, you can set the sampling intervals for each data set too. Figure 5.31 shows a program where the light sensor is logged with the red data set (the default data set when none is specified) and touch sensor 3 is logged with the blue data set. The red data set is started first and has a sampling interval of 0.75 seconds. Ten seconds later the blue data set starts with a sampling interval of 0.5 seconds. The red data set is logged for a total of 14 seconds and the blue is logged for 8 seconds. How many data points would you expect to have in each data set?

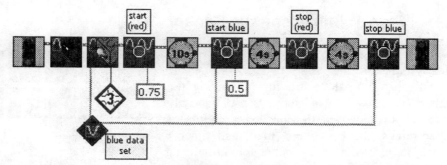

Figure 5.31. You don't have to start and stop sampling all data sets at the same time. Plus, data sets can be sampled with different sampling intervals.

5.5.4   Uploading Data

Uploading data is exactly the same as described in Chapter 3. If you log more than one data set, each data set will be uploaded to a separate data page. If you want to see how to skip this step, then jump ahead and read section 5.7.2.

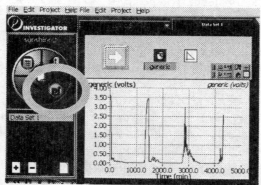

Figure 5.32. Upload data using the upload area as described in Chapter 3.

5.5.5 New Data Logging Functions and Modifiers

 The *Points Container* is used to record the number of data points in a particular data set. It's the same as filling a container using the **Pad Size** of the data set (container #26 though #28).

 The *Data Points Fork* works the same as all the other forks. It compares the current number of data points in the data set specified to the threshold.

 We'll show an example of the *Loop While Points in Data Set is Less Than* function in a little while in Figure 5.35. Like other loops, the loop executes as long as the number of data points is less than the threshold.

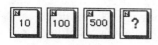 We also have some new *wait for* commands, which are pretty self explanatory. They are the most common way to control the number of data points collected. They are much more accurate than using a *wait for time*, like we did in Figure 5.31.

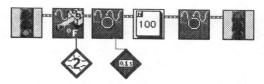

Figure 5.33. By waiting for a specific number of points, we can determine exactly how many points will be collected.

 There are also 6 modifiers that we haven't discussed yet. Three of them will be covered in the next section. The other three are called the value of the red, blue and yellow data sets, which is a little misleading because they are actually the value of the last data point recorded. They are the same as the value of containers #23, #24, and #25. It's the only way to access the data that is being logged. There currently isn't any way to access the rest of the logged data until you upload it to your computer.

5.5.6 Sampling at Irregular Intervals

When you sample at regular intervals then the time between samples is constant (for a given data set). Engineers call this *periodic* sampling. However, we also have the ability to sample at irregular intervals, which is called *aperiodic* sampling. We have three options for sampling at irregular intervals. The first is to take a data point whenever touch sensor 2 is pushed by using the *touch sampling* modifier. This is quite handy for conducting experiments in the field.

Figure 5.34 shows a simple program for taking 25 temperature measurements at irregular intervals. When you use the *touch sampling* modifier, the LCD is automatically set to display the total number of touches so you know how many data points you've collected.

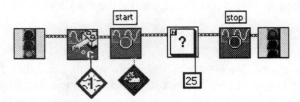

Figure 5.34. *Touch Sampling* allows you to collect data at irregular intervals.

Free Sampling and *Free Sampling with Time Stamp* represent the other two choices for irregular sampling intervals and are nearly identical. The only difference is that one records the time (like all other data logging methods) and one does not. If you don't care about the time each data point was taken, which is often the case when taking field measurements, then use *Free Sampling*. If you need to know the time, then use *Free Sampling with Time Stamp*. Of course, recording the time as well as the data takes more memory.

In both cases, you need to use the *Write Data Point to Data Set* function to let the RCX know when to record a data point. In Figure 5.35, we write a data point each time touch sensor 1 is pushed. Of course, this is basically *touch sampling* except that we're using touch sensor 1 instead of touch sensor 2. But we could have data logged a myriad of other things based on other conditions. Perhaps you want to data log the time each time an event occurs or data log a container value after each *Access Control Landing*. There's no limit with *Free Sampling*.

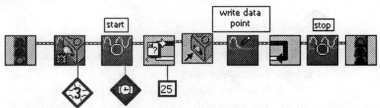

Figure 5.35. When you use *Free Sampling*, each data point is logged when the *Write Data Point* function is reached.

As a side note, when you data log a touch sensor like we did in Figure 5.31, the data set logs either a one or zero depending on whether the touch sensor is pressed or not pressed *at the time the data point is logged*. When we log clicks or releases as in Figure 5.35, the *cumulative number of presses* (or releases) is logged.

5.5.7   Data Analysis: Compute Tools 4 and 5

Compute Tools 4 and 5 introduce a new concept in ROBOLAB. Thus far all the programs you have created have been to control the RCX. However, you can also write programs to analyze your data (that's how Compute Tools 1-3 were created). To do this, you have to use the **G Code** sub-palette.

As the name implies, the **G Code** sub-palette deals with G Code. What is G Code? We'll go into it in more detail later in this chapter, but you've been using one form of G code all along. "G" stands for "graphical." It's the name of the graphical programming language that ROBOLAB and LabVIEW use.

Let's start off with some basic concepts and data analysis functions. The data bucket (a.k.a. data bin) is often confusing at first. It's important to realize that each *data bucket* can contain several *data sets*. For example you can upload 3 data sets into the red bucket in the Upload Area as shown in Figure 5.37.

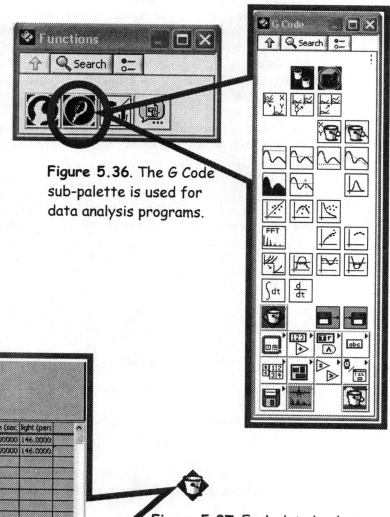

Figure 5.36. The G Code sub-palette is used for data analysis programs.

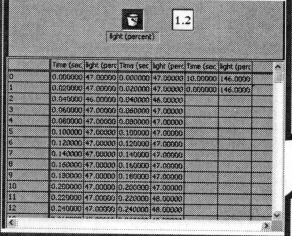

Figure 5.37. Each data bucket can contain multiple data sets. This one has three data sets.

ROBOLAB starts numbering the data sets at zero. So the 1st data set is data set #0, the second data set is data set #1 and so on.

Since there are 10 colored data buckets available, you have the capacity for lots of data sets to be stored. Each data set is comprised of 2 columns, which represent the X and Y components respectively. In most cases, the X component is *time* and Y component is the sensor data (like in Figure 5.37). However, this isn't always the case after we manipulate the data. For example, if we were trying to correlate temperature and solar radiation, we may end up with temperature for the X component and Voltage (from the solar cell) for the Y component.

So now you've got the basics of how data is stored in ROBOLAB. Now we have to discuss how to manipulate data buckets, data sets, and the X & Y components. Entire data buckets are represented with brown wires (just like the ones used for containers). One or more data sets are represented with pink wires (like the ones used for character strings before). The individual X or Y components are represented with orange wires. Got it? Okay, now we're ready to introduce the basic data analysis functions.

 Extract – This function allows you to separate out one data set from the specified bucket. You then have access to both the X and Y components separately (orange wires) and the one data set (pink wire).

 Bin Plots – This function takes in a data set, either from a plot or from another function, and puts it into the specified container. In the example below we've extracted just the 2nd data set (data set #1) from the red bucket, plotted it and stored it in the olive data bucket.

After you create a data analysis program, you push the white run arrow (which we normally use download programs to the RCX). The data analysis program runs and the results are shown on the graph.

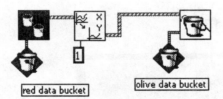

red data bucket   olive data bucket

Figure 5.38. Extracting the data set #1 from the red data bucket, plotting it, and putting it into the olive data bucket.

 Combine – This is the opposite of the extract function. It allows you to create a single data set from individual X and Y components.

 Combine Bins – This function allows you to combine two individual data sets into one group (that is represented by a single pink wire). In the example below, we've ***extracted*** just the first and second data sets from the red data bucket and then used ***combine bins*** to group them together. Finally we've used ***bin plots*** to plot the data sets and put them into the olive bucket. Note, since we are using G we are allowed to join the pink wires together. In normal ROBOLAB we could only do this with the green and blue wires.

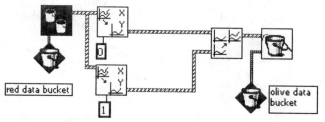

Figure 5.39. This program extracts the data sets #0 and #1 from the red data bucket and puts them both into the olive data bucket.

 XY Plot – This function allows you to take individual X and Y components and add them to a data bucket and plot it. Note the X and Y components can come from different data sets. In the next example, we've taken the Y component of the 2nd data set (data set #1) and used it as the X component for the data set that we add to the olive data bucket. The Y component from the first data set (data set #0) is multiplied by 3.14 before adding it to the olive data bucket.

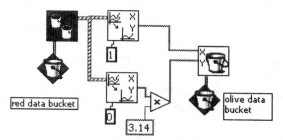

Figure 5.40. Here we've used the Y component from the data set #1 as the X component of our new data set that is added to the olive data bucket.

There are also several statistical functions available which should look familiar from Compute Tools 3 (they also appeared in the Measure Template in the View and Compare Area). It's pretty obvious how each of the functions operate. Our only word of warning is to be careful when you input multiple data 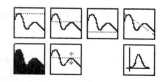 sets. The *mean, average, slope,* and *area under the curve* functions will all calculate the statistic for each data set individually and then average the results. The *maximum, minimum,* and *standard deviation* combine all the data sets before calculating the statistic. The *histogram* will produce a separate result for each data set.

The result of each function can be plotted using the *Bin Plots* function. The icons indicate what the plot will look like. For the *max, min, mean,* and *slope* you'll get two points with a line between them. If you superimpose this line on the original graph, you'll see it's the corresponding statistic (just like the icons show). The *area under the curve* doesn't produce a plot, just a numerical output (the graph is empty if you try to plot it). The *standard deviation* produces a plot with two lines, representing ±1 standard deviation centered on the mean. The *histogram* produces, not surprisingly, a plot of the histogram.

Since the outputs of these functions are data sets, you can manipulate them just as any other data set (the number of points in the data set will depend on the statistical function). In the following example, we've combined the results from the ***maximum*** and ***minimum*** functions into one data set and plotted it as the orange data bucket.

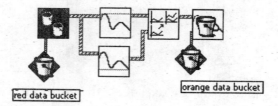

Figure 5.41. This will produce a single plot of both the maximum and minimum of all the data sets in the red data bucket.

Other than the ability to perform multiple statistical operations at the same time, we really don't get too much beyond what was available to us with Compute Tools 1-3. The real power of Compute Tools 4 and 5 lie in the rest of the functions on the central part of the **G Code** sub-palette. With the exception of the ***integrate*** and ***differentiate*** functions, these will take a little explanation.

There are five curve fitting functions available. ***Fit Line*** curve fits the data with a straight line (presumably with a least squares fit). ***Fit Curve*** uses an nth order polynomial to curve fit the data (n=1 is line, n=2 is a parabola, etc). ***Fit Exponential*** and ***Fit Ln*** can be used to fit the data set with exponential and logarithmic functions respectively. Finally, ***Fit Spline*** will use a spline curve consisting of the specified number of points (the default is 100 points). For each of the curve fitting functions, if you input multiple data sets, you'll get a separate curve fit for each data set.

In Figure 5.42 we've written a short program to curve fit all the data sets in the red bucket with 10th order polynomials. We've also used the **combine bins** function so that we can see our original curves along with the curve fits on a single graph. Finally, we've also used an **indicator** to show the coefficients for the curves on the **Front Panel**. Just a small preview of the G Code section that we'll discuss later in this chapter.

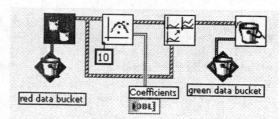

Figure 5.42. Curve fitting all the data sets in the red bucket with a 10th order polynomial.

The ***FFT*** function is used to perform a Fast Fourier Transform of the data set specified. We can't even begin to scratch the surface in terms of the theory. Suffice to say that the FFT is used to determine the *frequency content* of a data set. For many signals (data sets) we are looking for the most prominent frequency, such as the natural frequency of a pendulum swinging back and forth or the frequency of black-white transitions for a spinning disk. In these cases the FFT can be used to determine the dominant frequency to a very high accuracy.

An example will help clarify things. Figure 5.43 shows the light sensor data for a pendulum swinging back and forth (stored in the brown data bucket). In Engineering, this is called the *time series* data.

Using a simple data analysis program, we perform a FFT on the *time series* data to produce the *frequency domain* data, which is stored in the purple data bucket (Figure 5.44). When the purple data bucket is plotted (which happens automatically when you run the program), the natural frequency is clearly evident as the most prominent peak in the graph.

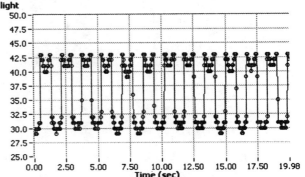

Figure 5.43. Light sensor data for a pendulum experiment (see Design Challenge 3.1.12).

It's totally misleading, but even though the horizontal axis title says "time (sec)," it's really "frequency (Hz)" (Hz is short for Hertz, or cycles per second). For this example, the dominate frequency is at 0.60 Hz, which corresponds to a natural frequency of 1.67 seconds. You might have been able to deduce this from the time series data, but the FFT is much more accurate than counting the time between peaks and valleys.

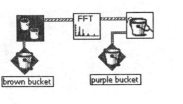 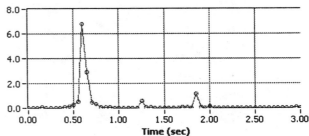

Figure 5.44. The FFT data analysis program and resulting frequency domain data. The horizontal axis label is actually frequency (Hz).

The next three function are all similar. The functions *Peak Time* and *Well Time* are used for determining how long a signal was above or below the cutoff value. As both their names and icons imply, they are to be used on peaks and valleys (wells). The important thing to remember is that both functions won't return any data if the cutoff value doesn't cross the data set twice (i.e. has to cross either a peak or a valley). The example below shows the Peak Time function used to determine the time the light data is above 55. The graph shows that there were 5 peaks above 55. The Y axis indicates the time each peak was above the cutoff value: 0.70, 0.52, 0.60, 0.04, and 0.02 seconds.

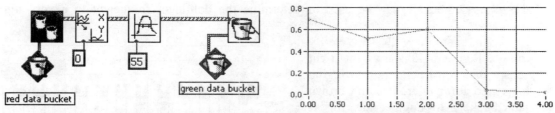

Figure 5.45. Results from performing a *Peak Time* analysis indicates that there were 5 peaks above 55. The first peak was above 55 for a total of 0.7 seconds.

The third function, *threshold*, is used to extract portions of the data set that lie between two cutoff values. One neat feature is that you can use one data set to extract a portion of a second data set. If you are only using one data set, then simply wire the same data set to both inputs, as in the example below.

The last features we are going to cover are the ***load data*** and ***save data*** functions. These are pretty straightforward but very useful. Rather than plot the results, we can save the data to a text file. Be sure to include the axis labels if you want them in the text file.

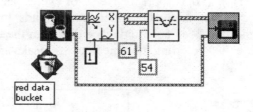

Figure 5.46. Saving the results of the *threshold* function to a text file.

5.6 The Camera Badge

A camera is a unique device. In many ways it is very intuitive to understand because we are so accustomed to processing visual information. To build a *camera sensor*, we need both a camera and a computer. This is equivalent to our eyes working with our brains. The camera (or our eyes) takes the picture and the computer (or our brain) does the *Image Processing*.

In order to be useful to us, the computer must take the picture provided by the camera and convert it into a single number – the *camera sensor value*. Stop and think about the difficulty of that task for a minute. Look around and imagine reducing everything you see into a single integer number. Counting is an obvious choice – how many red things or how many lights are there. Thus, while the camera sensor is intuitively easy to understand, it is also very difficult to use because we are accustomed to the incredible efficiency of our eyes and brain. The camera and computer are a long way from replacing our biological vision system. Figure 5.47 depicts the overall operation of taking a picture and converting it into the number 10, which is stored in the red container. The *image processing* step is where all the action is, so we'll spend most our time talking about it.

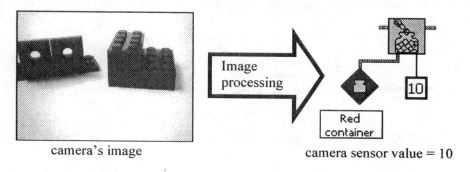

camera's image   camera sensor value = 10

Figure 5.47. The camera sensor must take a picture and then convert it into a single number, which is stored in either the red, blue or yellow container.

5.6.1   Launching the Vision Center

Vision Center is the ROBOLAB camera sensor program. To launch the **Vision Center**, go to the **Project menu** and select **Vision Center**. You can **select camera** from either the **Project menu** or from within the **Vision Center**. Any web cam can be used.

Figure 5.48. Launch the **Vision Center** from the **Project Menu** in Inventor.

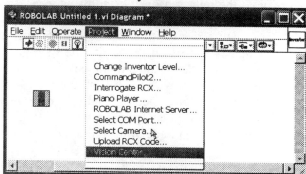

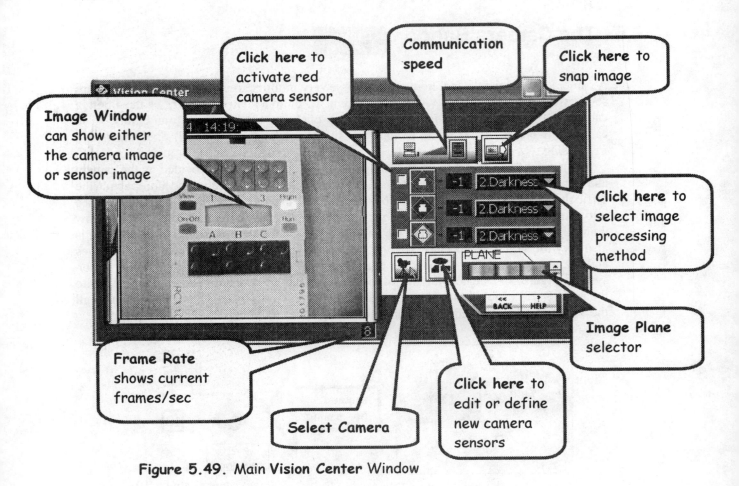

Figure 5.49. Main **Vision Center** Window

There are a lot of controls shown in Figure 5.49. Normally it would be a good idea to go over them before jumping into some sample projects. However, going over all the details is going to take quite a few pages. Instead, let's take a more inductive approach. Before getting into all the nuts & bolts of how to use the Vision Center, let's do some examples. After that, if you have more specific questions you can read the rest of this chapter.

5.6.2 An Electronic Cookie Jar

Roommates eating your food? Little brother pilfering your sugar stash? Here's a simple program that you can use to keep watch over your cookies. Figure 5.50 shows the VI which waits for the camera sensor to increase to 70 or above (this is just like using *wait for light* with the light sensor). Once this happens, the program tells the camera to *snap image* and then plays the default sound and starts over.

In order for this to work as planned, the camera sensor has to be set up correctly, which is shown on the right side of Figure 5.50. At the top, we've selected *slow RCX communication* – the only mode which allows the RCX to tell the camera to take pictures. Just below that we've activated the red camera sensor by clicking on the checkbox next to the red container icon. Finally, we've selected pre-defined sensor number 6, *Motion Location*, for the image processing method. This method (which is described in detail later) stores the magnitude of the motion detected in the red container.

When we download and run this program on the RCX, together the camera, the computer, and the RCX form an *integrated system* that takes a picture whenever the level of motion exceeds 70. Using 70 as the threshold in the program was determined through trial and error.

Figure 5.50. Electronic cookie jar program (left) and corresponding vision center settings (right).

Let's review what we've learned so far. The camera sensor is comprised of the camera, which takes the pictures, and the computer, which does the image processing. We used the Vision Center to tell the computer what type of image processing we want done – in this case we wanted it to measure the amount of motion (a number between 0 and 254). The camera sensor stored the amount of motion in the red container. Finally, just like all the other projects we've done so far, we needed to write a program for the RCX to run. The only thing that's a little different here is that the RCX must remain in constant communication with the IR tower so that the computer can keep updating the value in the red container.

Figure 5.51. Snapped image of the thief's hand in action.

5.6.3 Seek the Brightest Spot

The challenge was to find the brightest spot in view and then slowly move towards it. We might have been able to complete this challenge using just the standard light sensor, but we thought it would be cool to use the camera. So here it goes.

Our solution uses another one of the pre-defined camera sensors. The first thing we do is to set up the camera sensor in the Vision Center, as shown in Figure 5.52. This time we have selected *fast RCX communication* speed. We're using the red camera sensor again with pre-defined sensor #3, *Bright Location*, selected as the image processing method. This method actually uses all 3 containers; it stores the intensity of the brightest spot in the red container, the vertical (Y-location) in the blue container, and the horizontal (x-location) in the yellow container. That's all there is to setting up the camera sensor.

Next, we have to write the program that makes use of the camera sensor we've just defined. The algorithm we are going to implement is fairly simple. If the brightest spot is on the left side of the image, turn left. If it's on the right, then turn right. If the brightest spot is in the center of the image, then drive straight forward for a little while.

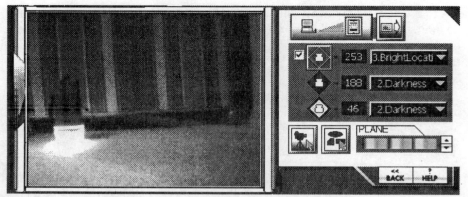

Figure 5.52. Setting up the Camera Sensor

The program we came up with is shown in Figure 5.53. We start by storing the horizontal (x-coordinate) of the brightest spot in generic container #3. Since the picture is 320x240 pixels in size (width x height), we subtract 160 from the x-coordinate (see Figure 5.66 for a definition of the coordinate system). This makes the center of the picture x = 0, left edge x = -160 and the right edge x = 160 (in engineering terms this is called *biasing* the signal). If the brightest spot is near the center of the picture (i.e., the x coordinate is between -10 and 10), then we drive forward for 1 second. On the other hand, if the brightest spot is not near the center of the picture, then we turn towards the brightest spot for 0.1 seconds. We've use a bit of proportional feedback control in that the motor speed is directly proportional to how far off center we are. (*Note: we've used a new advanced motor command, motor forward or back, that is only available in ROBOLAB version 2.5.4 and above. If you don't have it, you can make it as described in the Advanced Output skill badge in section 4.7*).

The wait for 0.2 seconds at the start of the program was added after we had tested this program a few times. We found that the robot was much faster than the camera sensor! The robot would turn, but the camera sensor wasn't updating very fast. This caused all sorts of problems, so we added the wait for 0.2 seconds to give the camera enough time to acquire and process a new image.

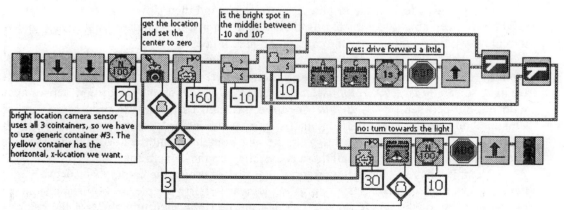

Figure 5.53. Light seeking program.

5.6.4 Counting non-Red Bricks

In this example, we'll show how to create your own camera sensor definition using a combination of image processing steps. The challenge is to design a camera sensor that can count the number of non-red bricks in the image.

To accomplish this task, we will define a new camera sensor that uses the red color plane to "filter" out the red bricks, thresholds the image, inverts the image, and finally uses a blobs analysis to count the number of items. Again, we'll go through this fairly quickly. The idea is to give you an overall view of how everything goes together to make a camera sensor. All the gory details are covered later in this chapter.

To define your own sensor, click on the **define sensor** button in the main **Vision Center** window (see Figure 5.49). This opens a new window, as shown in the figure below. In this example, the camera is looking at two bricks, a black 2x2 and a red 2x4. The first thing we are going to do is use the red color plane to eliminate the red brick from the image. Similar to the picture on your TV, the camera image is actually made up of red, green, and blue colors. Using the red color plane uses the information from only the red part of the image – you can think of it as a red filter.

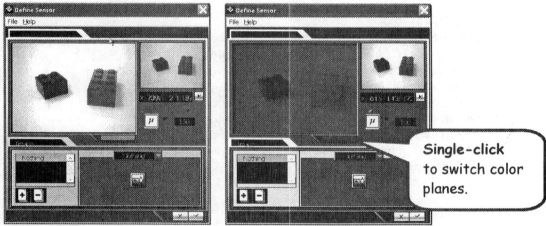

Figure 5.54. LEFT: a new (blank) sensor definition. RIGHT: the red image plane makes the image look like it is tinted red.

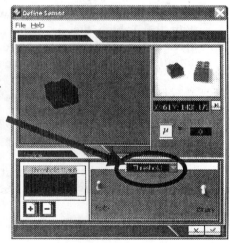

Figure 5.55. Thresholding the image.
Next, we select *threshold* as the **image operation** and choose *automatic*, *binary* as the type of threshold. This converts the image into a binary (two) color image: black and red. Everything within a certain range of intensity is colored black and everything else is colored red. Notice that the red brick has now disappeared from the image.

Figure 5.56. Inverting the image.

A sensor definition is made up of one or more **image operation** pages (steps). To add another page, we simply click on the "+" icon. Then we select *invert* as the 2nd image operation. This changes black to red and visa-versa. Why do this? Well, it turns out the next step only works if the background is black.

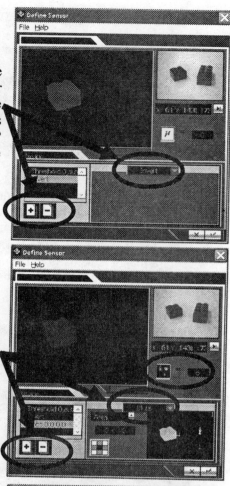

Figure 5.57. Blobs analysis.

Finally, we add the 3rd and last page to our sensor definition, select *blobs* as the **image operation**, and set the **sensor operation** to *blob count*. Note the size (number of pixels) of each blob is indicated on the image in the lower right. In the image shown, we have 6 blobs, 5 small ones and 1 big one. The big one is the 2x2 black brick and the small ones are remnants of the red 2x4 brick and are all 1 or 2 pixels in size.

Figure 5.58. Adjust the blob size filter.

To make the sensor ignore all blobs smaller than 100 pixels and larger than 10000 pixels, we set the min = 100 and max = 10000. Now we are only left with the 1 blob that is associated with the 2x2 black brick. The last step is to save our sensor definition by clicking on the green checkmark.

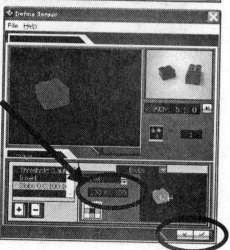

We now have a sensor that will count the number of non-red bricks. In Figure 5.59 our new sensor correctly picks out 4 non-red bricks (i.e., the red container = 4).

Figure 5.59. Our new camera sensor correctly counting 4 non-red bricks.

By using the **Image Plane Selector**, we can select the red container. This displays the processed sensor image. This is VERY useful for debugging your custom camera sensors. For example, here we can see that the sensor is only counting 3 non-red bricks because two of the bricks "overlap" and are being counted as only 1 blob.

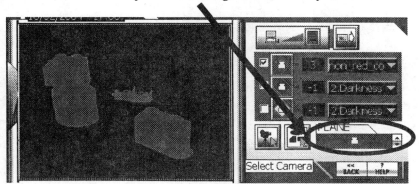

Figure 5.60. Viewing the processed sensor image.

Let's recap one more time what we know. The camera sensor is comprised of the camera and the computer. We use the **Vision Center** to tell the computer what type of image processing we want done. We can either select one of the eight pre-defined image processing methods or make up our own. Each image processing method is made up of one or more **image operations**, such as *threshold, invert,* and *blobs*. We select which camera sensors we want by clicking on the checkbox next to the red, blue or yellow containers. The camera sensor stores the sensor value in the corresponding container for use in our program.

We didn't do it for this example, but normally you would needed to write a program for the RCX to run. Don't forget to make sure the RCX is in view of the IR tower at all times. Or you could just carry the IR tower around as shown in Figure 4.64.

That should be enough to get you started. Go ahead and start playing around and having fun. If you get stuck or need information about a specific command or setting, we'll go over all the details for the **Image Window, Communication Speed, Image Processing Methods,** the **Image Plane,** and how to define a new sensor in the next dozen or so pages.

5.6.5   The Image Window

The Image Window can show the camera image as shown in Figure 5.49 or, by using the **Image Plane Selector**, the processed image, as shown in Figure 5.61.

The Image Window can also be blanked out, as shown in Figure 5.62. Why do this? Well, it turns out that image processing is a fairly computationally intensive operation, which means it takes a lot of computer power to do it. By blanking out the Image Window you make the computer's workload a little lighter and, thus, it can work a little faster.

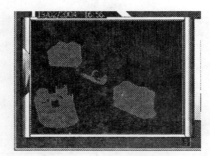

Figure 5.61. A processed image being shown in the Image Window

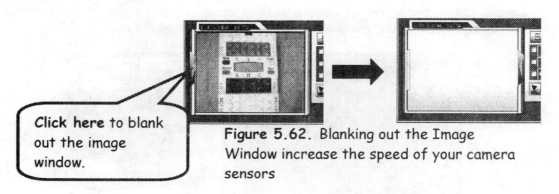

Click here to blank out the image window.

Figure 5.62. Blanking out the Image Window increase the speed of your camera sensors

5.6.6   Communication Speed

The computer reduces the camera image to a single number – the camera sensor value. This is exactly the same as the light sensor reducing the intensity of the light to a single sensor value except doing this for a picture is much more difficult.

Since processing the camera image is too difficult for the RCX to handle, it has to be done on the computer. Once the computer does this, it has to tell the RCX what the sensor value is. It does this by beaming the sensor value to the RCX via the Infrared Tower.

How often you want the computer to send the sensor value to the RCX will depend on the task. You can set the communication speed between the computer and RCX by clicking on the Communication Speed icon (Figure 5.63).

Just as the name implies, *No RCX Communication* means that the computer doesn't tell the RCX anything about the camera sensor value. With *Slow RCX Communication,* the computer sends the RCX the sensor values (in the red, blue and yellow containers) a few times a second. This mode also allows 2-way communication, meaning the RCX can ask the computer to snap an image, which it stores in the ROBOLAB>My Data>Vision> Pictures directory as sequentially numbered bitmap (BMP) images. With *Fast RCX Communication*, the computer sends the RCX the container values almost instantly. This mode is one-

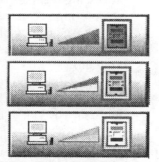

Figure 5.63. From top to bottom: No communication, slow, and fast communication

way, meaning the RCX cannot ask the computer to take images.

If the RCX is out of range of the IR tower (or the RCX is turned off), the error message shown in Figure 5.64 will show up in the main Image Window. Once the RCX is back in range, communication between the RCX and the computer will resume. Thus, it is possible for the RCX to receive the camera sensor value, leave and complete some tasks, and then return for more camera sensor data.

Figure 5.64. This error message appears in the Image Window when the RCX is out of range of the IR Tower.

5.6.7   Image Processing Methods

The main point of the **Vision Center** is to use a camera as a sensor. As mentioned earlier, we have to convert the camera picture into a single number. This conversion process is called *image processing*. The computer takes a picture, processes it, takes another picture, processes it, and so on. How often it takes a picture will depend on how hard the image processing task is, how fast the camera is, and how fast your computer is.

There are eight pre-defined image processing methods in ROBOLAB as shown in Figure 5.65. As you create your own image processing methods, they are added to this list (in alphabetic order). Let's go over each of these eight pre-defined methods quickly.

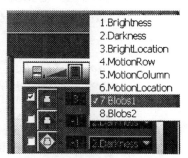

Figure 5.65. Image Processing Methods

> ***Brightness*** – This finds the value of the brightest spot on the image, with 0 = dark and 254=bright. This is a fairly simple image processing method, which means this camera sensor is quite fast.

> ***Darkness*** – The opposite of **Brightness**, this finds the value of the darkest spot on the image, with 0=dark and 254=bright.

> ***Bright Location*** – This is actually three image processing methods rolled into one. *It should be used only with the red container*. The red container is filled with the value of the brightest spot (same as the ***Brightness*** image processing method), the blue container is filled with the Y-location, and yellow container is filled with the X-location of the brightest spot. As shown in Figure 5.66, the image is 320x240 pixels in size. X represents the horizontal location and Y represents the vertical location. X=0, Y=0 is in the upper left corner and X=320, Y=240 is in the lower right corner.
> Though somewhat confusing, the labels for the blue and yellow containers do not change. But rest assured, that the blue container does contain the Y-value and yellow container contains the X-value of the brightest spot. Since this is actually three image processing methods combined, it is a little slower than either ***Brightness*** or ***Darkness***.

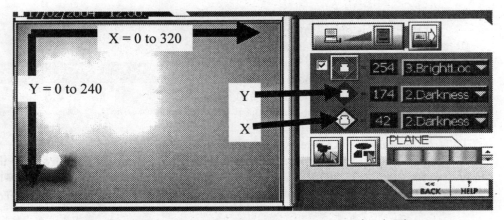

Figure 5.66. Bright Location image processing method. The image processing labels for the blue and yellow container don't mean anything. *It should only be used with the red container.*

Motion Location – This is another sensor that is actually three image processing methods rolled into one and, thus, is a little slow. It finds the magnitude of the motion (a number related to the amount of change), and the X- and Y-locations of the detected motion.

In general, all the motion image processing methods return noise (garbage) when nothing is happening. This is because of slight fluctuations in the camera and/or light levels. Fortunately, the noise is usually low - the camera looking a stationary scene typically results in a motion magnitude of around 10-15, whereas even the slightest motion of a tiny object results in magnitudes well over 100 (the maximum is 254). In Figure 5.67 below, a slight movement of the light resulted in a motion magnitude of 147.

The X-location of the motion is stored in the yellow container and the Y-location is stored in the blue container. As with the *Bright Location* method, the labels for the blue and yellow containers do not reflect the actual processing method. As usual, X=0, Y=0 is in the upper left corner and X=320, Y=240 is in the lower right corner.

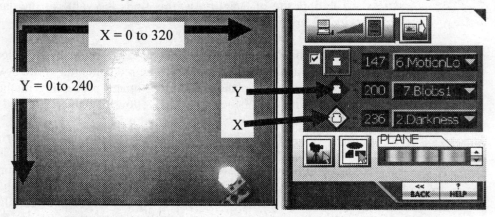

Figure 5.67. Motion Location image processing method. The image processing labels for the blue and yellow container don't mean anything. *It should only be used with the red container.*

Motion Row – This finds the Y-location of any detected motion. It is the same as the blue container for the ***Motion Location***.

Motion Column – This finds the X-location of any detected motion. It is the same as the yellow container for the ***Motion Location***.

Blobs1 – This image processing method finds the total number of objects (blobs) in the picture. The blobs can be of any size and any shape as shown in Figure 5.68. This method actually contains several image processing steps, called pages (see Figure 5.69). We'll get into more detail on *sensor definitions* later, but here is a little preview.

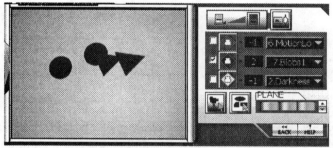

Figure 5.68. Here we are using the blue container. Blobs1 doesn't care what shape or size the objects are. If the objects overlap, they are counted as a single blob. This image has only 2 blobs.

First it takes the picture and applies a ***mask***, which tells the computer to ignore the edge of the picture. You can tell the size of the mask in Figure 5.69 by looking at how the bricks are cut-off around the edges – it looks as is there is a big black picture frame around the edge. The 2nd step is to ***invert*** the image, which changes black to white and visa-versa. The 3rd step is to ***threshold*** the image. This changes the grayscale image into a black and white one. Finally, a ***blobs*** analysis is performed which counts the total number of white objects in the picture, regardless of size or shape.

Figure 5.69. Blobs1 uses 4 image processing steps (pages).

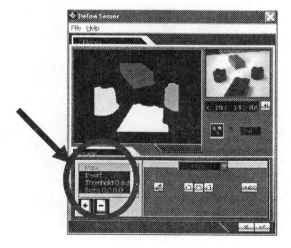

Blobs2 – this is very similar to *blobs1*, except this image processing method only counts blobs (objects) that are bigger than 500 pixels and less than 1500 pixels in size. How small is 500 pixels? How big is 1500 pixels? Remember, the image is 320x240 pixels, which is 76,800 total pixels. In other words, 1500 pixels is less than 2% of the total image – that not very big! Figure 5.70 shows the range of blob sizes that *blobs2* will count. Like *blobs1*, *blobs2* also has a *mask*, so objects at the edge of the picture won't be counted either.

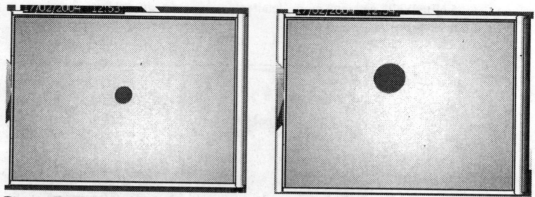

Figure 5.70. The dot on the left is 500 pixels and the dot on the right is 1500 pixels in size. **Blobs2** will only count objects between 500 and 1500 pixels in size.

5.6.8   The Image Plane

The Image **Plane** is kind of like a filter. You can use the image plane to view the red, green, and blue components of the image (the full color image is made up of the red, green, and blue images combined). You can also use the **Image Plane** selector to look at the processed image for the sensor associated with the red, blue, or yellow containers. In Figure 5.71 we see the original camera image, the red plane, and the processed image for the sensor associated with the red container.

Figure 5.71. This figure shows the original camera image (top), the red plane image (middle) and the processed image being used for the camera sensor associated with the red container (bottom).

5.6.9   How to Define a New Sensor

The eight pre-defined image processing methods will be enough to accomplish many tasks. However, sooner or later you're going to want to define your own camera sensor just as we did in section 5.6.4. To define a new sensor, click on the **Define Sensor** button (see Figure 5.49). This will open the window show in Figure 5.72. In general, there are 5 steps to creating a new sensor definition:

1. Select the **Image Plane**
2. Select the first **Image Operation** and the settings for this operation
3. Add more pages for additional **Image Operations** and their settings
4. Select the **Sensor Operation**
5. **Save** your new Sensor Definition

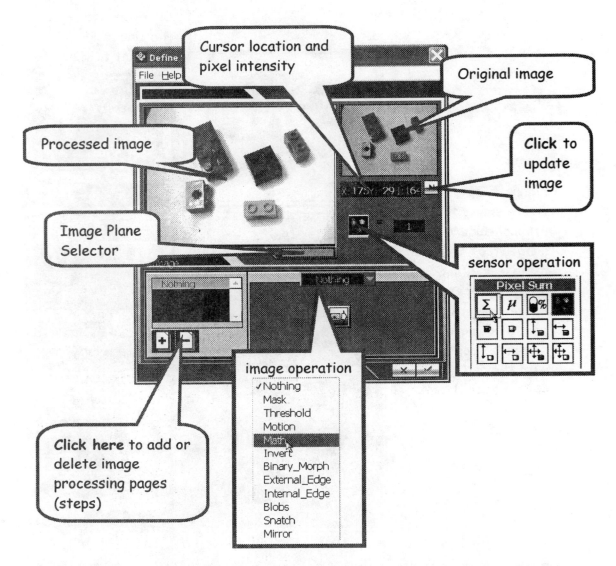

Figure 5.72. The **Define Sensor** window. Lots of options to choose from!

Step 1: Select the Image Plane

The **Image Plane** is basically a filter. You can use the filter to either filter out a certain color or look for a certain color. For example, in section 5.6.4 we showed how the red plane was used to filter out the red bricks – it made the red brick blend in with the background. However, the red plane can also be used in exactly the opposite way – to detect a red brick. One of the **Sensor Operations** that we'll discuss later is the **Pixel Average**. It basically tells you the average intensity (brightness) of the image. If we use the red plane to look at a green brick, the average intensity (the redness) is low because the green brick isn't very red. However, if we look at a red brick through the red plane, the average intensity (redness) is quite high.

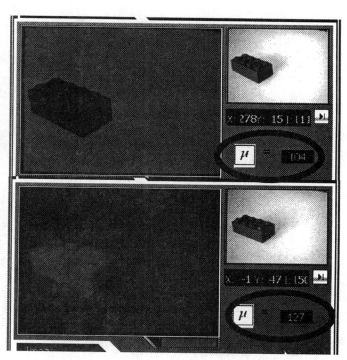

Figure 5.73. Looking through the Red Plane. The top image is of a green brick. The bottom image is of a red brick.

The green brick results in a lower average "redness" than the red brick (μ = 104 compared to 127).

Step 2: Select the first Image Operation

There are 13 different **image operations** and one of them, **Binary *Morph***, is a conglomeration of 9 related image operations. That gives you a lot of options! We'll quickly go over each of them now, but the best way to see how each of these works is just to play with them.

Nothing – as the name implies, it does nothing to the image. This is the default image operation for a new sensor.

Figure 5.74. Mask.

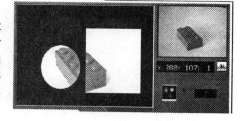

A mask is used to select the parts of the image that you don't want to process. It can be particularly useful for eliminating objects such as lights or an annoying background. You can use multiple masks on top of each other. This figure shows two masks applied.

Figure 5.75. Threshold.

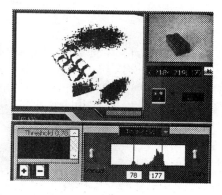

An image is normally grayscale, meaning the each pixel has an intensity between 0 (black) and 255 (white). When we threshold, define a threshold range. Everything inside the range forced to white (255) and everything outside the range is force to black (0).

There are 2 settings under threshold. Binary turns the picture black and white (black = 0, white = 1). Grayscale turns everything outside the range black (zero), while leaving everything inside the range the original grayscale value. You can either threshold manually or automatically. Using manual gives you more control, but auto works best for varying lighting conditions. Auto is used most of the time. In Figure 5.75 we are using a **manual, binary threshold** with the limits of 78 and 177. Thus, any intensities lower than 78 or greater than 177 are turned black and everything is else is turned white.

Figure 5.76. Motion

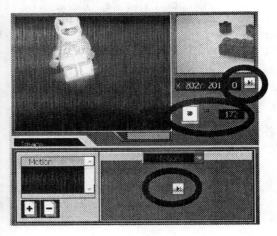

This image operation detects where the image is changing. It does this by comparing (subtracting) two sequential images. The snap image button in the upper right sets the first image. The snap image button in the lower middle sets the 2nd image. In this example, we added a mini-fig next to the 3 existing bricks for the 2nd image. When the 2 images are subtracted, anything that has not changed is black. Anything that has changed is white. The **sensor operation** is set to return the value of the brightest spot (172 in this example).

Figure 5.77. Noise levels for Motion.

Just as a comparison, this figure shows what happens when we snap the first and second images without changing anything. Notice that even though the two images were taken only a second apart there are some minor differences. However the intensity of the brightest spot is only 14 as compared to the 172 from the previous example. In engineering terms, 14 would be the *noise level*.

Figure 5.78. Math.

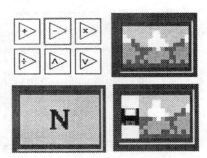

This image operation allows you to conduct simple math on images. You can add, subtract, multiply or divide all intensities by a number (N), another snapped image or from an image file. For example, for a grayscale image the intensities range from 0 to 255 (0 = black). You could lighten an image by adding 20 to it.

Invert – This image operation "inverts" all the image intensities of a grayscale or binary image. For a binary image, black becomes white and visa-versa. For a grayscale image, all intensities are flipped around 128. Thus, 127 would become 129 and 150 would become 106 and so forth.

Binary Morph – This is actually a collection of 9 different image operations that can be performed on a binary image. Since this will not work on a grayscale image, you always have to do a **binary threshold** operation before any of the binary morph operations. All of the binary morph operations have a connectivity setting as shown in Figure 5.79. This defines how pixels are "connected" to each other. On the left, the center pixel is only connected to 4 of its neighboring pixels. On the right, it is connected to all 8 of its neighbors (e.g., it has more influence on its surroundings).

Figure 5.79. Connectivity settings

Dilation – This operation increases (dilates) the size of white objects, which is the same as decreasing the size of black objects. It is shown in center of Figure 5.80. Compared to the original image (top), all of the white spots have grown slightly. The overall size of the brick has also shrunk.

Erosion – This is the opposite of dilation. It decreases the size of white objects, which increases the size of black ones.

Open – This is an erosion followed by a dilation. Why do this? The erosion and dilation negate each other for big objects, which retains their size. But it gets rid of small white dots and effectively "despeckles" an image. The result is shown at the bottom of Figure 5.80.

Close – This is the opposite of open. It's a dilation followed by an erosion. It gets rid of small black dots while keeping the size of the objects unchanged.

Proper Open – This is a close followed by an open followed by another close. This eliminates small white spots and smoothes the large white spots.

Proper Close - This is an open followed by a close followed by another open. This eliminates small black spots and smoothes the large black spots.

Thin – Removes white pixels from the image based on the connectivity setting.

Thick – Adds white pixels to the image based on the connectivity setting.

Figure 5.80. Original image (top), after a *dilation* (center), and after an Open (bottom)

Auto-Median – this is a proper open followed by a proper close. This operation reduces details, making simpler objects.

External Edge – This operation creates a 1-pixel thick edge outside all white objects. Only works on a binary image and uses the connectivity settings as shown in Figure 5.79.

Internal Edge – This operation creates a 1-pixel thick edge inside all white objects. Only works on a binary image and uses the connectivity settings as shown in Figure 5.79.

Blobs – Picks out the number of white objects (blobs) in a binary image. You can filter the selection process by area, orientation, aspect ratio or diagonal of the blobs. Most commonly we filter based on area by ignoring really small or really large blobs. Blobs only works on a binary image and uses the connectivity settings as shown in Figure 5.79.

Snatch – This operation picks out the biggest white blob and then outputs the area, orientation, aspect ratio, or diagonal of the blob.

Mirror – As the name implies, this operation produces a mirror image of the original, flipped about the central vertical axis (x = 160).

Step 3: Add more pages for additional Image Operations

Most camera sensors will require more than one image operation, the most common being *mask*, *threshold*, and *invert*. To add more image operations, simply click on the "+" icon. To delete an image operation, click on the "-" icon. You can also change the order of the image operations by simply selecting an operation and then dragging and dropping it in the list.

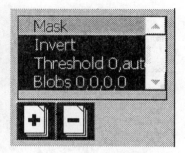

Figure 5.81. Image Operation pages.

Step 4: Select the Sensor Operation

This is where you set what information you want from the sensor you've defined. You have 12 choices. This is a very important step because often you want a specific piece of information from the image operations you've set up (e.g. such as the size of biggest blob).

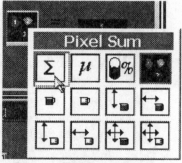

Figure 5.82. Sensor Operations.

- **Pixel Sum**: adds the sum of all the pixel intensities (up to the largest number allowable for a container, 32767)
- **Pixel Average**: returns the average pixel intensity, rounded down to the nearest integer (remember all math in ROBOLAB is integer math). For a binary image, it is almost always zero.
- **Amount Filled**: returns the percentage of the image filled with white for a binary image. For a grayscale image, it's the sum of all pixel intensities divided by 76,800, expressed as a percentage (e.g. 16%= 16).
  [Note: Pixel Average = (Amount Filled) ÷ 100, rounded down to the nearest integer]
- **Blob Count**: returns the total number of blobs (even if blobs is not one of the image operations selected)
- **Max or Min**: returns the maximum or minimum. Which maximum or minimum depends on the image operation. It can be max or min intensity, area, orientation, etc.
- **Max/Min Row or Column**: these return the row or column of the max or min. Again, this will depend on the image operations selected.
- **Max/Min Info**: these two use all three containers to output Max/Min the row (y-location) of the max/min and the column (x-location) of the max/min.

Step 5: Save your new Sensor Definition

The last step is to save your new sensor definition by either clicking on the green checkmark or selecting *save* from the file menu. That's all there is to it!

5.6.10   Additional Vision Center Help

In case all this isn't enough for you, Tufts University (the creators of ROBLOLAB) maintains an excellent self-tutorial on image processing on the web at:

http://www.ceeo.tufts.edu/robolabatceeo/College/tutorials/image_cli/index.htm

The tutorial covers the basics, like we've done here, and then goes about 10 miles beyond that (or 16 km if you live outside the US). It's by far the best (and only) resource we've found. Both instructions and additional Challenges are posted.

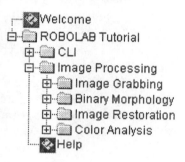

Figure 5.83. Online tutorial for image processing .

5.7 The Basic G-Code Badge

Welcome to Oz, you're about to get a look behind the curtain. You've probably realized by now that ROBOLAB is based on LabVIEW, Laboratory Virtual Instrument Engineering Workbench. LabVIEW is a graphical programming environment developed by National Instruments (Austin, TX) that uses a PC to replace traditional laboratory instruments like oscilloscopes, Voltmeters, etc. The concept is to use a standard low-cost PC as a virtual instrument, hence the term VI. The graphical programming language that is used in LabVIEW (and ROBOLAB) is called "G" for graphical. Programs written in G are called virtual instruments or VI's. ROBOLAB was written completely in LabVIEW using G by the folks at the Tufts University Center for Engineering Educational Outreach (www.ceeo.tufts.edu).

We're not going to even try to pretend that we can teach you G in this one section. If you are truly interested, we suggest you get a LabVIEW book such as *Learning with LabVIEW 7 Express* or *LabVIEW for Everyone*. Both books are excellent resources and pretty easy reading. While you won't become an expert in G, we will show you a couple of neat tricks.

Way back in Figure 2.22, which we've reproduced here, we introduced the **front panel** and the **block diagram** windows. We told you that all your programming would be written in the **block diagram** window. That was basically true, yet not completely true now that we're going to introduce you to G.

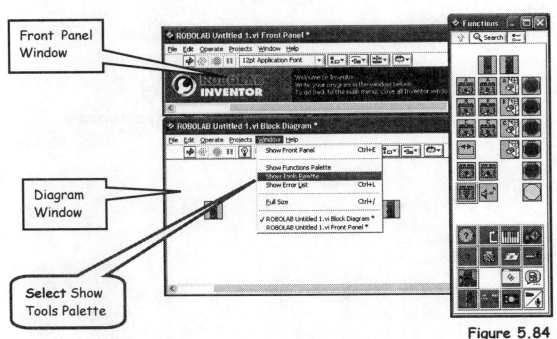

Figure 5.84
Inventor mode windows.

Thus far you've written programs on the **Block Diagram** but never actually done anything with the **Front Panel**. It may be a bit surprising but the **Front Panel** is supposed to be the user main interface. That's because it contains the **controls** (knobs, buttons, etc.)

and **indicators** (displays, graphs, etc) that are at the heart of a virtual instrument. The **Block Diagram** is where the program that runs the virtual instrument is written.

5.7.1   Your First VI

You can only access G-Code through Programmer levels 4 and 5 in Investigator, so be sure you're there before trying the following example.

With G-Code you have access to various data types: Boolean (true/false), integer, floating point (real numbers), and character strings (text) which are represented with green, blue, orange, and pink wires respectively. Let's start with an example of doing some simple math. Say you wanted to create an instrument which could add two numbers together (okay, you would probably call it a calculator). We can start by placing the *add* function (which is on the **numeric** sub-palette) in the **Block Diagram** and creating a couple of **controls** for the inputs as shown in Figure 5.85. To get the pop-up menu, simply right-click on the *add* icon while your mouse is over the wire terminal.

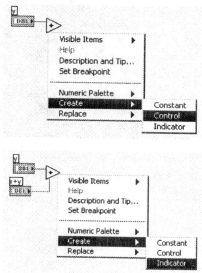

Figure 5.85
Adding a **control** to the *add* function.

If you look at the **Front Panel**, you'll see these controls on it now. Next, let's add an **indicator** so that we can see the output of the *add* function on the Front Panel (again, by right-clicking over the terminal).

Figure 5.86
Adding an **Indicator** to the *add* function

Once we've got our two **controls** and **indicator** we can rename them to something meaningful. This can be done with the text tool in either the Front Panel or the Block Diagram. Note, the default color for text is black, which happens to be the background color of the ROBOLAB Front Panel so the text may look like it's missing. In Figure 5.87 we've already changed the color, renamed the **controls**, and are in the process of selecting the **indicator** label (text box).

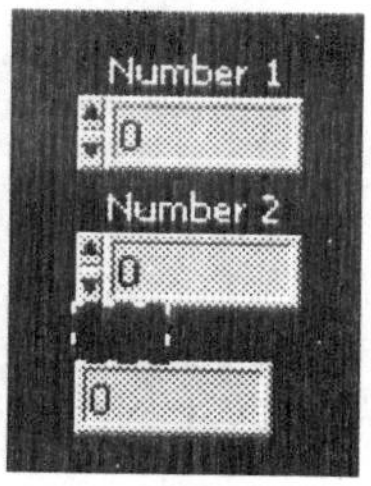

Figure 5.87
Renaming the labels (text boxes). The default text color is black, so the text for the indicator isn't visible.

Either the operating tool or the text tool can be used to change the values of the controls, now labeled number 1 and number 2. Hit run (white arrow) or Ctrl+R and you'll see the indicator display the result.

We can add another math function, like *multiply*, as shown. Note, the same two controls are now wired to both numeric functions.

Figure 5.88. Adding a second math function, *multiply*.

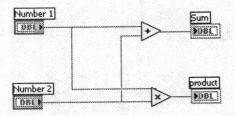

After changing the label and doing some additional font manipulations, we have the final version of the **Front Panel** for our simple calculator.

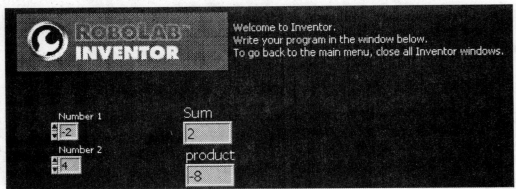

Figure 5.89. Our calculator **Front Panel**.

Okay, let's recap what we've learned so far. A VI is a Virtual Instrument. **Controls** are things that the user can adjust in our VI using the operate (or text) tool on the **Front Panel**. The **Indicators** are outputs (results) from our program and are displayed on **Front Panel**. The program that governs the behavior of the **Front Panel** is written in the **Block Diagram** window using G.

This is a pretty boring looking calculator, so let's spiff it up a bit by changing the look of the control and indicators. If you right-click on the **indicator**, you can change its appearance. Here we're selecting a meter that resembles and the output on an old fashioned analog Volt meter.

We can also change the appearance of our other **indicator** and **controls** to produce a much snazzier looking **Front Panel**. It doesn't function differently, just looks cool. You can use the **Run Continuously** command so that you can twiddle the knobs and watch the results change in real time.

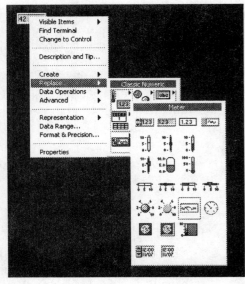

Figure 5.90. Replacing the standard indicator with a neat looking one.

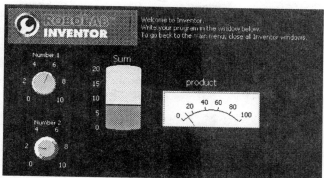

Figure 5.91. Our cool looking calculator **Front Panel.**

Though we haven't discussed it, there are tons of additional functions you can play with to make other VI's. There are also a plethora of controls and indicators that you can use to spice up the look of your VI's.

One obvious use for the **front panel** comes directly to mind: to display the sensor, container, and timer values real time. To do this you have to use the RCX in **direct mode** (in combination with G) and that is covered in Chapter 6.

5.7.2   Using the Front Panel in Compute Tools 4 & 5

This may be neat, but you're probably wondering what this has to do with the RCX. It turns out you can create a **Front Panel** for your ROBOLAB program the same way we just created that nifty calculator. Let's start with creating a Front Panel for our data analysis program (see section 5.5.7). Just as we did for the calculator, we can add some **indicators** and **controls** to our Compute Tools 5 program by right-clicking on the appropriate wire terminal.

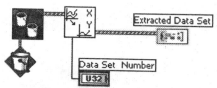

Figure 5.92. Using indicators in a Compute Tools 5 program.

Here we've used a **control** to allow the user to select which data set from the red data bucket he/she wants to view. The extracted data set is then shown as a graph (the default for this data type) when you run the program. Simply use the operate tool to change which data set you want and run the program again to update the graph. Unlike the standard graph in Inventor, you have complete control over the appearance of the indicator.

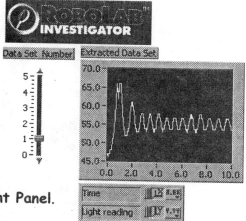

Figure 5.93. Our Compute Tools 5 **Front Panel.**

By now the reason why the **Front Panel** is called that should be obvious. Our **Front Panel** is starting to look a lot like the controls for a scientific instrument. A slightly different variation on the program shown in Figure 5.92 is shown in Figure 5.94. We've decided to bypass the Upload Area completely and create our own program that uploads the data from the RCX and plots it directly on the **Front Panel**.

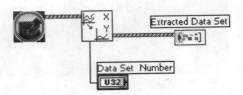

Figure 5.94. We've skipped the Upload Area with this program, which uploads the data and plots it directly on the **Front Panel**.

5.7.3   Using the Front Panel in Programmer 4 & 5

Using the **Front Panel** for data analysis is much more common than using it for normal ROBOLAB programs, simply because there isn't anything really to see (after all, nothing is happening with the RCX until you download and run the program). The exception to this is when you are using **direct mode**, in which case you can control the RCX in real time. But alas, you'll have to skip ahead to Advanced RCX Communication in Chapter 6 to read about that.

Indicators don't do much in normal ROBLAB programs, but you can add controls to your program. These can be handy when you want to change your program but don't want to re-wire it. For example, we can add two controls to the standard *Motor Forward* function, as shown in Figure 5.95.

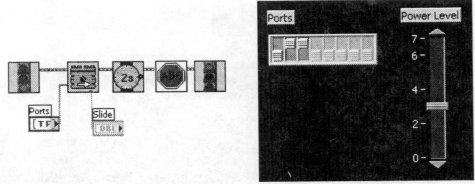

Figure 5.95. Adding **controls** to a standard ROBOLAB program (left). The controls as they appear on the Front Panel (right)

The control for the Ports modifier appears as a series of simple switches. Only three are active because there are only three motor ports for the RCX (A, B, and C from left to right). The other 5 are used when you are programming the Control Lab Interface, which is covered in Chapter 6. A switch up is equivalent to wiring that port modifier. Thus, in Figure 5.95, Motor A is off and Motors B and C are on. We've used a simple slider to adjust the power level (the default control is a numeric box like those shown in Figure 5.87).

Instead of re-wiring our program to add or remove ports or to change the power level, we now can adjust those parameters using the **controls** on the **Front Panel**. Of course we still have to download the program as we always have to the RCX before anything actually happens. Note, from the RCX's point of view, nothing different has happened. We haven't actually changed the program at all. We've only changed the way we specify the modifiers.

CHAPTER 6
RED LEVEL

Skill badges available in this Chapter

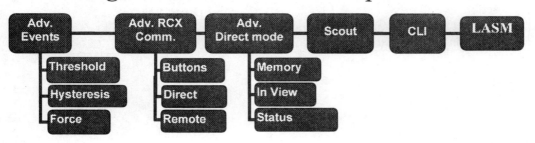

6.1   Red Challenges

6.1.1   Simon Says (revisited)

Challenge: You know the rules of the game. Now we want you to make a robot that plays it as well as you do. Unlike the Challenge in Chapter 4, this time you play the part of "Simon," and your instructor's robot has to do is exactly what you say.

Skill Badges:

Procedures:

Experimental Setup: The instructor will have a robot that everyone can examine. It will not be programmed to do anything because that is your job!

Robot Design: Since the RCX can't decipher voice commands (yet) your Simon will be "talking" to your instructor's robot over the IR port. There are no requirements for your robot other than the ability to send IR signals. In other words, the design of your robot only counts towards aesthetics.

Program: Your Simon should send out complete programs to the instructor's robot.

Hints: Try to make your motions as precise as possible since having your IR port in view of Simon's is essential to lasting the whole round. In order to make two motors behave the same (to drive straight forward without curving, for instance), you may need to run them at different power levels. Experiment.

Grading:

Your grade will be based 80% on performance and 20% on creativity and aesthetics.

Performance	Creativity & Aesthetics
A: You have complete control of the instructor's robot (5 or more actions) B: You get the instructor's robot to perform three actions in a row (without intervention) C: You get the instructor's robot to perform one action D: You get the instructor's robot to move F: You don't show up to class	A+: Best of show A: Outstanding B: Good C: Okay D: Nothing special F: Divert your eyes!

6.1.2 Psychic SumoBot

Challenge: You're probably familiar with SumoBots that try to push their opponent out of the ring. In this competition, in addition to pushing your opponent out of the ring, you can also try to program him to drive out of the ring.

Skill Badges: Adv. RCX Comm.

Procedures:

Experimental Setup: The competition arena is a white circular area 3-4 feet in diameter. The outer edge of the competition arena is lined with silver (mirror-like) tape. Approximately 6 inches inward is a concentric ring colored black.

Robot Design: Anything that moves is allowed. Your instructor may place a limit on the size of your robots.

Program: Anything for your own robot is fair game. However, when it comes to sending commands to another robot, only **direct mode** commands are allowed (i.e. no reprogramming your opponent by sending a remote program). Also, you are not allowed to use any of the button commands (no turning off your opponent or changing which program they are using).

Grading:

Your grade will be based 80% on performance and 20% on creativity and aesthetics.

Performance	Creativity & Aesthetics
A+: Undefeated champion	A+: Best of show
A: You win more than you lose	A: Outstanding
B: You win more than once	B: Good
C: You battle and have fun	C: Okay
D: You have something that moves	D: Nothing special
F: You don't show up to class	F: Divert your eyes!

6.1.3 Remote Controller (revisited)

<u>**Challenge:**</u> This is similar the Challenge back in Chapter 2, except this time you have to build a wireless remote controller. You will use your controller to drive your vehicle through an obstacle course or maze as fast as you can. Since this takes 2 RCX's this will be a multi-team project.

<u>**Skill Badges:**</u>

<u>**Procedures:**</u>

Experimental Setup: An obstacle course or maze is also required for students to demonstrate controlled driving of the vehicle.

Robot Design: Nearly any vehicle will suffice for this Challenge. You should consider designing a controller that can control both speed and direction. Each team should make a car.

Program: Your program will have to use Advance RCX communication. No sending just mail! **Warning**: there is going to be a lot of IR traffic. There is a high probability that your RCX will be the unwilling recipient of an unsolicited program if you are not careful.

<u>**Grading:**</u>
Your grade will be based 80% on performance and 20% on creativity and aesthetics.

Performance	Creativity & Aesthetics
A+: You make it through the fastest	A+: Best of show
A: You make it to the end	A: Outstanding
B: You make it more than ½ way	B: Good
C: The robot is under your control at some point in time	C: Okay
	D: Nothing special
D: You wander aimlessly	F: Divert your eyes!
F: You don't show up to class	

6.1.4   Fast Line Follower

Challenge: This is a slight twist on an old favorite. By now you've almost surely made a line follower using either *wait fors* or light sensor *forks*. This time around, you'll use only light sensor *Events*.

Skill Badges:

Procedures:

Experimental Setup: The course should be constructed using black electrical tape on a white background (the floor). The line will curve gently and be approximately 5-6 feet long. The instructor will use a stop watch to time how long it takes your robot to follow the line.

Robot Design: For this exercise, you need to design and construct a basic car with at least two wheels and a light sensor facing down.

Program: Detect the line and/or background using only *Events*.

Hints: Hysteresis is great for ignoring small fluctuations in light levels.

Grading:

Your grade will be based 75% on performance and 25% on creativity and aesthetics.

Performance	Creativity & Aesthetics
A+: You follow the line the fastest	A+: Best of show
A: You follow the entire line	A: Outstanding
B: You follow the line more than 2 feet	B: Good
C: You car zig-zags	C: Okay
D: Your car runs when turned on	D: Nothing special
F: You don't show up to class	F: Divert your eyes!

6.1.5   Whistling Brothers

Challenge: The goal of this challenge is to place five RCX's down on the table and have to each whistle a specific tone. Press **run** and the leftmost one should sing 220 Hz, the next 440 Hz, and so on. Now, take the RCX's and rearrange them - when you hit run again, the leftmost one should still sing 220 Hz, etc. This means that each RCX must determine where it is in the order and play the correct note.

Skill Badges:

```
Adv. RCX
Comm.
```

Procedures:

Experimental Setup: Nothing special is needed (except a lot of RCX's)

Robot Design: No requirements. You may want the RCX's to pivot so that the IR ports can face each other.

Program: You will have to decide how the RCX's are going to communicate (i.e. handshaking protocol) and how they will determine their positions in the line (i.e. whether is it the 1st, 2nd, 3rd, 4th, or 5th RCX in the line).

Grading:

Your grade will be based 75% on performance and 25% on creativity and aesthetics.

Performance	Creativity & Aesthetics
A: All 5 whistle correctly, even when randomly rearranged	A: Outstanding
B: Almost got it, but an occasional mistake.	B: Good
C: All 5 whistle in order once	C: Okay
D: All 5 whistle	D: Nothing special
F: You don't show up to class	F: Divert your eyes!

This challenge is based on a robot that was built at Tufts University. You can find pictures (and perhaps a movie) on the Internet if you want to see one solution to this challenge.

6.2 The Advanced Events Badge

By now we're pretty sure that you have found events pretty useful. When using multiple events, students often want to know how to determine which event occurred. We'll discuss two different ways: using the *Event Fork* and the *Event Container*. In this section, we'll also get into some of the subtleties of events. That is, how to control the event triggers. We'll even show how to remedy the problem that our LEGO® cockroach had way back in Chapter 4 (Figure 4.11).

6.2.1 Event Fork and Event Container

The Event fork is used to check whether or not a particular event has already occurred. The only modifier needed is the color of the event that you want to check (the default is the red event).

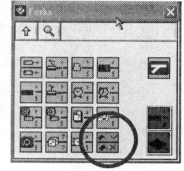

Figure 6.1. The *Event Fork* is located, not surprisingly, on the **forks** pallet.

Unless the *event landing* is at the end of your program, you often can't be certain whether or not the event has occurred. In the next example, the robot is programmed to simply drive forward for 10 seconds unless it bumps into something first. When we get to the end of the program, we can't tell if Motor A stopped because the 10 seconds elapse or because we've bumped into something. This could make a big difference if driving forward was only the first step in a long chain of maneuvers. The *event fork* is a convenient tool for determining if an event has occurred. Here we play a beep if the motor was stopped by the event.

Figure 6.2. We've used the *event fork* to let us know if the robot stopped because it bumped into something.

The next example can best be described as a LEGO® robot that needs CPR. In this case, we're using the *event fork* to check whether the one event we're monitoring has occurred at all. Why does it require CPR? If you don't push the touch sensor every 2 seconds, the motor turns off and the program ends!

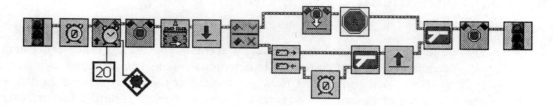

Figure 6.3. This robot needs CPR. If the touch sensor isn't pushed at least once every 2 seconds, the robot dies!

While this is one use of the *event fork*, it's more common that you are using multiple events and want to know which event occurred. Since all events in a given task share the same landing, it can get a bit confusing. The *event fork* can come in handy for this.

In figure 6.4, we've shown a simple method of displaying which combination of touch sensors has occurred. Try it out. You'll not only learn how to use *event forks* and brush up on nested forks (chapter 3), but you'll also get a feel for how close together two events have to occur in order to be considered simultaneous.

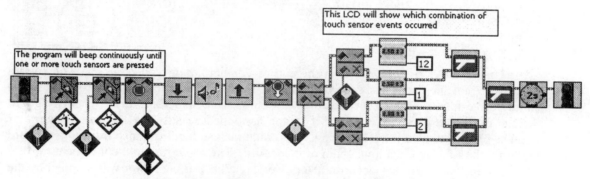

Figure 6.4. Event forks can be used to determine which events have occurred.

If you have more than three or four events, using nested *event forks* can get cumbersome (remember you can have up to 15 events). Another method of determining which event has occurred is to use the *event container* (figure 6.5).

The *event container* allows you to determine which event, or combination of events, has occurred. It's a bit tricky since you have to know how to translate a decimal number into a binary number or visa-versa.

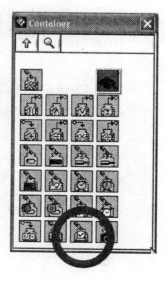

Figure 6.5. The Event Container is located at the bottom of the container pallet.

Figure 6.6 shows an example of using the event container to figure out which combination of touch sensors was pressed. If the event container had the number 6 in it, you would know that events 2 and 3 had occurred (i.e. touch sensors 2 and 3 were pressed). If the event container had the number 2 in it, that means only the blue event occurred (touch sensor 2 was pressed).

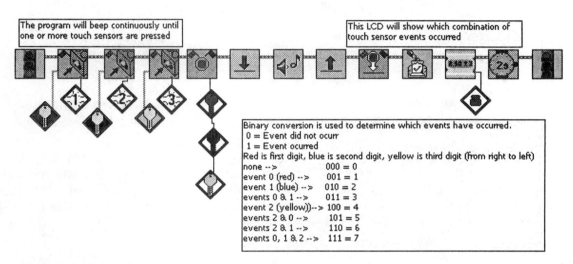

Figure 6.6. The event container can tell you which events have occurred. Each event represents one of the binary digits (from right to left) which is then converted to the decimal equivalent.

In this example, we've only used the three standard events (red, blue, and yellow), but you can actually have up to 15 events (don't forget events are global – meaning you can't use the red event in two different tasks). This means that you can have up to a 15-digit binary number. Everything from 000000000000000 to 111111111111111, which correspond to no events and all 15 events respectively. Thankfully, ROBOLAB converts this binary number into a decimal number before storing it in the *event container*. Thus, our 15 digit binary number becomes a decimal number ranging from 0 to 2^{15}=32,768.

To use the *event container* you have to convert the decimal number back into its binary equivalent. Then the 1's and 0's indicate whether each event has occurred. For example, if the *event container* has the value 312, then the binary equivalent is 100111000 (we've left off the 6 leading zeros to save space). Reading the binary number from right to left, this would mean that events 4, 5, 6, and 9 occurred. Get it?

Note, we're not masters at doing binary conversions. We did the conversion using a Java-based converter we found on the Internet. Microsoft Excel also has a conversion function (DEC2BIN) that is part of the Analysis ToolPak (which is not installed by default). Unfortunately it can only handle up to 10 digit binary numbers. ROBOLAB can also do binary to decimal conversions (see Figure 6.36 for an example).

Just as a side piece of trivia, you can also make use of the decimal - binary number relationship to start monitoring multiple events. Rather than wire the red, blue and yellow event modifiers to the *start monitoring for an event* function, we can simply wire the number 7, since it is the binary equivalent to 111. Figure 6.7 shows the exact same program as in Figure 6.6 except we've started monitoring using the number red container, which has the number 7 in it.

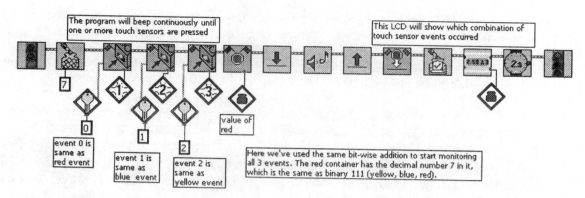

Figure 6.7. You can start monitoring for events with the numbers rather than the event modifiers by making use of binary conversions.

Is this just trivia or useful information? Depends. Have you ever thought about a case where you might want to decide which events to monitor depending on what happens earlier in the program? If you were to use the event modifiers, you wouldn't have any choice. If you use a container value, like Figure 6.7, you could decide which events to start (or stop) monitoring on the fly.

6.2.2   Forcing and Clearing Events

Two useful commands are *force an event* and *clear all events*. As their names imply, they are used to make your program either think an event has occurred and to delete all events. When you *force an event*, the RCX thinks the event has occurred. It stops whatever it was doing and jumps to the *event landing* just like usual. You can even use the *event container* or *event fork* to see if the event occurred and the RCX will tell you it has.

The main difference between *clear all events* and *stop event monitoring* is that once you clear all events, you can't start monitoring for them again. In the example shown below, even though we attempt to restart the event monitoring, nothing happens (we're stuck in the jump/land repeat forever). After the *clear all events*, there is no event to re-start monitoring!

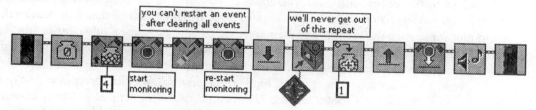

Figure 6.8. After clearing all events, it is impossible to start monitoring for events again.

6.2.3 Advanced Event Characteristics

When you define an event (the first of the three steps, as described in Chapter 4), you are really using a combination of two functions to define all 7 event characteristics:

- *Type of event* – high, low, or normal
- *Event* – which event key (i.e. what color event or which generic event number)
- *Event source* – the port number, container number, timer, etc
- *Upper threshold* – the value of the event source that must be exceeded to trigger the event (for high and normal event types only)
- *Lower threshold* – the value the event source must fall below to trigger the event (for normal and low event types only)
- *Hysteresis* – the event source must cross the hysteresis line to cause an event to trigger (see Figure 6.11 below).
- *Duration* – how long the event source must be above or below the threshold before the event is triggered.

Figure 6.9 shows what the ***set up light event*** function really is doing. First, the type of event is defined with the ***set up enter hi event*** function and then the remaining 6 characteristics are defined using the ***define event*** function.

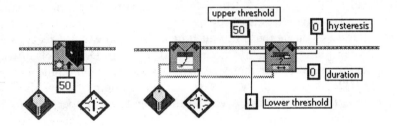

Figure 6.9. When you set up an event (left), you are really defining all the event characteristics with two functions (right).

Reading about the event characteristics is definitely not the best way to learn about them. We've found that the program shown in Figure 6.10 is a great way to teach students how the different types of events work. We use the rotation sensor because it's easy to control the sensor readings. If you don't have a rotation sensor, then you can make a similar tool using a container and 2 touch sensors, one to +1 and the other to -1 from the container.

In Figure 6.10 we've shown the "high" event, but you can easily replace it with either a "low" or a "normal" to get a feel for how each type works. If you're really clever, you can use **controls** (as discussed in section 5.7) rather than numeric constants for the upper and lower thresholds, hysteresis, and duration. That way you don't have to keep typing in new numbers when playing around with the tool.

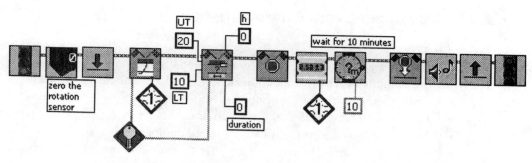

Figure 6.10. A simple "events tool" that you should copy and play with to get a better feel for how events work.

With your "event tool" in hand, let's discuss one characteristic at a time. We'll start with the type of event since that's the easiest to comprehend and lays the foundation for the rest of the characteristics. Using your "event tool" set both the hysteresis and duration to zero (we'll get those later). Set the lower threshold (LT) to 10 and the upper threshold (UT) to 20.

 A "high event" is one where the sensor value has to exceed a certain value before the event is triggered. The value that must be exceeded is the *upper threshold* (UT). If you look at the icon, the sensor value must go from the white area to the green area (on top). Try it. You'll find the sensor value starts at zero (because we reset the rotation sensor at the start of the program), and as you increase it, you'll hear the beep when it reaches 21 (i.e. exceeds 20). You can keep going higher but nothing will happen. Drop back down to 20 and then go back up to 21. You'll hear the beep again. The beep will sound every time you go from below the UT to above the UT. You can try dropping below the LT, but nothing will happen since this is a "high" event. Referring to the upper part of Figure 6.11 (lighter arrows), the event is triggered for cases 1, 3 and 5.

 A "low event" is just the opposite, meaning the sensor value must drop below the *lower threshold* (LT) before the event is triggered. Again, the icon gives you a visual cue; the sensor value must drop down from the white area to the green area. Replace the *set up enter hi event* with a *set up enter low event* on your "event tool" and begin experimenting again. You'll find a similar behavior as last time. You'll hear the beep when you drop down from 10 to 9. Referring to the lower part of Figure 6.11 (darker arrows), the event is triggered for cases 1, 3, and 5.

 A "normal event" is one where the sensor value either drops below the upper threshold or exceeds the lower threshold. The icon shows a central green region with upper and lower white regions. Set up your tool again and begin playing. What you should find is that there are now 2 cases that trigger and event, when the sensor goes from 9 to 10 (crossing the LT) and when the sensor goes from 21 to 20 (crossing the UT). In Figure 6.11, this is case 4 (both the light and dark arrows).

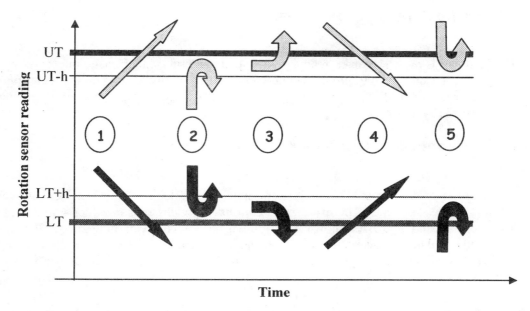

Figure 6.11. Five possible scenarios for our "event tool." Some of these will trigger an event and some will not, depending on the type of event (high, low or normal). UT=upper threshold, LT=lower threshold, h=hysteresis.

Let's turn our attention to the first of the two remaining characteristics, the duration. Go ahead and use the program in Figure 6.10, except set the duration to 100 instead of zero. The duration is the length of time, in hundredths of a second, that the sensor value must exceed the threshold before the event is triggered. By using a value of 100, we're saying that the sensor reading must stay at 21 or higher for 1 second before the event is triggered (for a "high" event). [**Note: at the time of writing, ROBOLAB 2.5.4 had a bug which prevented the duration setting from working. The bug has since been reported and may be fixed on your version. If it hasn't, download the latest patch**].

Finally, we come to hysteresis, which we've saved for last because it's the most confusing for most students. Again starting with the program in Figure 6.10, change the hysteresis value to 2 (leave the duration at zero). Download this to your RCX and play around. What you should find is that the beep plays the first time you reach 21, but if you toggle between 20 and 21, no sound is played (this corresponds to case 5 in Figure 6.11). By adding hysteresis, you're not only requiring the sensor value to exceed the UT but you are also requiring it to dip below UT-h (the UT minus the amount of hysteresis). So now you have to go from 18 to 21 in order to hear the beep. In Figure 6.11, only case 1 will trigger the event (UT-h = 18 in this example).

You can also try adding hysteresis to the "low" and "normal" events. For the "low" event, you should find that you have to go from 12 to 9 in order to get the event to trigger (again, case 1 in Figure 6.11). Similarly, for the "normal" event, you have to go from either 9 to 12 or from 21 to 18 to trigger the event. This is case 4 again in Figure 6.11, but in this circumstance, the event isn't triggered until you cross UT-h or LT+h.

6.2.4   Checking Your Progress

The hard part is over. However, reading with understanding is much easier than thinking on your own. To check your progress and see if you're really getting it, try determining whether or not each of the cases in Figure 6.11 would trigger a high, low or normal event when there is hysteresis.

6.2.5   Event State Container

The *event state container* allows you to peer inside and look at what the RCX is seeing when it comes to events. The *event state container* divides sensor values into 3 ranges: low, normal, and high. As shown in Figure 6.12, low is everything below the lower threshold (LT), high is everything above the upper threshold (UT), and normal is the range between the LT and UT. Hysteresis is not shown because it changes the story a little (see below).

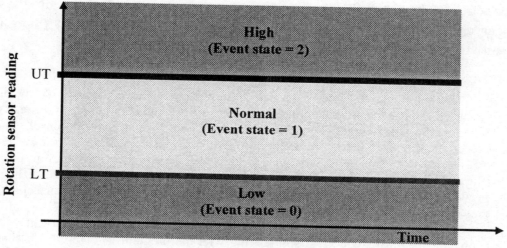

Figure 6.12. The event state container divides the sensor reading into 3 basic ranges: low, normal, and high.

The *event state container* shows which range the sensor value is currently in by returning a 0 (low), 1 (normal) or 2 (high). The only trick is how the hysteresis is handled. Figure 6.13 shows how a "high" event handles hysteresis. The low range is extended by the hysteresis on the way up. When we exceed the UT, the event is triggered, and we enter the high range. On way back down, the transition to the normal range is delayed by the hysteresis again. Eventually we can enter the low range again by going below the LT.

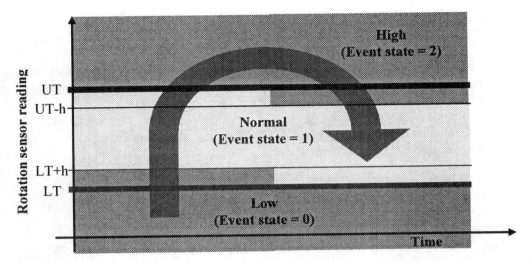

Figure 6.13. The event states for a "high" event when there is hysteresis. The transition between states is delayed by the hysteresis.

While we have only shown how a "high" event handles hysteresis in Figure 6.13, the "low" and "normal" events handle it in a similar fashion. You should try and draw a picture similar to Figure 6.13 for yourself for the "low" and "high" events based on Figure 6.11 and what you know.

Figure 6.14 shows program similar to the "event tool" we used earlier except that we've added the *event state container* in a couple of places so that we can see what the RCX is seeing. Note, this program will only work until the event is triggered for the first time. If you want it to repeat, you'll have to add another jump/land pair. [**Note: at the time of writing, ROBOLAB 2.5.4 had a bug which prevented event state container from working. The bug has since been reported and may be fixed on your version. If it hasn't, download the latest patch**].

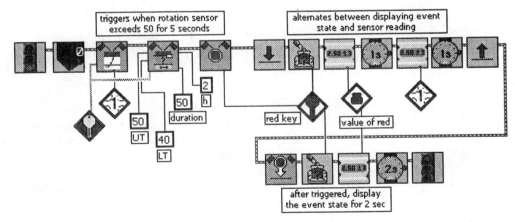

Figure 6.14. Similar to our "event tool," this program makes it easy to see what the *event state container* does.

6.2.6   The LEGO® Cockroach

Remember the LEGO® cockroach that we tried to implement with events back in Chapter 4 (Figure 4.11)? Well, now we have a way to fix the problem we were experiencing. If you recall, the problem was that the light event never triggered if we already had a light sensor reading above the upper threshold (40 in this example). Now that we know a little more about events, we can use the force event function to make the event occur if the light sensor reading is initially greater than the UT. We've also played Darwin a bit and let our cockroach evolve by adding a bit of hysteresis. This cockroach won't be as sensitive to minor variations in light levels.

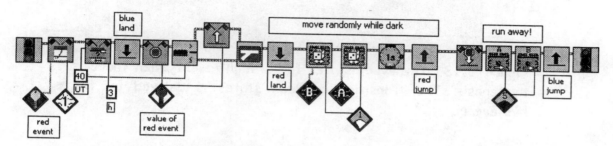

Figure 6.15. A corrected version of our LEGO® cockroach that successfully uses events.

Can you improve upon this design? How about making a cockroach that learns? Each time the lights come on it gets more sensitive to the light. Each time it has to be a little darker before it will start wandering around again. Or how about building in some self preservation? If a long time elapses with the lights on, it starts to go hungry and will venture out into the light.

6.3 Advanced RCX Communication

Students always seem to want to know how to create the "killer" program that will turn off another student's RCX. Teachers always want to know how to prevent the "killer" program. While we will get to it (soon), we also want to cover some other useful advanced communication features.

Before we get started, we want to give you a quick reminder about the nomenclature we'll use. When we talk about RCX's sending programs to each other, we'll often use the labels "sender" and "receiver" for obvious reasons. We'll also use terms "local" and "remote," which we introduced back in section 4.6. The local and remote RCX's will correspond to the sending and receiving RCX's in all cases (i.e. the terms are interchangeable). Finally, programs that are downloaded and run on the RCX are called **remote mode** programs and those which run on the PC are called **direct mode** programs.

6.3.1   The Button Commands

The four button commands, like *set display*, do not really have much to do with RCX communication other than being located on the **RCX Communications** sub-palette. Nonetheless, this is probably the best place to discuss them since a couple of them are quite useful when sending remote programs.

All four functions are pretty straightforward. The *view* function allows you to view any of the three inputs, three outputs, or internal clock. Ever notice that whenever you use a *wait for light* or *wait for dark* function, the LCD automatically displays the light sensor reading? Well, if you look inside the *wait for dark* code, you'll see that the *view* function is used.

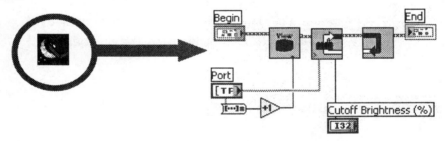

Figure 6.16. The *wait for dark* function uses the *view* command.

 The *change program on RCX* function is similar to the **Prgm** button on the RCX but has one small, but important, difference: after it changes to the specified program, the program is automatically started. The *change program on RCX* function only has this peculiar behavior when used in a local program (one running on your RCX). As we'll see in a little while, when you send this command to another RCX, it acts just like pushing the **Prgm** button (i.e. changes the program, but does not execute the program).

 We've already used the *turn RCX power off* function in a few previous examples in this book. Not surprisingly, when this function is executed, the RCX turns itself off. It's the primary component of the "killer" program. If you send this command to another RCX, it will turn itself off! Now, if we could only figure out how to turn the RCX back on...

The *run* function is the same as pressing the run button – it starts the program. Since you need to be running a program in order to execute the *run* function, it may seem a bit useless at first. Why would you want to run the program that is already running? In Figure 6.17 we show part of the hidden power. The run function essentially starts the program over from the beginning. Thus, in the example below, the RCX will beep continuously until the touch sensor is pressed. While this is simplistic example, can you think of any cases where you might want to start the entire program over from the beginning?

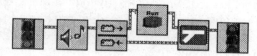

Figure 6.17. This program will beep until the touch sensor is pressed.

The other great feature of the *run* function will be discussed a little later. It ends up being invaluable for starting a program on another RCX.

6.3.2 Fill Remote Container

Quite simply, the *fill remote container* function does just that. Rather than storing a number in one of your own containers, you can store a number in another RCX's container. The peaceful use of this function is to share information with other RCX's. The diabolical use of this function is to fill your competitor's containers with random numbers so that his program doesn't work correctly. Note, this function will fill the container of <u>every other RCX in range</u>. It doesn't distinguish between friend and foe.

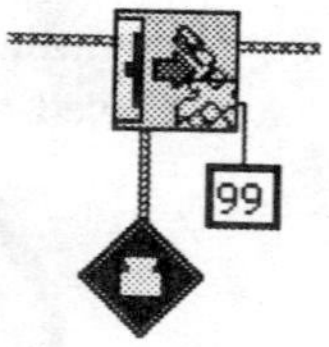

Figure 6.18. This will fill the blue container of every RCX in range with the number 99.

6.3.3 Direct Communication

Direct communication acts just like **direct mode** (Chapter 4) except instead of your PC sending your RCX commands, your RCX sends the commands to another RCX. There are a couple of key points to keep in mind when using direct communication:

- Every RCX in range will execute the direct commands you broadcast.
- If you are on the receiving end, you don't have a choice. Your RCX will execute any commands that are sent.
- Direct mode commands are essentially a new task, meaning the program currently running will continue to do so (see section 4.5.6).
- No structures (loops, jumps, forks, etc.) can be sent via direct mode.

Every time we hold a robot competition, at least one student figures out the "killer" program on his/her own. By adding three simple icons to your program, you can effectively "kill" every other RCX in range! We've taken it one step further and used a **control** (chapter 5) on the ***RCX tower power function*** to set the IR power to high just to be extra evil.

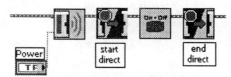

Figure 6.19. The "killer" code

In all fairness, we are obliged to share with you a couple of ways to protect yourself from the "killer" program. The most obvious way is to cover your IR port with tape. We've found this to be the most effective method. Simply building a LEGO® wall in front of the IR port doesn't effectively block the IR signal and, thus, is not a reliable mode of protection.

Beyond covering your IR port with tape, we've found that the next best way to defeat the "killer" program is to continually send mail, as shown in Figure 6.20. Because sending has a higher priority than listening, by continually sending mail, you effectively prevent your IR port from ever accepting any input. As it turns out, one RCX continually sending mail actually works as an effective jamming signal and can protect any RCX in range from the "killer" program. The only known loophole we've experienced occurs in large programs with several tasks running. In these cases, there can be brief periods where the RCX is busy doing something else before it gets around to sending mail again. This leaves a short window of opportunity for someone to sneak in the ***turn RCX power off*** command.

Figure 6.20. How to protect yourself from the "killer" code

Getting back to direct mode communication in general, anything you put between the ***start direct*** and ***end direct*** functions will be sent out and sequentially executed by all RCX's in range. In Figure 6.21, we send a series of 4 commands. The important thing to remember is that, like **direct mode**, the commands are executed sequentially; before a command is sent, the previous command has to finish. In the example below, it is very likely that the robot will drive out of range before the ***stop A*** and ***turn RCX power off*** commands are ever sent.

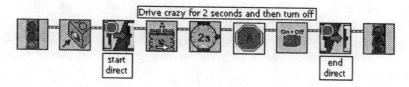

Figure 6.21. The intention is to get our opponents RCX to drive crazy before turning them off. However, this will most likely backfire because their robot will probably drive out of range before we turn them off.

The next example shows a simple remote controller. If touch sensor 1 is pressed, motor A runs in the reverse direction. If touch sensor 2 is pushed, motor A runs in the forward direction. If neither is pushed, no commands are sent. Again, in order for this to work, the RCX receiving the commands would have to remain in IR contact with your RCX (the sender).

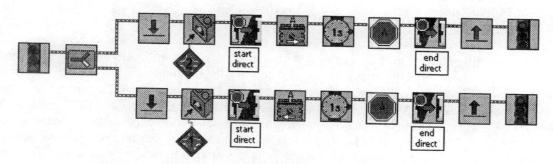

Figure 6.22. A simple remote control program.

All the examples thus far may seem a bit simplistic, but remember you cannot send any type of structure (fork, loop, jump, etc.). This severely limits what you can make another RCX do. Other than structures, almost anything goes. In the Figure 6.23 we fill the red container with the value of sensor port 1 and display it to the LCD before playing the red music scroll. Both the red container and the value of senor port 1 refer to the receiving RCX. Thus, the receiving RCX will display the value of its sensor port 1 to its LCD. As for the music scroll, each note is transferred one at a time from your RCX (the sender) to the remote RCX (the receiver). Naturally, this implies that the red scroll that is played is the one stored on your RCX (the sender).

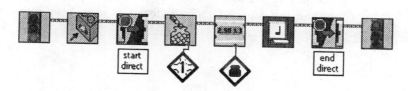

Figure 6.23. The music scrolls play the local scroll. Each note is transferred one at a time.

Some functions seem like they should work fine but don't for some unobvious reasons. The ***wait for dark*** in the next example cannot be sent as a direct command because it contains a loop inside (see Figure 6.16). Since structures cannot be sent and the ***wait for dark*** uses a structure, this program generates an error (something about a jump without a land, which at first doesn't seem obvious).

Figure 6.24. This program generates an error because the ***wait for dark*** contains a loop inside (see Figure 6.16).

Another interesting note is that in Figure 6.24 we had to specify the light sensor as port 2 because ROBOLAB generated an error saying that we had two sensors on the same port. It wasn't smart enough to realize that the touch sensor is on the local RCX and the light sensor is on the remote RCX. In Figure 6.25 we've circumvented this problem by using the ***reset sensor ports*** function (which is located on the **reset** sub-palette). Now we can use sensor port 1 on both RCX's with different types of sensors.

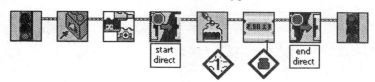

Figure 6.25. In order to use sensor port 1 on both the local and remote RCX's we have to use the ***reset sensor ports*** function.

6.3.4   Remote Programming

The **remote programming** icons look nearly identical to the **direct mode** icons (in black and white they are indistinguishable). The direct mode icons have a blue background while the remote programming icons have a brown background. This tiny distinguishing feature belies a major difference between the **direct mode** and **remote program** functions: **remote programs** are not executed until the program is run.

Just like in **direct mode**, there are a couple of key points to keep in mind when sending **remote programs**:

- Every RCX in range will be reprogrammed by your broadcast.
- If you are on the receiving end, you don't have a choice. Your RCX will be reprogrammed.
- Any program that is currently running is stopped <u>and erased</u> when you receive a remote program (just like when you use your PC to program your RCX).
- Structures are allowed (jumps, forks, loops, etc) but task splits are ignored.

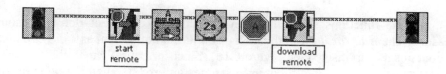

Figure 6.26. This will download a 3 icon program to all RCX's in range, but the green run button must be manually pressed in order to execute it.

Sending a **remote program** is exactly like downloading a program from your PC to the RCX. The program doesn't run until you press the run button. Figure 6.26 shows the same code that was sent in Figure 6.21 (sans the *turn RCX power off* command), except this time it is sent as a **remote program**. The program will not be executed until you either physically press the green **run** button on the RCX or it is sent the *run* command, as described in the next example.

In Figure 6.27, we've shown how to both specify which program slot to use (slot 3 is the default) and how to start running the program after you've sent it. Notice we've used a combination of **direct mode** and **remote programming** to accomplish the task (since the icons look identical in black and white, pay special attention to the comments).

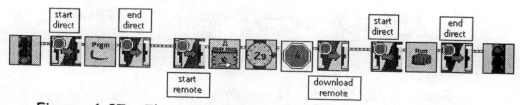

Figure 6.27. This will change to program 3, download the program, and then run it on all RCX's in range.

As mentioned earlier, unlike **direct mode**, when you use **remote programming** you can send programs that contain all the normal structures like loops, jumps, and forks. You can also use containers, timers, etc. The program shown will run for 5 seconds, beeping while the touch sensor is not pressed. Since we haven't sent the *run* command using **direct mode**, the program won't run on the remote RCX until manually started.

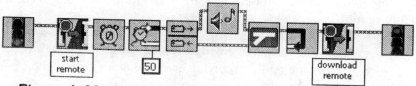

Figure 6.28. Remote programs can contain all the normal structures like loops and forks.

While structures are okay, tasks are not. Trying to send a multi-task program will not generate an error, but any tasks other than the primary one will not be downloaded. This also holds true for subroutines. You cannot send a subroutine to another RCX, but you can send a program that executes a subroutine.

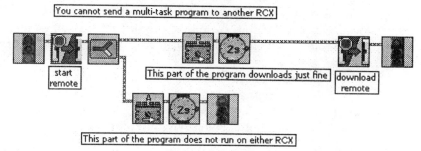

Figure 6.29. This program doesn't work as intended. ROBOLAB doesn't allow you to send multi-task programs to another RCX. If you try, only the primary task is sent.

6.3.5 Putting it all Together

In Figure 6.30, we've gone a bit overboard, but it's a pretty cool concept. "Tell me, what do you see over there?" is the basic premise for this program. The local (sending) RCX sends a very simple program to the remote (receiving) RCX and then runs it. The trick is that the program fills a remote container. Since the remote RCX is filling a remote container, that means the local RCX's container gets filled! You can essentially use another RCX's sensors as your own. Cool, eh?

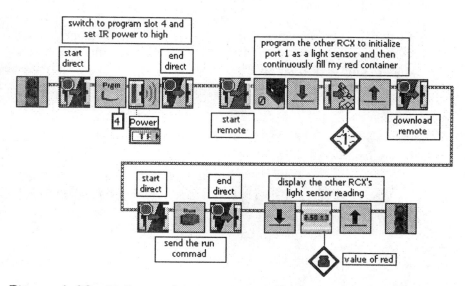

Figure 6.30. Tell me what you can see! This program makes the remote RCX fill the local RCX's red container with the value of the remote RCX's port 1.

6.4 The Advanced Direct Mode Badge

As we mentioned way back in Chapter 4, the real power of **direct mode** is the ability to run programs both on the RCX and your PC simultaneously and have these programs share information. However, before we delve into distributed computing, there are a couple of new **direct mode** functions that we want to cover: *delete subroutine*, *delete tasks*, and *memory map*.

As we mentioned in section 6.3, we'll use terms "local" and "remote" interchangeably with "sender" and "receiver" when talking about RCX's. Additionally, we'll refer to programs that are downloaded and run on the RCX as **remote mode** programs and those which run on the PC as **direct mode** programs.

6.4.1　Delete Tasks & Delete Subroutines

The *delete task* and *delete subroutine* functions are both located on the **structures** sub-palette but neither can be used in a normal **remote mode** program. If you've tried to use them, then you've seen the error message that indicates they can only be used in **direct mode** programs.

The *delete task* command is used to either delete one specific task or to delete all tasks in a given program. The neat feature about this function is that when you delete a task, the remaining tasks continue to function just fine. And it's not like stopping the task. When you restart the program the task that was deleted will not run (because it's gone). If you delete all tasks, you will not only stop the program, but you will also erase it completely from memory. [**Note: at the time of writing, ROBOLAB 2.5.4 had a bug which caused the default of the *delete task* function to do nothing instead of delete all tasks. The bug has since been reported and may be fixed on your version. If it hasn't, download the latest patch**].

In the example below, we first download and run the **remote mode** program as usual. The beep will play continuously and motor A will switch direction every second. When we run the **direct mode** program, the beep keeps playing and the motor stays on but it no longer switches direction. If we stop the program and run it again, only the beep is played. The motor is never turned on because task #2 was deleted from memory.

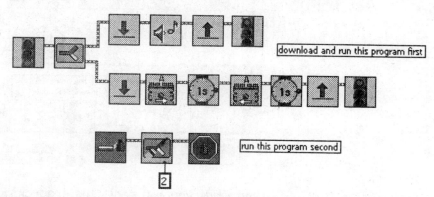

Figure 6.31. When we delete task #2, only the lower task will stop running. The beep will continue to play and the motor will stay on.

Note that the delete task function only applies to the current program. In other words, the **direct mode** program in Figure 6.31 would not delete task #2 from any of the other 4 programs stored on the RCX.

We introduced subroutines in section 5.2.2. Remember that subroutines are stored in a separate section of memory, apart from the rest of the 5 programs, and that you can have up to eight subroutines (numbered 0 through 7). One of the neat features was that a subroutine can be called by any task in any program. If you haven't used subroutines yet, you can probably skip the next few paragraphs.

The ***delete subroutine*** function is similar to the ***delete task*** function in that it is used to erase a subroutine from the RCX's memory (i.e. there is no getting it back once you delete it). However, unlike the ***delete task*** function, you can only delete one subroutine at a time (the default is to delete subroutine zero). In Figure 6.32 we're deleting subroutine #3.

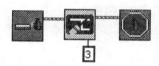

Figure 6.32. This is the only way to delete a subroutine from memory.

Interestingly, the ***delete subroutine*** function is the only way to erase a subroutine from memory. If you've used **Interrogate RCX** (on the **projects** menu), you've seen that you can delete all tasks. But there isn't (yet) an option to delete all subroutines. Since deleting one subroutine at a time, as shown in Figure 6.32, can be a bit tedious, we'll show you a quick way to do it. In Figure 6.33 we've used a bit of G code to delete all 8 subroutines.

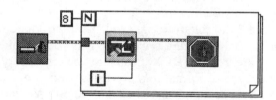

Figure 6.33. A bit of G code provides us with a quick way to delete all 8 subroutines at once.

In case you're thinking about it, you cannot send either the ***delete task*** or the ***delete subroutine*** functions as **direct mode** commands from one RCX to another RCX. Imagine the havoc you would cause if you only deleted certain tasks from your competitor's robot! That would be a really cruel trick if it were possible.

6.4.2   Memory Map

Need to know how much memory you've got left in your RCX? The ***memory map*** function can tell you. You have to use a bit of G code (see Chapter 5) in order to use it because you need to set up an **indicator** for the output (the memory allocation). The program shown in Figure 6.34 shows the use of the *memory map* and the resulting **indicator** on the **front panel** (after the program is run). All RCX's will have the same total memory, 6143 bytes, which is the amount left after the firmware is installed. The amount of memory used (Mem Used) is the sum of the memory used for the programs (Prgms) and data logging (log). Note, the log indicates the amount of memory (bytes) used, not the number of data points stored. As shown, 1536 bytes equates to about 500 data points.

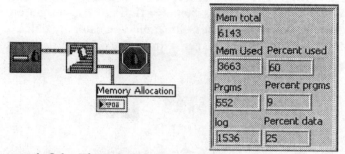

Figure 6.34. The *memory map* function outputs the current memory statistics to an **indicator** on the **front panel**.

6.4.3 Read Value

We first saw the **read value** function back in Chapter 4 where we mentioned that we would see a better use for it once we learned a bit of G code (Chapter 5). Well, now we're ready to show you what we were alluding to.

If you've used **Interrogate RCX** (which can be found on the **projects** menu along with **Vision Center**, **Select COM port**, etc) then you are already familiar with the *read display* function. **Interrogate RCX** basically makes use of a bunch of *read display* functions with some pretty formatting. By using **indicators** on the **front panel**, we can create our own VI that accomplishes the same thing. We can even paste pictures on the **front panel** to make it look fancy.

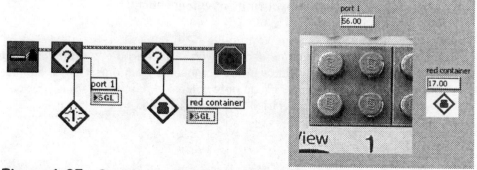

Figure 6.35. Our custom version of Interrogate RCX made with a couple of *read display* functions and **indicators**.

Figure 6.36 shows another example along the same lines. This time we are displaying the value of the red container, which was filled using the *event container* (see Figure 6.6). Since the *event container* returns an integer value, we've converted it into a Boolean (binary) array and displayed the array as a series of switches indicating whether or not each event has occurred.

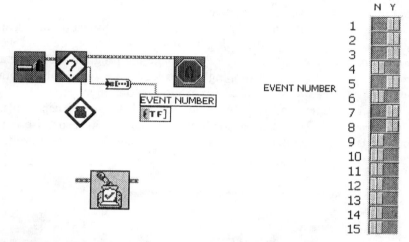

Figure 6.36. This **front panel** (right) shows which events have already occurred. The red container is set in the program running on the RCX (which is not shown) using the *event container* (Figure 6.6).

6.4.4   Using Direct Mode with G-Code

In our opinion, the real power of **direct mode** is the ability to use it in conjunction with G code. We've already shown you some of this in Figures 6.33, 6.35 and 6.36. Basically we are saying that you can run a program on your PC in **direct mode** while also running a program on the RCX in **remote mode**. While we can poll the RCX using the read display function, as we showed earlier, more importantly we can do things that the RCX can't do alone, like complex math. In Figure 6.37 we take the value of sensor port 1, take the sine of it, and then display the result to the LCD on the RCX. We also do a little math so that the result is displayed to the LCD as a floating point number.

Since **direct mode** programs can run on top of **remote mode** programs, we could just as easily filled a container with the result. Then the program currently running on the RCX could do whatever we wanted. Viola! We can now do complex math with the RCX (with a little help from your PC).

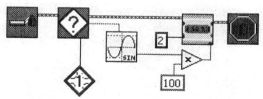

Figure 6.37. Take the value of port 1 and take the sine of it before displaying it to the LCD.

If we want the program in Figure 6.37 to run more than once, we have a couple of choices. The first, and easiest, is to just use the **run continuously** mode instead of standard **run** mode (the double arrow instead of the single white arrow). If we took the program in Figure 6.37 and ran it continuously, we would get a continual update on the LCD.

The second method is much more powerful but it takes quite a bit of research on your part simply because it involves programming in full-blown G. In Figure 6.38, we have used the *read run status* function and a *while loop* to make the program loop over and over as long as there is a program currently running on the RCX. As soon as the remote program stops on the RCX, sound #3 plays and our **direct mode** program stops.

This method is better than running continuously because we can implement more than one type of structure (while loop, for loop, etc) and we have precise control of the terminal conditions (i.e. when the loop stops). The downside is that you have to learn G in order to take full advantage of it.

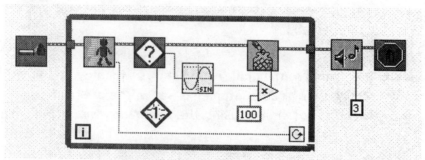

Figure 6.38. The main part of this program loops while there is a program running on the RCX. As soon as the program ends, the direct mode program plays a sound and then ends.

As we mentioned back in Chapter 5, we aren't going to pretend to be able to teach you G code in this book. There are plenty of good books out there that will do a much better job. Fortunately, the context help is pretty good for the basics. You can also find a lot of material on the Internet that various professors have posted for their engineering courses.

What can you do if you learn G code? The sky is the limit. For example, if you think about it, the **Vision Center** is essentially a **direct mode** program that incorporates G. When you selected all those image processing settings in the **Vision Center**, you were using the **front panel** of the **Vision Center** VI.

You now have the power to create you own custom VI's that take full advantage of the front panel. You can have the user adjust multiple parameters and develop an interactive program that works in conjunction with **remote mode** programs running on the RCX. Have fun!

6.5 The Scout Badge

Figure 6.39. The Scout programmable brick

The Scout brick is often referred to as the RCX's little (blue) brother. In many ways, this analogy is quite appropriate. In terms of size, however, the Scout and RCX are nearly identical. Since ROBOLAB can program the Scout brick and a lot of people have requested information about it, we've decided to include a short section in this book. We mentioned way back in Chapter 1 that the Scout brick is one of the three LEGO® programmable bricks (the RCX and the Microscout being the other 2). We also mentioned that you can no longer buy the Scout brick from LEGO® since they discontinued it a few years back. However, there are a lot of them out there, and you can still find them for sale occasionally on Internet auction sites (mostly used ones now).

Let's go over some the unique features that differentiate the Scout from the RCX. First off, the Scout has only 2 output ports, A and B. Sending the command ***Motor C forward*** won't generate an error in ROBOLAB, but it also won't do anything on the Scout. Secondly, the scout has two sensor ports, 1 and 2, and a built in light sensor. Only touch sensors can be used on the input ports. If you try to wire any function that uses another kind of sensor, ROBOLAB will generate an error.

While we don't have the ability to display to the LCD, the Scout does have several indicator lights to indicate the status of the various ports and sensors. As shown in Figure 6.40, there is a green LED that lights up when the IR port is active. There is a yellow LED that lights up when either the upper or lower light threshold is reached. There is also a yellow LED for each of the touch sensor ports. If a program is not running, a sound is played when either touch sensor is pressed or released. Touch sensor 2 will play a slightly higher pitch tone when activated. The sounds are not played while a program is running. Finally, there are four green LED arrows that light up to indicate motor activity (not shown in Figure 6.40).

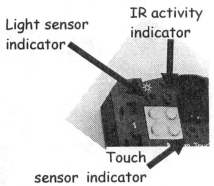

Figure 6.40. Indicator lights on the Scout

When it comes to programming, the Scout brick has two modes of operation: **stand alone** and **power mode**. In stand alone mode, you "program" the scout using the 4 buttons – no computer is required. Whether or not this is actually programming is topic of much debate that we will endeavor to avoid. Using the buttons, you can select how the Scout will move, react to light, and react to the touch sensors. You can also select speed (time scale) and several special effects (FX). The instructions that come with the Robotics Discovery

Set (LEGO® kit #9735) provide an excellent description for using **stand alone** mode, so we won't attempt to duplicate it here. Rather, we shall cover the basics of using the Scout brick in **power mode**.

6.5.1   Power Mode with ROBOLAB

To program the Scout using ROBOLAB, you have to put the Scout in **power mode**. To do this, hit the **select** button until the icon of the Scout brick above the big white word SCOUT is flashing. Then hit the **change** button and you should see a little lightning bolt (⚡) appear next to the scout icon. The lightning bolt indicates you are in **power mode** (Figure 6.41).

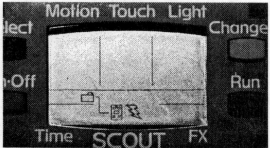

Figure 6.41. The Scout LCD indicating you're in **power mode**.

All the Scout functions are located on the **Scout Commands** sub-palette and the **Scout subroutines** sub-palette.

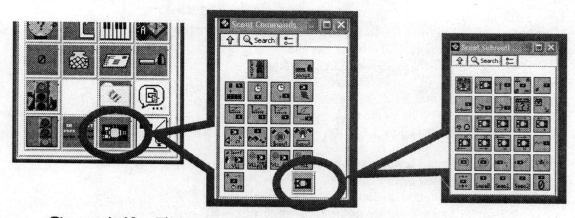

Figure 6.42. The Scout functions are located on the **Scout Commands** sub-palette at the bottom of the **functions** palette.

All regular Scout programs start with the *begin scout* function, which is the Scout's version of the green light. Scout programs end with the standard red light. The Scout differs from the RCX in that only 1 program can be stored at a time. The program can have a maximum of 6 tasks.

We tend not to use very many of the specialized Scout commands. Almost all of the standard RCX commands will work. You can play the usual system sounds and music (individual notes or entire music scrolls). All three timers function. All the standard structures (loops, jumps, forks) are allowable, with the exception of subroutines, events and data logging. You can even send and receive mail. There are also 10 global variables, but unfortunately they cannot be accessed through the normal container commands. Figure 6.43 shows a sample program that utilizes a lot of familiar RCX functions.

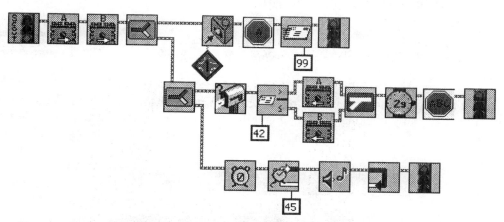

Figure 6.43. A sample Scout program that shows the variety of RCX commands that can be used with the Scout.

6.5.2   Direct Mode

Earlier we said there are two modes (**stand alone** and **power mode**). Strictly speaking, **direct mode** is a third mode, but you must be in **power mode** on the Scout brick in order to receive **direct mode** commands. **Direct mode** programs end with the ***end direct mode***, just like the RCX **direct mode** programs. Also like **direct mode** for the RCX, you can run a **direct mode** program on top of a **remote mode** program that is currently running on the Scout.

Figure 6.44. A simple Scout direct mode program that can be run on top of another Scout program.

6.5.3   Using the Scout Events

Probably the most commonly used Scout-specific functions are related to **Events**. There are 15 predefined events that can be used on the Scout. Unlike the RCX, there are only two functions required to setup and monitor a Scout event: ***start monitoring for a Scout event***

and *Scout event landing*. As with RCX events, all events in a given task share the same landing. You can monitor up to 15 events simultaneously.

Setting up a Scout event is a little more complicated than it was for the RCX. To setup the event(s) to be monitored you have to right-click on the events terminal to create a **constant**. You select the event number using the up and down arrows on the indicator on the left <u>using the operate tool</u> (the little hand). You select the type of event to be monitored using the pull down menu (again, with the operate tool). If the event isn't being monitored (because you haven't defined the type of event), then the description will appear grayed-out, as in Figure 6.45 (event #1 is shown).

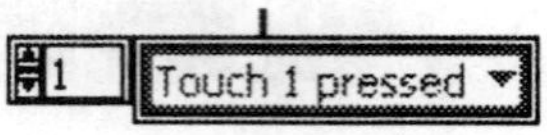

Figure 6.45. The Scout event "constant."

Figure 6.46 shows event #0 being set up to monitor touch sensor 1. You can set up multiple events by clicking on the up and down arrows on the indicator, to the left of the event description, and then selecting the type of event you want to monitor.

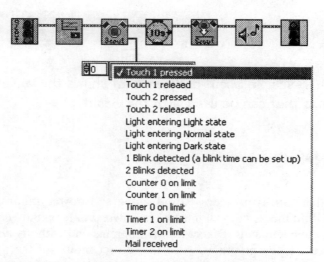

Figure 6.46. Event #0 is being set up to monitor for a press on touch sensor 1.

Let's run through the 15 type of events quickly. The touch sensor events are pretty straightforward. The light sensor events are similar to those described earlier in section 6.2. The entering light state, normal state, and dark state are equivalent to the high, normal, and low events described earlier (see Figure 6.12). You can change the upper and lower thresholds and hysteresis using the appropriate Scout commands.

The blink events are triggered when there is a rapid change in the light sensor reading. You can set the sensitivity of the blink (i.e. how fast the blink must be) using the *Scout light sensor blink time* function. You can also set up events that are triggered when either of the two internal counters or three timers exceeds the limit set with the *set counter value* and *set timer limit* functions. Finally, you can set up a mail event that is triggered when any non-zero value of mail is received by the Scout.

6.5.4   Scout Subroutines

The Scout brick has a whole bunch of built in subroutines that are normally accessed while using the Scout in **stand alone** mode. However, we can also use the subroutines in our ROBOLAB programs to save ourselves some programming. Some of the ROBOLAB help files are quite confusing when it comes to the Scout commands. The best way to see how they work is to play with them (which is what we did). The next best thing is to see a couple of examples.

The two programs shown below are identical in function but making use of the built in subroutines saves a lot of programming steps. How you specify the duration is not consistent among Scout subroutines. Sometimes the duration is in milliseconds (ms), while other times it is in 10ms intervals. In the example, below 200*10ms = 2.00 seconds.

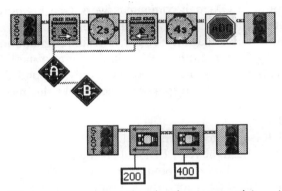

Figure 6.47. These two programs do the same thing. Using the Scout subroutines can save you a lot of programming effort.

In the next example, the Scout will zigzag 5 times (5 loops) with 2 seconds (duration = 200) between each change in direction. After that, it will turn right <u>forever</u>. Why forever? Because the duration is set to zero and, according to the help file, that means it will loop forever.

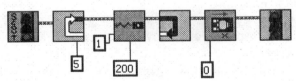

Figure 6.48. This program zigzags 5 times and turns right forever.

In the next example, we've combined several Scout subroutines and a Scout event to create a nice little program that doesn't use any of the standard RCX functions. The event we are monitoring is the pressing of touch sensor 1. We start out by doing a 2 second zigzag with the *basic motion sub.* This subroutine lets you choose from the seven basic movements (same choices available under Motion in **stand alone** mode). Then we simply drive forward forever (duration = 0). When touch sensor 1 is pressed, the event is triggered and we stop driving and do a 3 second avoid left maneuver (since touch sensor 1 is on the left side). Finally, we do a little song and dance using the bug feature.

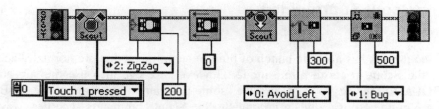

Figure 6.49. A complete program that doesn't use any RCX commands.

6.5.5   Using Mail

While in **power mode**, the Scout brick can send and receive mail from any other Scout or RCX. All the normal RCX mail commands work (see Figure 6.43). Mail is probably the easiest way to share information between an RCX and a Scout.

A little know fact is that the Scout's internal programming actually is already set up to accept remote commands from an RCX in the form of mail. The trick is this only works when running in **stand alone** mode. The Scout only responds to mail values 1 through 15. As far as we can tell, this is the response to each mail value received:

1: Avoid left
2: Avoid left (seems to be same as #1)
3: Play music, flash the red LED, and zigzag
4: Go forward for 1 second (both motors A and B)
5: Go backwards for 1 second (both motors A and B)
6: Turn right for 1 second (motor A forward, B reverse)
7: Turn left for 1 second (motor A reverse, B forwards)
8: Motor A forward for 1 second
9: Motor A reverse for 1 second
10: Motor B forward for 1 second
11: Motor B reverse for 1 second
12: Stop both Motors A and B
13: Send VLL forward continuously
14: Send VLL reverse continuously
15: Stop VLL

The last 3 responses are really cool since you can use the RCX to send a message to the Scout, which then sends a VLL (Visible Light Link) command to the Microscout. Again, these mail responses are generated only when you are currently running a **stand alone** mode program.

6.5.6   Programming the Microscout using VLL

VLL stands for Visible Light Link. It uses the red LED on the front of the Scout brick to send commands to the Microscout's light sensor. To send a command, use the *Scout VLL commander micro scout* function, as shown in Figure 6.50. Like the Scout events, you need to right-click on the VLL command terminal and either create a **constant** or create a **control**. Either a pull down menu will appear on the block diagram (Figure 6.50) or a control will appear on the font panel.

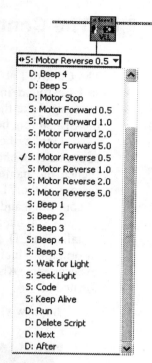

Figure 6.50. The available VLL Microscout commands.

The "D" before the command indicates a direct mode command (i.e. the Microscout will execute the command immediately). An "S" indicates that a "script" program is being sent. Script programs can be up to 15 commands in length. Figure 6.51 shows a 4-command script program being sent to the Microscout. The program is not executed until either the **run** button is pushed or the direct command *Run* is sent.

Note, the Microscout has to be within a few inches of the Scout's red LED. Also, the Microscout has 7 built in programs and one programmable slot labeled "P." The Microscout needs to be on P in order to receive a program from the Scout. If you want to delete the current program, you need to use the *Delete Script* direct command.

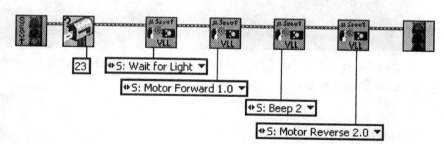

Figure 6.51. This will send a script program 4 commands long to the Microscout after the Scout receives a mail value of 23.

One really annoying feature of the Microscout is that it always plays a complicated beep before starting the motor. Plus, the motor only has one speed and will coast to a stop rather than just braking. Despite these minor drawbacks, the potential for creating a hierarchal robot community is pretty cool. You can have RCX's in charge of Scouts which are in turn in charge of Microscouts.

6.6 The Control Lab Interface (CLI) Badge CLI

The Control Lab Interface (CLI) is another LEGO® product that is no longer sold but can still be found in significant numbers at many schools (because it was a very popular product). Like the previous section on the Scout brick, we're including a short section on the CLI simply because many people have asked for it.

Unlike the smart bricks (the RCX, Scout, and Microscout), the CLI has to be continually connected to your computer in order to function. The CLI is simply an interface (hence the name) between the LEGO® motors/sensors and your computer. The coolest feature of the CLI is the ability to use 8 sensor inputs (4 powered, 4 passive) and 9 outputs (8 controlled and one always-on output).

If you happen to have an older version of ROBOLAB (2.5.2 or earlier), then on your installation CD, there is a folder called RCX-Control Lab, which contains a lot of useful information including sample ROBOLAB programs for a lot of the old Control Lab experiments. Also, for additional information there is a great online tutorial for the CLI located at:

http://www.ceeo.tufts.edu/robolabatceeo/College/tutorials/image_cli/index.htm

Figure 6.52. The Control Lab Interface (CLI) has 8 inputs and 9 outputs!

6.6.1 Setting up the CLI

As mentioned earlier, the CLI needs to be connected to your computer in order to function. Being an older style device, it uses a serial port connection. The serial cable needed is called a "null modem" or "computer-to-computer" serial cable. A standard serial extension cord won't work.

We've used the cable that comes with the older-style LEGO® serial towers with a gender changer (male-male) quite successfully.

Figure 6.53. Using a gender changer on the end of a serial tower cable works fine.

You also have to supply power to the CLI (sorry, no battery option). Any AC adapter that works on the RCX will also work on the CLI (same Voltage requirements and same size adapter plug). You can tell when you've got it connected correctly because the red LED next to the emergency stop button and the green "on" LED both light up.

6.6.2   Programming the CLI

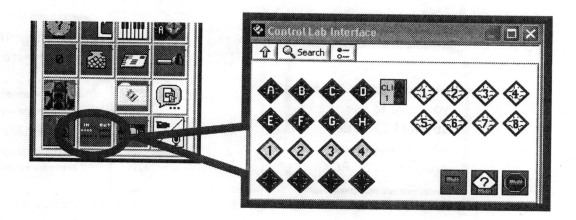

Figure 6.54. The **CLI** sub-palette is located at the bottom of the **functions** palette.

The CLI uses all the same RCX commands, except that you now have 8 input and 8 output ports to utilize. There is also a 9th output port at the bottom center of the CLI. This port is always on at full power.

   All CLI programs start with the ***begin control lab interface*** function and end with the standard stop light, as shown in Figure 6.55. The only significant difference between the RCX and the CLI is that the CLI distinguishes between powered (blue) and unpowered, or passive, (yellow) sensors. Fortunately, LEGO® has been kind enough to color code all of their sensors. The light and rotation sensors are blue and, thus, can only be used on the 4 blue input ports. The touch and temperature sensors are yellow and can only be used on the yellow input ports. You shouldn't complain about this limitation – you have four of each, which is one more than the RCX!

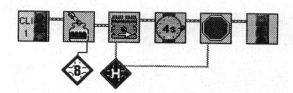

Figure 6.55. Here are a couple of commands that you won't find in an RCX program.

When you run a CLI program by clicking on the usual white run arrow, you'll get a special **Start CLI** pop-up window (Figure 6.56). The window will indicate whether or not the CLI is connected properly, the current status of the CLI (idle or running), and a warning that if you want to download a program to an RCX while the window is open, you have to use the special *begin RCX* command. If you don't, ROBOLAB will try to send your RCX's program to the CLI (which will generate errors).

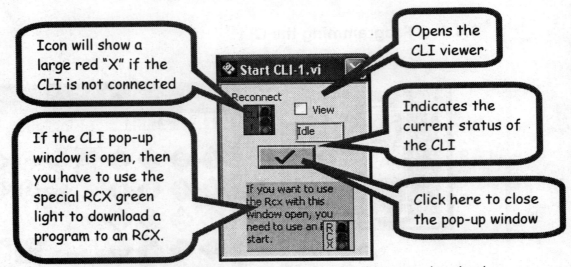

Figure 6.56. The Start CLI pop-up window opens when you download a program to the CLI.

If you click on the check box next to "View" the **CLI viewer** will open. The **CLI viewer** is CLI's version of the **Interrogate RCX**. While this window is open, you can see the status of the various sensors, motors, and containers (variables). You can also see the LASM commands (discussed later in this chapter) that are being sent. The current command is highlighted as shown in Figure 6.57 (the program in Figure 6.55 currently running).

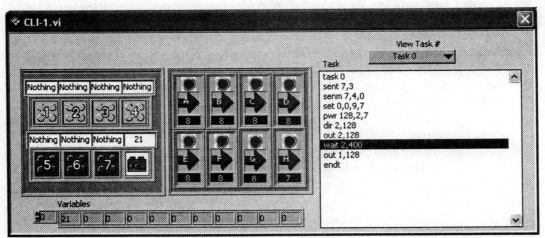

Figure 6.57. The CLI Viewer allows you to see current status of input and output ports as well as the LASM code as it is executed.

Which functions can be used with the CLI? Since the CLI doesn't have a speaker, you cannot play any system sounds or music. Also, since it doesn't have an IR port, you cannot use any mail functions. Events and subroutines are also not possible. Other than these few exceptions, all the normal RCX functions work with the CLI.

6.6.3   Data Logging

Data logging with the CLI is nearly identical to data logging with the RCX. In Investigator, you have to be using **Programmer** level 5 because level 4 doesn't have the **CLI** sub-palette. We have also found that you cannot sample very fast over the serial connection. The shortest sampling interval we can reliably get is around 0.8 seconds.

Figure 6.58 shows a simple data logging program that collects ten light sensor readings with a sampling interval of 1.5 seconds.

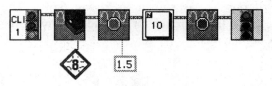

Figure 6.58. A simple data logging program using the CLI.

In order to upload data from the CLI, you need to have the CLI pop-up window open (Figure 6.56). If you close the CLI pop-up window (because the program is done running) and try to upload data, Investigator will automatically attempt to upload data from an RCX.

After uploading the data, you may notice that the data logging didn't start right away. In the example below, the sampling interval is 1.5 seconds, but it took 0.4 seconds to initialize the light sensor and start data logging.

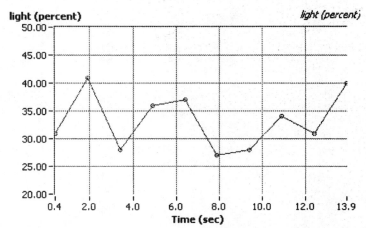

Figure 6.59. Sample data for the program in Figure **6.58**.

As a side note, the data you log is not actually stored on the CLI (it has no internal memory). Rather, it's stored on your computer. Thus, the term "upload" is a bit of misnomer since you already have the data on your computer – you are simply accessing it. You'll find that the CLI data is "uploaded" nearly instantaneously because all you are doing is opening a text file on your computer. If you think about it, you'll also realize that you can store nearly unlimited amounts of data!

6.6.4   Direct Mode

Unlike the RCX and Scout, **direct mode** with the CLI cannot be run on top of another program. If you think about it, all programs using the CLI are really **direct mode** programs since the CLI has no internal processor. So the inability to run a **direct mode** program on top of another program is not too surprising.

Like all **direct mode** programs, you cannot use any structures (jumps, loops, forks, etc). The only new command that we need to introduce for **direct mode** is *poll interface box*, which is the CLI's version of the RCX's *read value* (see section 6.4.3). By creating an **indicator**, we can display the value of any input port (or container value) to the **front panel** of our VI, as shown in Figure 6.60. The **CLI Viewer** (Figure 6.57) is essentially a fancy **front panel** for a hidden **block diagram** that uses a bunch of *poll interface box* commands.

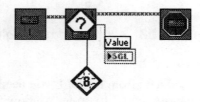

Figure 6.60. The *poll interface box* command is the only function specific to CLI **direct mode**.

6.7 The LASM Badge

LASM stands for LEGO Assembly Language. When you write a program in ROBOLAB, you are actually creating a set of LASM codes that is sent to the RCX via the IR tower. The firmware on the RCX interprets and executes these commands. What makes ROBOLAB so nice is that you don't have to remember all the LASM commands. Instead you get to memorize icons, which we find much easier (most people remember pictures better than text).

There is at least one other popular programming environment that uses LASM. Not Quite C (NQC) also uses the same LEGO firmware and, thus, also generates LASM code. In this case, the NQC code is converted into LASM and then sent to the RCX. The RCX can't tell whether it's receiving a program from ROBOLAB or NQC. In fact, you can download a program in NQC and then upload it back to ROBOLAB, using the Ask RCX program (located on the **projects** menu).

6.7.1   The Begin LASM Command

 When you write a program, ROBOLAB takes the icons you wire together and converts them into text – the LASM code. Normally in ROBOLAB, you don't ever see the LASM code that is generated. If you want to see and/or edit the LASM code, simply replace the standard green light with the LASM green light, which is located on the **Advanced** sub-palette.

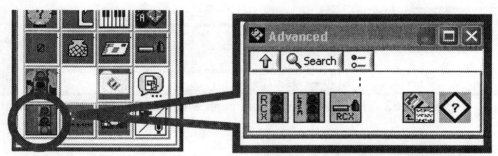

Figure 6.61. The *begin LASM* function is on the **Advanced** sub-palette.

You don't need to have an RCX or even an IR tower connected to your computer to run a LASM program. When you run a LASM program, like the one shown below, the program is not downloaded to the RCX. Instead the **VBrick** window opens, as shown in Figure 6.63.

Figure 6.62. A simple LASM program.

The **VBrick** window has a lot of features, which will be discussed in detail in the next section. For now, we're just going to examine the LASM code that is shown on the left half of the **VBrick** window. If you click on a LASM command on the left, the dialog box on the right will provide a brief description of the command. In the example shown below we see that *delt 0* is used to delete all the tasks in the current program.

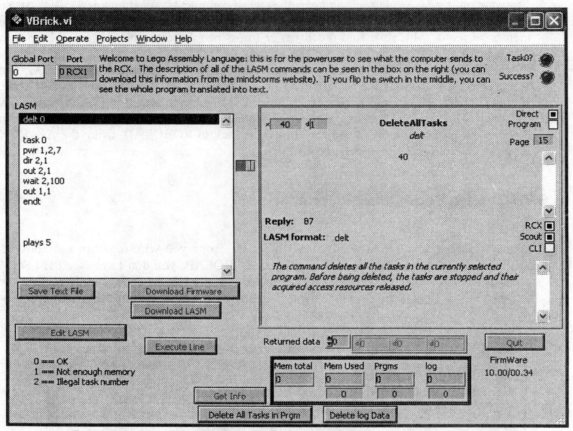

Figure 6.63. The **VBrick** window opens when you run a LASM program.

As shown in Figure 6.63, the program in Figure 6.62 generated 9 lines of LASM code, which we've repeated here:

delt 0	deletes all tasks in the current program
task 0	defines the start of the first task (we've been calling it task #1)
pwr 1,2,7	sets the motor power for port A to power level 7 (full power)
dir 2,1	sets the direction of port A to forward
out 2,1	turns on port A
wait 2,100	waits 1 second
out 1,1	turns port A off
endt	defines the end of task #1 (equivalent to the red stop light)
plays 5	makes the RCX beep after it downloads the program.

Remember back in Chapter 4 we said that ***Motor A Forward*** is actually a combination of three functions (see Figure 4.66)? The LASM shows this also. We can see the three functions ***pwr***, ***dir***, and ***out*** are used to turn on motor A. Hopefully, you also realize how nice it is to program with icons rather than text.

6.7.2   The VBrick window

Now that you've got the basic idea of how ROBOLAB converts the icons into text programs, let's investigate the **VBrick** window a little closer. We'll need a program that is a little more interesting than our last example. Figure 6.64 shows part of the LEGO® cockroach program (Figure 6.15) redone with the ***begin LASM*** command and the corresponding **VBrick** window.

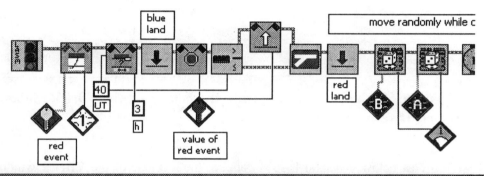

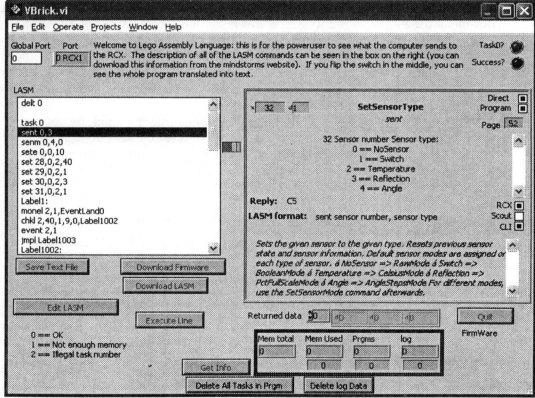

Figure 6.64. Part of the LEGO® cockroach program redone with a ***begin LASM*** (top) and the corresponding **VBrick** window (bottom).

Right in the middle of the window, between the two main text boxes, there is a small switch. When you click on it, the right text box changes into a somewhat translated version of the LASM that is a little easier to understand. All of the common LASM commands are translated into English, but some of the less frequently used commands remain unintelligible.

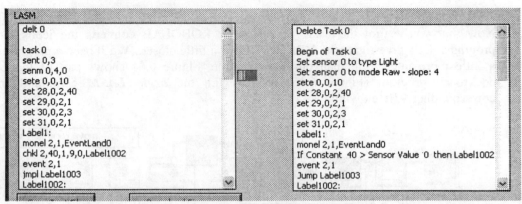

Figure 6.65. Click on the switch in the center of the **VBrick** window to change the right text box.

Just below the main LASM code on the left side of the **VBrick** window, there are several buttons. You can save the LASM to a text file, download the firmware to the RCX, download the LASM to the RCX (i.e. download the program), edit the LASM (a pop-up window will open – see below), or execute (download) just the selected line of LASM.

There are three more buttons at the bottom of the **VBrick** window that allow you to look at the memory map (see section 6.4.2), delete all tasks (i.e. erase the current program) and clear the data log buffer. The last button, near the bottom right, quits (exits) the **VBrick** window.

The small check boxes along the right side indicate the valid uses of the LASM command selected. In Figure 6.64 we've selected the *sent 0,3* command and see that it can be used in either **direct mode** or **remote mode** (program) and that it is a valid command for both the RCX and the CLI, but not the Scout.

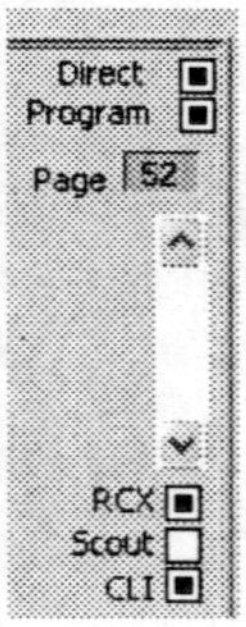

Figure 6.66. The check boxes along the right edge pertain to the currently selected LASM command.

We've nearly reached the end of our lengthy journey (i.e. the end of this book). There's one last feature we want expand upon before we say goodbye. If you click on the **Edit LASM** button, a new pop-up window will open (Figure 6.67). Here you can edit the LASM directly. Try deleting the very last command (plays 5) and you'll find that your RCX doesn't beep after receiving the program.

Probably of more interest for users new to LASM is the text box on the right side. You can scroll through all the LASM commands by clicking on the indicator at the very top labeled "LASM Defs." You can also search for a particular LASM command using the search box at the bottom of the screen.

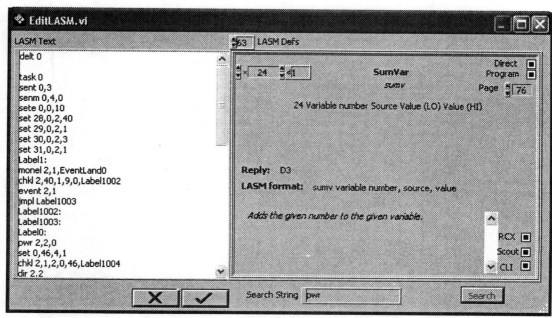

Figure 6.67. The Edit LASM pop-up window.

APPENDIX A
Information about LEGO® Kits

There was a recent newspaper article that stated there have been nearly 400 billion LEGO® bricks sold over the past five decades (LEGO® was founded in 1934, with the first LEGO® brick being sold in 1949). That's a whole lot of bricks! To put it in another perspective, according to LEGO® (the company) children spend a combined total of approximately 5 billion hours per year playing with LEGO® bricks. That's a whole lot of time!

What does this trivia have to do with engineering and ROBOLAB? First, it gives you a feeling for the number of LEGO® kits that are sold each year. Second, it provides a clue for the amount of time that instructors and students will spend using LEGO® bricks. This is especially true if you're the poor bloke who has to sort a Team Challenge kit. You are going to personally contribute significantly to the total number of hours spent "playing" with LEGO® bricks!

A.1 The Future of the Mindstorms Product Line

When the folks at LEGO® read this paragraph, they are probably going to be a bit surprised (and we must acknowledge that LEGO® had nothing to do with it). Nonetheless, we thought it is worth writing because many educators have asked us about the future of the *Mindstorms for Schools* product line. There was a nasty rumor circulating in early 2004 that LEGO® was going to discontinue the *Mindstorms* product line. While we're not sure whether or not LEGO® has ever released an official statement, our sources at LEGO® have indicated that the *Mindstorms for Schools* product line is here to stay. Heck, we wouldn't have invested the time to write this book if that wasn't the case!

A.2 RCX-Based Kits Available

There are a variety of RCX-based kits available. This section will briefly describe the more popular ones. We are also going to stick our necks out a bit and give you our opinions about the advantages and disadvantages of each kit. See section 1.8.3 for a list of places to buy the kits.

A.2.1 Team Challenge Set

This set comes in two varieties, depending on the type of IR tower: serial (#9793) and USB (#9794). This is the "standard" kit that most schools and colleges use. We've used this kit for years without trouble.

Advantages:
- It comes with nearly 1000 pieces.
- Everything a student team will need is in the box.
- Convenient storage and transport.
- Accepts a 9V DC adapter.

Disadvantages:
- Inventorying and sorting the kit is <u>very</u> time consuming.
- A bit expensive at $199.
- No rotation or temperature sensors included.

A.2.2 Retail RIS 1.0, 1.5, and 2.0

RIS (Robotics Invention System) has evolved from version 1.0 to 1.5 and now to 2.0. This is the popular retail box set found in stores. It can be found priced for as low at $100 (on sale) up to the MSRP of $199.

We don't recommend using this kit because the RCX lacks the 9V DC adapter port. With that said, many of our students have successfully used it for our courses. They just end up replacing/recharging batteries quite often. Rechargeable high-capacity (2000+ mAh) NiMH batteries are highly recommended.

Advantages:
- Over 700 pieces.
- Everything a student team will need is in the box.
- Programming software included (this is **not** ROBOLAB)

Disadvantages:
- Inventorying and sorting the kit is <u>very</u> time consuming.
- No rotation or temperature sensors
- Only 1 light sensor
- Programming software is not ROBOLAB
- RCX 2.0 and 1.5 do not have an DC adapter port
- Big box that is not very durable.

A.2.3 ROBO Technology Set

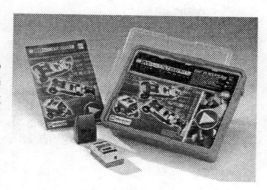

The ROBO Technology Set (#9785) appears to be a pared down version of the team challenge kit. It includes just over 200 pieces, including the RCX, IR tower, 2 motors, 2 touch sensors, 1 light sensor, and 1 lamp element.

This kit seems to be aimed at educators who want to try out the RCX for the first time. We've used it quite successfully for outreach programs for grades K-6. There are clear building instructions for several simple cars. Plus, there are few enough parts that the students can sort the kit in a reasonable amount of time at the end of each class period.

For more advanced students, we find that there are not enough pieces for them to make their robots. Robot competitions will definitely require additional parts. This kit can easily be supplemented with extra parts to make a really good set (e.g. Technology Resource Set or Scenery Resource Set).

Advantages:
- Enough parts to make simple robots is in the box.
- Costs about $45 less than the Team Challenge Set (MSRP: $152)
- Inventorying/sorting is fairly easy (includes sorting tray)
- Convenient storage and transport.
- Accepts a 9V DC adapter.

Disadvantages:
- No rotation or temperature sensors
- Only 1 light sensor
- Only enough pieces to build simple robots

A.2.4 Other Bundled Sets

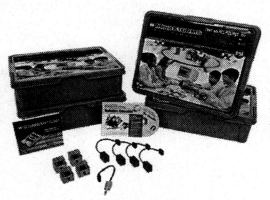

There are other various sets that bundle one of the kits above with the ROBOLAB software and/or a LEGO® camera. These bundles save a little money over buying the components individually.

There also some combination packs that bundle several items together, like the Robotics Educator Start-up Pack ($1,250). It includes 4 Team Challenge kits, 4 rotation sensors, 4 extra motors, a temperature sensor, the ROBOLAB software, and the Robotics Educator software. This bundle saves you about $100 over individual components and is worth getting if you are starting from scratch.

Finally, there are several "theme" packs that are aimed at specific themes like an amusement park, an intelligent house, Mars exploration, Alien encounters, and race against time. These sets include classroom activities (lesson plans) and specialized assortments of pieces to go along with the theme.

W990690

W979795

A.3 Who Should Buy the Kits?

When using LEGO® bricks and ROBOLAB, there arises an interesting question: who should buy the kits? For a teacher (grades K-12), this isn't really an issue. However, for a college/university, either the institution or the students can buy the kits.

A.3.1 Student Owned

The main reason for requiring students to purchase their own kits is to relieve the institution from having to inventory and/or maintain the kits. Requiring students to purchase the kits is logistically the easiest but also can be costly for the students. We do not prefer this method because it is expensive for the student.

The Team Challenge Set is the set of choice when students purchase their own kits. Including an RCX, an assortment of sensors, motors, and enough parts to suitably build robots, the set costs approximately $200. This cost is feasible in the context of how much students pay for textbooks, especially when students work in teams of two or more and can share the cost. Experience has shown that a market for used kits develops just as the case for used textbooks, which partly reduces the cost to the students.

When students buy the kits, the issue of start-up costs is also negated. Meaning, you can start a course or project that uses LEGO® bricks without having to worry about securing start-up funds for the initial investment in the hardware.

A.3.2 Institution Owned

When the institution owns the sets, dealing with stolen, damaged, and missing parts is THE major issue. Many instructors have found it is not uncommon to sacrifice one or more kits as a source of spare parts, which adds to the overall cost.

Below we list three possible methods for distributing the institutionally-owned kits to the students:

1) Maintain a dedicated laboratory (or classroom space) with all the necessary kits. This method works well for traditional classrooms/laboratories. This method is difficult if any robot construction, out-of-class, or at-home activities are conducted. Either the Team Challenge Set or the ROBO Technology Set works well, depending on the complexity of the activities.
2) Loan or rent kits to students. The institution purchases and owns the kits and then either loans or rents the kits to the students for the duration of the exercise or term. For experiments which only require the RCX and a few sensors, a "core" kit can be used quite effectively. However, for courses which involve extensive robot construction, inventorying kits at the end of term can be a major issue since some kits contain over 800 pieces. Again, either the Team Challenge Set or the ROBO Technology Set works well, depending on the complexity of the activities.
3) Hybrid: loan/rent a "core" kit (with the more expensive parts such as the RCX and sensors) and have student purchase their own "bricks." This method works well for courses which involve robot competitions. The "core" kits are easily inventoried and

the students are burdened only with the cost of the bricks. The Technology Resource Set is a very cost effective way for students to buy bricks (includes over 1100 pieces for $57).

For teachers (grades k-12), option 1 above is really the only viable method. The only choice is whether to use the Team Challenge Set or the ROBO Technology Set. We recommend the Team Challenge Set simply because you won't need to buy additional parts in the future (except for spare parts and/or sensors not included in the set). As we mentioned previously, inventorying the set is the most difficult task. We wouldn't wish the task of inventorying an entire class of kits on any teacher! Rather, most teachers have the students' team inventory and/or sort the kits. Teams should report which pieces are missing so that they can be replaced. Some teachers never inventory the kits and simply give out spare parts as they are needed.

Keeping students from stealing parts is another major issue for teachers (motors are the most common part to "walk away"). Probably the most creative solution we have heard came from Brian Pinches, a teacher from Kurnai College, which is a high school in the Latrobe Valley of Victoria, Australia. At the end of each class he weighs the kits on a digital scale. By knowing how much each of the major components (e.g. the RCX, a motor, etc) weighs he can quickly determine if something is missing. The hidden beauty of this method is that the robots don't have to be disassembled, making multi-day projects viable.

For college/university instructors, the most difficult scenario is for a course in which a single experiment or exercise is conducted. In this case, it is economically unfeasible to make the students purchase their kits or even their own bricks. This leaves only options 1 and 2 above, which both require the kits to be sorted and inventoried periodically. Experience has shown that even after a single experiment the inventorying process can be very time consuming and pieces are often missing and/or damaged.

A.4 The Other Programmable Brick Kits

We've mentioned the Scout and Microscout several times throughout this book, so we'll take a moment to describe the kits they come in. Note, that all the kits described have been discontinued and, thus, are no longer available through retail stores.

The Scout brick can be found in the Robotics Discovery Set (#9735). The kit has about 400 pieces and used to retail for $150, but can be found for as low as $50 on Internet auction sites now.

The Microscout was actually available in two different kits, the Droid Developer Kit (#9748) and the Dark Side Developer kit (#9754). The Droid Developer kit has about 650 pieces and initially retailed for $100 but could often be found for half of that at discount stores. We've seen these for as low as $20 on Internet auction sites.

The Dark Side Developer Kit has nearly 600 pieces. The Microscout in this set is actually a little different than the one in the Droid Developer Kit. The Dark Side Microscout has a red plastic screen while the Droid one has a blue screen. This kit retailed for about $100 and, surprisingly, has retained much of that value on Internet auction sites.

APPENDIX B
Tips for Teachers

There are two great new resources to help you resolve common problems. The first is the **Quick Start Guide** that is available for free from www.legoeducationstore.com. The second new resource is the knowledgebase at the Tufts University ROBOLAB website:

---

http://www.ceeo.tufts.edu/robolabatceeo/activekb/

The dynamic nature of the knowledgebase will ensure that it's the most up to date resource and, thus, is the first place we recommend seeking advice.

It's not new, but very few people seem to know about it. The **ROBOLAB Reference Guide** is <u>303 pages</u> of all things ROBOLAB. It automatically installed in the ROBOLAB installation directory in the folder labeled "Support Material." The **Using ROBOLAB** book (or the electronic version) is also a great resource and is easier reading than the Reference Guide. There is also a great information area in the Training Missions (see Figure 1.12), which includes heaps of troubleshooting tips.

Even though we've pointed you towards these great resources, we still feel obliged to share with you some tips for resolving the most common problems we've encountered:

- No response from the tower or RCX.
    - The RCX isn't turned on.
    - The RCX is facing the wrong direction (the black plastic front has to face the IR tower attached to the computer).
    - Battery is dead in the serial IR tower.
    - Wrong COM port.
    - Fluorescent lights can interfere with IR communication (okay, the bulbs themselves don't cause interference, but the electronics in the high voltage ballasts do). Try turning off the lights or covering the IR tower and RCX with a piece of paper (to block the lights).
- The firmware downloads part way, but keeps getting stuck.
    - Be sure everything is connected correctly. ROBOLAB has a good multimedia setup guide (see Figure 1.10).
    - Rather than trying to continue, we've had more success canceling the download and starting the download over.
    - Overhead fluorescent lights also wreak havoc on the firmware download process. Try shielding both the IR tower and RCX with a piece of paper to block the fluorescent lights. The green box from the Team Challenge Set also works great to cover the RCX.
- Program doesn't work as expected
    - Did you remember to download the program? Students often forget to download the program after they make changes.

- o Is the run indicator (the little man) still running? Often the program has ended but you forgot to turn the motors off, so it just keeps going (see Figure 2.37). No wonder it won't stop when it sees the line!
  - o Low batteries can wreak havoc with light sensor readings.
  - o Wrong output port – make sure the motor port you are using matches your program.
  - o Wrong input port – make sure the sensor port you are using matches your program.
  - o You've downloaded someone else's program. The IR towers are very good transmitters, and in large classes with lots of computers, it's very easy to accidentally receive someone else's program.
  - o Make sure the program you are running is the same one you downloaded. Often you will accidentally hit the **Prgm** button and, thus, change which program you are running.
- Light sensor isn't detecting colors correctly.
  - o The light sensor doesn't detect color, it only detects the intensity of light! See section 2.3.5 for details on the light sensor.
- Light sensor cannot detect a line.
  - o Light Sensor may be too far from the surface. Try mounting the light sensor as close to the ground as possible. This minimizes the affect of ambient light while maximizing the reflected light. See section 2.3.5 for details on the light sensor.
- Motors won't turn off.
  - o Don't forget that you need to turn the motors off before the program ends. In Inventor and Investigator, the motors do not automatically turn off at the end of the program (see Figure 2.37).
- The ROBOLAB function does seem to do what it is supposed to (according to the help file).
  - o There may be a bug in ROBOLAB. Downloading patches from the Internet can solve a lot of problems: http://www.ceeo.tufts.edu/robolabatceeo/Resources/default.asp
  - o Try testing just the one function, separate from the rest of your program.
- Can't wire anything to a function.
  - o You may have accidentally wired the **begin** and **end** together (see Figure 2.74). Try removing bad wires (Ctrl+B).
  - o Sometimes just deleting the function (icon), putting it back in and rewiring solves the problem.
- Can't figure out the "spaghetti" code
  - o When student's get done with a program, it often resembles a bowl of pink spaghetti, which makes debugging really difficult. Try using **Ask RCX** (on the **projects** menu) to upload the program from the RCX back to the computer. ROBOLAB will format the program automatically for you.